I Won't Forgive
What You Did

I WON'T FORGIVE WHAT YOU DID

FAITH SCOTT

POCKET
BOOKS

LONDON • SYDNEY • NEW YORK • TORONTO

First published in Great Britain by Pocket Books, 2010
An imprint of Simon & Schuster
A CBS Company

1 3 5 7 9 10 8 6 4 2

Simon & Schuster UK Ltd
1st Floor
222 Gray's Inn Road
London WC1X 8HB

www.simonandschuster.co.uk

Simon & Schuster Australia
Sydney

A CIP catalogue record for this book is available
from the British Library.

ISBN: 978-1-84983-156-7

Typeset by Hewer Text UK Ltd, Edinburgh
Printed and Bound in Great Britain by
CPI Cox & Wyman, Reading RG1 8EX

PART ONE

CHAPTER 1

Though he was only in his sixties in 1963, when I was eight, Grandpops always seemed old to me. He had a bald head with just a little white hair remaining, which ran in a semicircle round the back of his head. He still had enormous black eyebrows, however, which sat above round tortoiseshell glasses.

He was short, and he always dressed the same – waistcoat, white open-necked shirt, no tie, battered black boots and baggy trousers. He also had a peaked cap that he wore everywhere. Even indoors it rarely came off. For some reason Grandpops always wore a suit jacket, often with another jacket over it. The pockets were filled with all manner of things: screws, pens, washers, filthy hankies, betting slips and, most importantly to me, sweets.

His hands seemed large, but then, when I was little, most men's did, probably because when they touched me that was what I noticed. Pops' were dark brown and dirty, just like his teeth, which were rotting and broken, with several missing. He had horrid breath, and fingernails that were broken and snagged. He always smelled of alcohol when he came to our house, because he'd spend several hours in the pub before he visited, intermittently leaving to visit the betting shop, to gamble on the horses. It was from here that he used to either stagger down the hill or catch the bus to our house, invariably laden with flowers and vegetables from his garden, which he'd bring for my mother. Sometimes, he was so drunk that he fell over on the pavement and at least once had to go to hospital for stitches to his head. Despite his appearance and manner my mother was very close to him. My father, conversely, seemed to hate him.

Pops always visited on Saturday; had done for as long as I could remember. We'd sometimes have to get the bus to see him in the week, too, more often than not at his house. Pops' house was just the same as Pops – filthy and full of junk, it smelled of wine and dirt, and inside the walls were covered in black mould. The huge table in the kitchen was always covered in dirty, half-drunk tumblers of wine, similarly half-consumed bottles, gone-off food – usually cheese, bread and fried eggs – and, on the Rayburn, there was often a saucepan of some unpleasant-smelling stew. There were various buckets, in which all kinds of things fermented: dandelion, rhubarb, parsnip, carrot, and every type of hedgerow fruit that could be used to make alcohol.

He had been a sniper in the war and was a good shot, and would stand by the door to his kitchen shooting blackbirds with his rifle. I couldn't bear seeing the poor blackbirds fall from the sky, fence or tree. He also had a menacing-looking handgun, which he kept under his pillow, and I always used to think that, if I upset him, one day he would use it on me. Ironically, he always used to try to stoke my fear, but in an entirely different direction. Keep away, he used to tell me, from 'bastard Ken', who lived next door. 'He can't be trusted around little girls.' He'd often shoo me indoors, and lock us both in for good measure, which scared me almost as much. Even if we just went down the garden, he'd lock the door, because he said Ken was a thief and would go into his house and steal his things. Pops also told me Ken would go into his garden, when Pops was out, and dig up his vegetables and flowers to give to women he fancied, pretending he'd grown them himself. And according to Pops, sometimes he put poison in Pops' garden, which was why his crop was poor at times. It was confusing listening to what Pops believed about Ken, and scary. Nowhere and no one felt safe.

I watched his arrival now, from behind the kitchen door, the place I habitually stationed myself on Saturdays, when he came to visit. My mother being her father's daughter in most ways, meant our house, only the second I had lived in, was every bit as filthy as his. It was bigger than our first home, quite large in comparison; if it hadn't been quite so full of rubbish – it had a sitting room, dining room and kitchen, all connected – I could have run around it in a circle. As it was, the dining-room doors always remained closed because it wasn't a room we could use. There wasn't any space left in it, because it was full of clothes and newspapers and crockery.

Back then, I didn't know why Pops frightened me so much, only that I felt the familiar anxiety well up as he tried to coax me from where I was standing. One Saturday, I remember, he was in the kitchen talking to my mother, who was making him his usual cup of tea. In his hand were the sweets, several packets, which he would have bought on the way. Sometimes it would be Fruit Pastilles, or maybe Love Hearts, and at Easter, an Easter egg, made from cheap, odd-tasting chocolate. But Fruit Gums were the ones I loved best, because I could hold them tightly in my hand to warm them up a little, which made them tastier and easier to chew. I could see one of the packets today was Fruit Gums.

'Come and get them, then,' he said. Pops never used my name. 'Come on. I'm not going to hurt you.' As was always the case, I felt crushed by indecision, unable to make up my mind. I couldn't work out what was the matter with me. Why did I hesitate? Why did I feel so much fear? I was only being offered sweeties, for goodness' sake. 'I'm not going to hurt you.' He said this a lot. But I needed to work out from the tone of his voice whether, this time, he actually meant it; whether he *would* 'get me', because if he did – and he mostly did – I felt panicked and trapped because I couldn't get away and, much as I was desperate to shout 'Help! Stop tickling me!' no sound would come out of my mouth.

I stood rooted to the spot, unable to act, and frustrated with my small self for being in such a state. On the one hand, I wanted to be with my grandad, enjoy his attention, have him laugh at me – something no one else did. And yet it also felt bad. *I* felt bad. But how could that be? He was Pops. Why on earth would he want to hurt me? He loved me.

I simply couldn't understand why I should so mind him tickling me, and wished I was not so pathetic and small. If I was bigger, I thought, it would all be all right. I glanced, as I always did, at my mother. Why was I so silly about Grandpops touching me? *She* knew what he was doing – she could see it for herself

– and if *she* thought it was okay, why didn't I? This is what grandads did, didn't they? They tickled you, all over, until it hurt. I felt upset when I thought about it, wanted to burst out crying, but I didn't. I felt bad that I didn't like it, and also sad about my mother. How badly I wished I could explain how I felt or, better still, that she somehow just knew what was happening and stopped it, without me having to say anything. But once again I reminded myself, this was what grandads were for. Grandads tickled, and all children liked being tickled. So it must be *my* problem, mustn't it? Must be *me* that was the problem. Why on earth did it make me feel so strange and bad?

Eventually, my anxiety overcome by my reasoning, I edged out from behind the door and walked to where Grandpops stood by my mother. I stretched my arm out as far as it would go so I didn't have to go too close.

'There,' he said, holding the sweets out. 'That's it. Come here, come on, that's it. Come closer so you can reach. Which one would you like? This one? Come on, that's it.'

I moved a little closer with my arm outstretched, keen to maintain my distance, already aware that the sound of his breathing was changing. But I was too late in noticing, and before I could escape, he had grabbed hold of my wrist and pulled me against him, hard between his legs, crossing one of his legs over me so that I was clamped and couldn't get away. The precious sweets, suddenly, were returned to his pocket, and his hands were now all over my chest, the stench of his breath wafting all round me. He was also now making the horrible scary noise he always made when he was tickling me, a sort of humming or buzzing, between tightly clenched teeth.

Within seconds I was lifted up and carried into the sitting room, to the chair he usually sat in, and placed upon his lap. Now his hands, always dextrous in containing my attempts to escape him, were moving all over me – up inside my skirt and then down my top, back up my top, and then down and then back up my skirt, as he continued to make the awful scary noise.

Sometimes, my mother, who was almost always there – either still making tea, or standing watching in the doorway – would say tiredly, 'Oh, leave her alone, Dad, for goodness' sake.' But she never said it in a way that convinced me she meant it, and he never took any notice of her anyway.

Right now, she said nothing, and he lifted me up and turned me round, so that we were now face to face, my legs between his legs, pressed tightly against him, my feet hardly touching the floor. He began tickling me, again and again, all over, his touch, always firm, became rougher and more frantic, his face close to mine, his eyes never leaving my bewildered face.

And then suddenly, just as I thought I was going to suffocate, it stopped. Pops looked breathless and was hot. The horrible noise had stopped too. He pushed a hand into his pocket and sweets appeared again.

'Go on,' he said hoarsely. 'Which ones do you want?' And I duly chose the Fruit Gums, took the packet, and walked away, feeling a terrible sadness and a great need to cry. I didn't know why, I just did. My mother brought him his tea then, and they continued to chat, as if nothing of importance had taken place.

I ate the sweets, because the sweets were the thing I most

wanted, yet I felt sick and hungry, but full at the same time – as if something solid was lodged at the back of my throat.

I looked again at my mother, but she had nothing to say. She'd just stood there watching him, laughing.

CHAPTER 2

Nowadays I take the view that my biological parents are only my parents because I chose them. Chose them to conceive me, to prevent anyone else having to have them – though I use the term 'parents' loosely. I was never 'parented' as such.

I also now know that my life probably began as a result of my father raping my mother. When I was older, she told me she didn't care for sex, but that my father, as in all his dealings with the world, wouldn't take no for an answer. If she didn't want sex, and most of the time she said she didn't, then he'd simply shout and threaten until she submitted. I was conceived in this fashion when my brother Phillip was six months old and my sister Susan – their first-born – just two. If my conception was inauspicious, the pregnancy was worse – at some point before my birth my brother developed gastroenteritis, was hospitalized, and nearly died. Naturally, the very last thing my mother wanted, she later told me, was another baby. Particularly a girl.

My brother survived, but the circumstances of my arrival were further complicated when my father was dismissed from his job as a farmhand. This was because it emerged that he'd been having an affair with the farmer's teenage daughter. As the family's house went with the job, they'd lose that as well, and when I was born they were about to become homeless.

He did eventually find another job that came with accommodation, working as a lorry driver for a haulier, ferrying farm animals – sheep, pigs and cattle – to market and to slaughter, with a little furniture removal on the side. The accommodation that came with this new job was in a tiny village close to where my father had grown up. It was rented by his employer, along with some land for his lorries, from a local aristocrat.

The village had about forty houses, two shops, a pub, three farms and a telephone box. It consisted of one through road, about two miles long, which could be accessed from the busy country roads at either end. Nobody ever came there. Why would they? Apart from the pub, which was really only for the locals, there was no reason to. Its inhabitants were either wealthy, and treated with awe by the locals, or old country folk, some of whom were dirty old men, who scared me, and who were employed by the farmers and upper-class people.

Like any other isolated rural community, everyone – superficially – knew everyone else's business. Enough, at least, for everyone to know we were poor and treat us accordingly. This sometimes meant a freshly baked roll for my siblings when they were on errands, or, more often, it seemed to mean that because we were poor we were unable to understand how to behave and had to be spoken to in a particular way. The villagers were kind to me, almost too kind, in some cases – to the point of leaving me feeling humiliated. It often felt as if they were patting me on the head and saying 'there, there', almost as if I belonged to a different species.

Most of the village homes were huge private houses with massive gardens, and their owners were rich and influential. We had a solicitor, a magistrate and a successful author, among others. Most of the other dwellings were tied cottages belonging to the big houses and farms.

Our new home was one such, a tiny mid-terrace dwelling, almost derelict and virtually uninhabitable. It had two small rooms upstairs and two small rooms downstairs, and no electricity, heating, hot water or bathroom. The narrow, unkempt garden sloped downwards towards a river, and the toilet was in a shed halfway down. There was a tin bath my mother occasionally carried into the house and filled, so we could all take turns to have a bath. By the time the youngest got in it was invariably cold and dirty, and there it would stay until my mother could be bothered to move it, which was usually hours, or even days, later. The house was filthy when we moved in and grew even filthier, and was also damp and very dark. The only real source of light was the picture window at the front, where I could watch the horses and hounds go through the village. It was the only home I knew in my young life and it was an unpleasant prospect. Aside from the physical manifestations of squalor, my home, whenever my father was in it, was a place I inhabited in fear.

My father was a terrifying person. A giant of a man, well over six feet tall, he had masses of wavy dark hair, a long face with a pointed nose, and both his hands and feet were enormous. He seemed to always wear the same clothes, a blue or green cardigan, checked shirt, navy trousers and brown shoes. He worked seven days a week, and from a very early age I felt enormous anxiety and fear when he was due home. Where I didn't understand why Grandpops made me so uncomfortable and distressed, with my father it was simple. I was terrified of him because he was a terrifying man, and I dreaded his arrival, all his shouting and swearing, the unthinkable prospect of upsetting him without meaning to, and so becoming the focus of his furious temper. My father frightened everyone who knew him, man, woman or child. Even Grandpops mostly avoided him.

Throughout my childhood, when he took off his shoes straw and hay would fall from his socks and trouser turn-ups. He always smelled of farmyard dung, and he'd doze in front of the fire with his feet on the mantelpiece – the steam rising from his wet socks smelled dreadful. He sat so close to the fire he gobbled up every last bit of heat, leaving just the sofa behind him, which is where I would sit, cold, and too afraid to make a noise in case I woke him up.

He also seemed to hate my attempts to clear up, which, as I grew old enough to try to make my environment nicer, was something I did all the time.

'Fucking little bastard,' he'd say to my mother. 'She's been fucking tidying up again, where's she put my fucking stuff? Fucking tidying, the fucking little bitch,' he would roar. 'Why can't she just fucking leave things alone!'

I was so terrified of him that, by the time I was eight, I real-ised the best thing to do when he threatened, called me names, raised his hands as if to wallop me, saying, 'Aah, I'll give you a fucking doughboy in a minute!' was to stand stock still and say absolutely nothing.

I took care, once I'd grown a bit, to never be undressed anywhere near him. If I was ever less than fully dressed – even if I was in a dressing gown – he'd shout and swear and demand I get dressed at once. As a child, I had no idea why he was like this. All I knew was that if he came into a room and I wasn't fully dressed, his reaction made me feel as if I'd done something terrible, and something equally terrible was about to happen, if I didn't immediately get out of his way.

My mother's physical form was the opposite of my dad's. She was short, and very tiny sometimes – a modern-day size 8 – but sometimes as large as an 18. She was always on diets, and either bingeing or starving, and knew the calories in every single foodstuff. She had very long, dark, wavy hair, and long fingernails, and seemed to exist in a parallel world, one that was impossible to penetrate. In the real world, at home, she seemed an almost ethereal presence, and as a consequence we lived in chaos. Every room was filthy and full of junk. The floors and the furniture were littered with dirty clothes, dirty nappies, dirty baby bottles and dirty crockery, and strewn with broken toys and rotting food.

In terms of squalor, it wasn't a lot different from Grandpops's house, where my mother had lived before marrying my father. She'd lived there all her life, a few miles from the village where we now were, and her family were real country folk – very poor – who were generally suspicious of outsiders.

She was the youngest of three; she had two older brothers whom she idolized and had always been close to. Both her brothers and her mother (my maternal grandmother, who suffered from chronic depression and who Pops treated appallingly) knew full well Pops sexually abused her. Today it's clear that whatever the roots of her strange behaviour, her brothers knew her escape from their father was vital and when she met my father, and marriage was on the cards, they couldn't get her out of the house quick enough. It would soon prove to be a case of frying pans and fires, but when, despite Pops' objections, they wed and she moved in with my father's mother and her husband, her brothers felt deeply relieved.

My parents didn't stay long with my paternal grandmother however, only until my father completed his national service. His work soon took them both to a tiny hamlet where my mother now lived a life of virtual isolation. She had two tiny children and a third on the way but was cut off, both physically and emotionally. She was no longer sexually abused by her father, but still abused, albeit differently, by her new husband.

By the time I was born, though I obviously didn't know it, my mother was suffering from anxiety and post-natal depression and seemed unable to function domestically. Though at this time she still sometimes dressed smartly and wore make-up, she was remote and unreachable and seemed to live in her own world.

More often than not, and particularly towards me, her 'attention' consisted of being cruel. One of my earliest memories is of the way she'd taunt me whenever the 'scissor man' was due to come. The 'scissor man' was a travelling knife grinder, who'd visit people's houses to sharpen knives and scissors.

'He's coming,' she'd tell me, 'to cut off your tongue. To cut off your tongue with his knife!'

She'd go on to expand on and intensify her attack, her descriptions becoming more and more lurid.

'He'll put his knife in your mouth,' she'd say. 'And slice right through your tongue, and it'll fall to the floor, and you'll never be able to speak again.'

She'd laugh then. 'He'll be here soon,' she'd warn, as I cringed in fear. Then she'd look out of the window. 'Is that him I can see coming?' Then she'd laugh a bit more. 'Unless,' she'd add, 'he's been held up on the way, cutting out another little girl's tongue.'

I'd be so frightened by now that I could hardly breathe. I'd run and hide, terrified I'd be sick on the floor or wet myself, and bring even more unspeakable horrors down on me. The eventual knock on the door would send me frantic, feeling trapped and defenceless and unable to think straight.

And that was the point at which she'd really laugh hard, throwing her head back in mirth and then watching my expression.

'Here he is!' she'd say, as she opened the door. 'Here he is to cut off your tongue!'

Then, as I hid behind the sofa, she'd tell the scissor man all the things she'd told me about his purpose in coming to our house. And when she passed him the knives she'd be laughing even harder. 'Which knife do you want to use?' she'd ask gleefully. 'Do you want the bigger knife, here, or the smaller, sharper one?'

My mother only ever really laughed for two reasons. When she was being disgusting – talking about wee or poo or 'blowing off', for instance – or, as with the scissor man, when she was being cruel.

But my mother wasn't just cruel on the spur of the moment;

she often seemed to want to be cruel. And the most devastating cruelty she inflicted when I was small was one that would stay with me for decades. She told me that because I'd been born on a Wednesday, I was therefore a 'Wednesday's child', and full of woe.

Just as I believed the scissor man would cut off my tongue, I absolutely truly believed this. Being born full of woe, she kept repeating, was my lot. It was used as the explanation for all of my feelings and, as a consequence, whatever feelings I had were dismissed, be they my terror of the scissor man or my fear of my father or the distress and revulsion I couldn't articulate or understand every time Grandpops tickled me. After all, went the reasoning, those feelings wouldn't have existed had I not been born on the wrong day.

For an adult who's been brought up in an atmosphere of love and care, it's obviously easy to realize such silly labelling cannot possibly matter. For me, though, as a small terrified child – *and* as an adult – it impacted on all areas of my life. I was so conditioned to believe it was a part of who I was, that it became an integral part of my being.

I hated being a Wednesday's child. I used to cry and plead with my mother for me not to be a Wednesday's child. Not to have this terrible burden to carry. To be a different child, a better one. A Monday's child, maybe – fair of face. I liked that. Or a Friday's child perhaps. If I was loving and giving like a Friday's child, then maybe my mother would love me better. I'd happily have been *any* child other than the one I'd been born. But no, I was born on a Wednesday and was woeful, and as a consequence it seemed I could never please her. I tried so hard, but it never seemed to work, and she always called me 'stupid, silly Faith'. Indeed, the only time she didn't seem indifferent to my presence was when she was telling people how stupid and silly I was. Naturally, I soon learned to play along and act in role when required. Anything was better than what I mostly had – her total indifference.

She used to remind me of my woeful status throughout my childhood; not only that I'd been born a woeful Wednesday's child, but also, wittingly or unwittingly (I didn't know which), that I was the only Wednesday's child in the whole world.

Not that the day of my birth mattered really. I had plenty to feel woeful about, whatever day of the week I'd been born, as I was about to find out.

CHAPTER 3

By the time I was four I was no longer the youngest, my mother having now produced two further children: my sister Karen – eighteen months my junior – followed by my younger brother Jack, who was now six months old. My older sister was at school, but that still left four of us at home, under five, and our house was in constant chaos.

Though externally we might have seemed like any other family, behind closed doors we were not. There was always muddle. All the rooms had dirty clothes on the floor and strewn on the furniture. There was washing on the kitchen floor and outside in the yard. My mother would sometimes throw things behind the sofa, so there seemed less of a mess before my father came home, but there was little she could do about the smell, even if she noticed – and there wasn't any evidence that she did. Mouldering food was left on crockery, next to soiled cotton nappies, which lay wherever she last changed a baby. These smelled horrible, as did all the dirty baby bottles, which had thick films of white lining their insides, where she'd added cereal to stop the babies crying.

My mother told me babies only cried for two reasons – because they needed feeding or changing. The trouble was that these two things were under her control, and she'd only attend to them when *she* decided. Most of the time, my siblings' cries went unheeded, bar her remarking they were being 'bloody little sods'.

If they persisted, and, being babies, they did, she'd sometimes pick them up and shake them to shut them up. Even as a little girl this evoked strong feelings inside me, for I knew this had been my treatment too. How she'd force food down my throat and, much as I was gagging, how grateful I'd feel I was being fed at all.

I was glad to be four now, and to be walking about. Glad not to be just lying there waiting for the sound of her footsteps, and whatever her mood meant she'd do.

Not that I had any understanding, at four, of just how appalling our lives were. I knew what I knew, and it was *all* I knew, and though much of what happened to me felt wrong – Grandpops' weekly sessions of 'tickling', for example – I persisted in the idea that this must be down to me, to my having been born so full of woe.

At that time, therefore, any moment of brightness was something I cherished, which was probably why a close friend of the family, Daniel, who was in his thirties, meant such a lot to me. Just as with Grandpops, there was never a time when Daniel was not part of it. He'd known me from babyhood and visited several times a year. As an adult, I would come to realize the horrible truth about him, about how carefully he groomed me so he could do what he wanted, but to the four-year-old me, a child desperate for attention, he was a light in the darkness of my emotionally cold world. He seemed to care for me, be interested in me, wanted to seek out my company. He seemed to love me, which made me love him.

Everyone seemed aware of Daniel's special interest in me, but no one appeared to think anything of it. I was simply his favourite, so no one thought it strange or unusual that he'd want to spend all his time with me.

I never knew much in advance when Daniel was coming. Sometimes I'd overhear my parents talking about when he was due. One day, however, I hadn't had even this prior notice, and the first I knew of his arrival was when I heard the sound of greetings coming from the front door, and him saying, 'Hello, Pamela, how are you?' to my mother.

Hearing this, I did what I always did when Daniel arrived. I ran off and hid behind the sofa. I wasn't ever really sure why I did this. I knew he'd come to find me as soon as he was able, even before my mother had made a cup of tea.

I sat on the floor, by the wall, against the back of the sofa, my legs bent and my knees clasped to my chest. The sofa was old and shabby, a big, musty-smelling brown thing, and I hid behind it, hating the anticipation, feeling 'on guard', even though I wasn't quite sure what I was guarding. It was confusing, feeling all this anxiety welling up, while at the same time there was a sense of such excitement. Despite my stress, I also wanted his attention. I knew I was important to Daniel, because his wife had always told me that I was 'the apple of his eye'.

I could hear him approaching and my sense of confusion about my anxiety increased. Why was I anxious? I *wanted* to see him – he was always so gentle and asked questions about what I'd been doing, and though I didn't answer – I always felt too shy – he didn't seem to mind at all.

Eventually, I emerged, my stomach churning, the anticipation of knowing he'd find me having become impossible to bear.

'There you are!' he said, beaming. He looked happy to have found me. 'You little minx! You've been hiding from me, haven't you?'

He was tall and thin, smartly dressed and slightly balding, with white teeth, and cotton wool in one of his ears. I liked lots about Daniel, but I didn't like the cotton wool. I never knew why it was there.

He reached towards me now, his arms outstretched, laughing as he pulled me towards him and picked me up. His face was so close I could feel his breath on my eyes as he moved to kiss my forehead and my hair. He sat down then, on the sofa, cuddling me tightly on his lap, his face close as he rubbed his cheek against mine. He was stroking my fingers, slowly, individually, while whispering: 'You little girl, why were you hiding from me? You funny little thing. You know I love you, don't you?'

When I was older, my mother told me that Daniel 'couldn't get enough' of me, and that whenever he came, he'd always ask, 'Where's that Faith?' upon which he'd pick me up and cart me off somewhere. By this time, I remember feeling rage, albeit subconsciously, at her pathetic acceptance of his behaviour. I would eventually come to realize it might be even more than that; I wondered if she secretly enjoyed the knowledge that something so disgusting was being done to someone else, just as it had been done to her all those years before – that somehow she felt a sense of sick revenge, or justice. Her own sickness, I came to understand, really was that bad.

But it wasn't just my mother who condoned his behaviour, all the adults in my life seemed complicit. It was as if by saying 'He really loves your girl, Pamela' it made what he did to me okay.

But seeing Daniel, and having Daniel give me all this attention, was at that moment the best feeling in the world. He stood up again now, and carried me out of the front door, up the road, through the field, then down a path that led towards the river. No comments had been exchanged between him and my mother; we just went out.

Daniel walked in silence till we came to the stile we always stopped at, and he sat me down on the step grown-ups would stand on if they wanted to climb over. He was now humming gently, and staring straight at me. I found it impossible to look at him, but I could feel his eyes on me. He never looked anywhere else at this point.

My feet dangled. I couldn't reach the grass below me, but he was standing next to me and I knew he wouldn't let me fall. My head was level with the top of his legs now, and he held it tight into him and began stroking my hair. He had his other arm around my shoulders and was hugging me. First tight, and then looser, and then tightly again, squeezing and unsqueezing with a rhythmical motion, and, after a bit, moving his body from side to side. As he moved, the middle part of him brushed across my face, and every so often he'd stoop a little to kiss my hair again. I didn't mind this – in fact, it felt nice; he was so gentle. The only thing that bothered me was the fabric of his trousers; the material brushing against my mouth felt all itchy.

All too soon, however, I felt anxious, the familiar anxiety I always felt at this point – a sense of 'badness' whose origins I didn't understand.

He stopped then, stood straight, and turned away from me, and when he turned back around, his hand was moving up and down on the thing I knew he would put in my mouth, even though it was too big and made me choke.

Sometimes, he'd only get it close to my mouth before stuff came out and made a big mess down my chin, but today he moved it slowly across my lips once or twice before staring straight at me as he pushed it between them.

At this point, being with Daniel no longer made me happy. Now it filled me with apprehension, fear and panic. I began to feel sick, and all wobbly and unsteady. I tried to scream – I always did – but no sound came out, and I knew I must try to open my mouth as wide as it would go. I didn't want it in my mouth but I was frightened that if I didn't let him, I'd choke on it and then I'd die. The feeling was horrible. I couldn't breathe with Daniel's thing in my mouth. I thought I would be sick and keep choking and then I'd definitely die. I knew about dying because I knew about kittens. Daddy would put them in a bag and throw them in the river and, because they couldn't breathe, they all died.

He was staring harder now, going: 'Look at me. You know I love you, don't you?' and I had to force myself to do it, because I really didn't want to. Looking at him made me feel even more afraid. But *why*? Daniel loved me and was kind to me. So why did I feel so desperate to scream and run away?

He made a sound in his mouth now, and took the thing out

of mine, holding on to it and making strange blowing sounds, before putting it back in again, more slowly this time, then keeping it very, very still.

I knew what came next because it *always* came next. He pushed it hard, suddenly – pushed it down my throat – and I was retching and retching, but terrified of biting it, as I needed to close my mouth. And then the bitter taste came, and made me retch even more, and when he took the thing out I bent down so he couldn't see, and spat the stuff into my hand. I wiped it down the sleeve of my pink jumper, because I didn't want to get it on my red tartan pinafore. I couldn't bear to eat it, but I couldn't let him see because I really didn't want to upset him. I knew I mustn't upset Daniel, because he *liked* me.

He plucked me up from the stile then, and we set off back for home, him cuddling me and telling me he loved me, but in a different, much less intense way.

Sometimes he'd take me to watch football or cricket, where the local teams played – but I didn't like being in the unfamiliar surroundings, and would be anxious to return to my mother.

Today we went back the way we'd come, and though Daniel seemed less and less interested in me as we did so, he still said 'You know I love you. You're my favourite. You're *very* special, as we made our way back to my house.

By now I didn't feel special at all. I felt all too aware he wanted to leave me, which left me sad, and feeling strange, and full of woe. I shut my eyes tightly to try to make it go away, and told myself everything was all right.

The adults barely looked up as we came in, and Daniel set me down on the red tiles. However upset I was, I at least still felt important. I'd been given special attention because I *was* special – different from my brothers and sisters.

I went back to where I'd been when he'd arrived – behind the sofa – and my mother went to make him his tea. By now, I didn't want to be around him any more, because I knew he'd start getting all anxious about leaving and saying what a long drive it was home. I also knew that once he went I'd be unable to sit still and would wander around, as if there was something missing and I was looking for it. I wouldn't find it, of course, because it was simply the anticlimax after all the excitement of his arrival.

And now he *had* gone again, and my mind was a muddle; I was relieved the bad bit of seeing him was over, but at the same time felt this great sense of loss. Daniel loved me and was happy to be with me, and I knew if I hadn't been a woeful Wednesday's child, I wouldn't be so stupid about it all.

CHAPTER 4

It would be many, many years before I would fully understand that Daniel's tenderness towards me was not an expression of love, but the conscientious grooming of a small child he wanted to abuse. All I knew, *as* a child, was that Daniel, who was so gentle, was one of the few welcome things in my life. It made no difference that I felt bad when he had me do things I didn't want to. Daniel was everything the rest of my life wasn't; he was kind, he seemed to love me, he wasn't violent. In contrast, life at home seemed very dark.

And also frightening. I cannot remember a time when I didn't spend significant periods of my day silent behind or by the side of my mother's chair. I was crippled with fear if I couldn't physically see her, afraid of what she might otherwise do to me or one of my siblings. I thought that if I could see her I could prevent this from happening, and also protect her from my father and his violence. That way, I reasoned, with my little-girl logic, neither of them would have to go to prison.

But whatever the squalid nature of my home and family – even my unhappy, dysfunctional one – it was the only thing I knew. It was no surprise therefore that when the time came for school I was absolutely terrified of leaving it.

By the time I was due to start my first day, my older sister had already painted a picture that left me feeling very fearful. The reality, however, was even worse.

That morning, at least, had started well. I was dressed in a grey pinafore and white blouse that were now too small for my older sister. Because this was a special occasion I had a pair of new white socks and black shoes that did up with buckles. I also had a new grey jumper, which my mother had knitted with wool she'd obtained by unpicking a jumper from a jumble sale. This made me feel very important. I had a jumper of my own, knitted especially for me, because I was going to school.

This was a big event, and one my mother had been warning me about for ages. 'Thank God,' she kept saying, 'that you're going to school soon and will be out of the way.' My older sister had also been telling me things. She told me I must behave and keep quiet, or else I'd be in trouble, because they wouldn't like me, and because she was the oldest. All of this sounded scary. I didn't know what form this trouble might take, but when I arrived at the gates and saw all the children in the playground it no longer mattered. All the pleasure of wearing my new grey school jumper disappeared. I just wanted to go home.

There were probably no more than sixty children – it was a village school – but to me it seemed like there were millions of them, all running around screaming. As a contrast to the dark, silent world I usually inhabited, it was more intimidating than I could ever describe.

I'd been walked there by Nan, my paternal grandmother,

having been dropped off by my father in his lorry, because the school was near her house. It was a long way from where we lived but it was the one I had to go to because it was the one my father had gone to and it had been decided.

Nan held my hand tightly and pulled me through the gate, then across the playground to my teacher. I looked down at the ground, feeling little and empty in my tummy and scared, and not wanting to see the children's faces or listen to their noise. She spoke to the teacher – she knew her because they lived close to each other – and then, suddenly, she was gone. I felt totally lost and unable to think; I simply couldn't understand what I was doing there.

My teacher was called Mrs Hope. She had glasses with semi-circular lenses stuck on the end of her nose, was stern-looking, and wore her hair in a bun. She showed me to a cloakroom which had a peg with my name written by it. I didn't want a peg with my name next to it. I wanted my mother and I burst out crying.

Everything about school made me cry that day. The classroom was so bright it blinded me. After the darkness of my home there was just so much going on. There were books, pencils, crayons, paper and building blocks everywhere. I was afraid to touch anything and felt totally overwhelmed.

I dealt with my anxiety by not speaking to anyone, either adult or child. While the other children chattered and ran around noisily, I closed in on myself, feeling completely out of my depth.

I continued like this all day. Not knowing what to say, or how to be or what to do, I just sat or stood up or put my hands together, according to what I was told. I didn't know the words to what we had to say before lunch, and I couldn't eat my lunch because I was afraid of making a mess and didn't want the other children to look at me eating. I felt clumsy and awkward and different from the other children, who all seemed to know what to do and how to do it and who I thought must think I was stupid. One of the older children put a bit of food on my plate and all I wanted to do was throw the plate at her, push over the table and run away.

When the time came for going home I was so relieved, because it felt as though I'd been there for ever. We had to put our chairs upside down on the little tables and were told to put our hands together again while Mrs Hope had us repeat words such as 'Dear Lord, thank you for keeping us safe today . . .' I didn't know who the Lord was and I didn't want to know. I'd already decided not to go again.

When I got home, having come back on a coach with my siblings, my mother didn't seem at all pleased to see me and just carried on peeling potatoes. I didn't expect a hug, because she never, ever hugged me, but I didn't think she'd even missed me at all, and I felt bewilderment, sadness and complete confusion, as if by going to school I'd lost all sense of myself, and couldn't work out where, or to whom, I belonged. I felt completely alone – expecting at any minute someone would suddenly appear and take me to where I was really supposed to be. That was reason enough not to go to school.

After the shock of my first day it took no time to confirm school was as bad as I'd imagined. This was, in large part, due to the fact that I was simply not prepared for it at all. What I realize today is that this was for obvious reasons – the only people allowed in our house were family, so I had no meaningful concept of what the outside world was like. And even had my mother been the sort who liked to socialize and hold tea parties for her children, it would still never have happened, because my father hated anyone being in the house. He'd be very aggressive and vocal about it, telling callers either to 'Piss off' or 'Fuck off' and slamming the door in their faces. The concept of having a 'friend round to play' was not something I ever thought about while my father behaved as he did.

Not that at five I had any notion of the word 'friend'. Because neither of my parents had ever shown any interest in me, I couldn't even speak properly. I didn't need to. I wasn't expected to have thoughts or opinions. I was just 'there'. On the rare occasions when my father did address me directly, it was always a scary business, fraught with stress. One Christmas, when I was small, I remember him holding out a tin of biscuits, and though I only hesitated for a second before deciding which one to take, he snatched the tin back angrily, snarling at my mother that I was an 'ungrateful little bastard' and could 'fucking go without' if what he was offering wasn't 'fucking good enough'.

I was also, as my mother liked telling everyone, 'cack-handed, left-handed and stupid'. Before school I can't remember ever having a book or pencil, and now I was expected to use such things every day, not knowing what to do with either. I didn't even know how to hold the latter in my hand, let alone how to write with it. I'd never had a book read to me, at bedtime or any other time, so when I encountered them, I used to start at the back and work backwards. When I did begin to write I was similarly confused. Being left-handed, it was natural for me to start on the right and work my way leftwards towards the middle. Straight away this reinforced just how different I felt. As did my mother. She told me, and anyone else who'd listen, she'd spoken to my teachers, and the school had informed her they couldn't teach me; they'd just have to 'leave me to sort myself out'.

Which I did try to do. But such was my panic when I was asked to copy out even the simplest words, I would make an appalling mess. Being left-handed *did* feel like a handicap. The only way I could hold a pen was with my fingers wrapped around it and as I wrote my left arm moved across the page, and the ink from the fountain pen – which every child had to use – smudged all the words I'd just written. The pages of my books were therefore covered in long blue lines and smudges, leaving my writing unrecognizable. The side of my left hand was always stained blue as well, and this would often end up down my face, and on my clothes.

It may well be that the school understood my difficulties as a left-hander – a significant minority of people are left-handed, after all – and, perhaps, had my family been like other families, it wouldn't have mattered very much. But I hated being left-handed. For me, it was yet another visible and humiliating reminder of how useless I was.

My sense of terror at being made to go to school – and therefore parted from my mother – did not diminish. I was in a constant state of anxiety about being away from home, and had been from my earliest years. I couldn't bear my mother being out of my sight, let alone having to leave the house without her. The enforced separation filled me with intense fear, reinforced, as it was daily, by her indifference to where I'd been, what I'd done, who I'd met, how I'd fared. I really thought if I went to school, that one day I would not have a home to return to. This thought, which was present throughout my childhood, caused me a sense of extreme dread. I thought I'd disappear, not be missed, and be replaced by another child without anyone even noticing I'd gone.

As a consequence, every morning I'd cry uncontrollably, filled with the most awful apprehension. Often I would run away, down the road, and hide behind the telephone box. If I breathed in, I could just about wedge myself into the space behind it and the wall and although it was dark, dirty, spidery and wet, I didn't care. It was from here that my father would drag me out and pull me along the road to his lorry, all the time shouting over his shoulder at my mother, 'I haven't fucking got time for this, the little bastard, fucking hell!' He'd then open the door, drop me inside the lorry and slam the door shut, while my mother stood on the door-step saying nothing. By the time my father had climbed into the driver's seat she would have already gone back in.

He'd always make sure he locked the cab door. If he didn't I'd try to climb out and run away again. He'd then drive the three miles to school in silence, while I sobbed, often picking up Mrs Hope if she happened to be walking as we passed. If she joined us, he'd immediately become someone else; charming, quietly spoken, laughing. The contrast was extreme. He was a completely different person, who didn't swear. But I was so used to his behaviour changing I didn't think to question it. I just thought that must be how all people were, and that his behaviour towards me must be my fault.

Once at school the routine never varied. He'd throw me over his shoulder again, and walk laughing across the playground, while all the children stopped running about to stare at me. Once I'd reached the classroom, and he'd deposited me, the children stopped staring and resumed their running around, as if nothing had happened. This behaviour seemed not in the least strange. I'd been told for so long I was silly, stupid Faith – why wouldn't they think I was?

Because we were poor we didn't have to pay for school dinners, so when the dinner register was called and the children had to pay their money, my name, of course, was never called. I felt the humiliation of this keenly. I always thought the other children would realize my name hadn't been called and that I was having a dinner I hadn't paid for.

Differences such as this were piling up. At dinner time I began to notice the children around me were fussy about food and left vast amounts on their plates. I desperately wanted to be like them, but I was always hungry, and grateful to have nice food to eat, that I couldn't ever help but eat it all. I ate very slowly though, hoping no one would notice. I couldn't bear the thought of them watching me eating. I didn't have any likes and dislikes; the concept didn't exist for me – but after the meal all pleasure in it was replaced by always feeling greedy and bad. Later I realized this was because I wasn't supposed to have any needs, even hunger.

My sense of difference grew at the same rate I did. The school was in a middle-class area, and many of the children attending were from nice, well-off families. Having nothing to offer and never feeling good enough, my behaviour was submissive from the start, and, having picked up on this, several children bullied me.

Looking back, it seems obvious my appearance didn't help. My hair was dull and untidy-looking, because it was washed with cheap washing-up liquid, proper shampoo being too expensive. And because the water at home was cold, it was hard to rinse out, plus there was only one hairbrush. Toothpaste was also too expensive so my teeth were discoloured. The only thing to clean them with was a saucerful of salt that my mother would put by the kitchen sink for us to use. It was brown most of the time – I didn't know why. Did salt go rusty? I usually had to force myself to use it because the taste of it made me retch and retch.

But, for all that, my appearance wasn't the main problem. For all the privations, I still looked tidy and clean – especially if the school photographer was coming, when I'd be kitted out in the best clothes possible. It was clear I'd come from a large, poor family – my clothes and shoes were sometimes too big, or too small – but practically, in terms of kitting us out well when she needed to, my mother could often be industrious. At such times, she'd sew and darn, knit and crochet, and there were always huge piles of clothes on the floor by her chair that she was going to mend at some point. There were also boxes and boxes of knitting patterns and needles, plus half-knitted teddies and dolls' clothes. There were piles of clothes from jumble sales and heaps of old knitted jumpers, waiting for her to unpick them.

But very little ever got finished. It was as if she lacked whatever it was she needed to see most of these tasks through and was simply stuck in this endless cycle of starting. She'd also, at such times, make piles of cakes. Many more than could ever be eaten.

Some things, however, did get done. During these phases she'd always, it seemed, knit pink cardigans, in several sizes, to be handed down to each daughter in turn. My younger sister, therefore, spent a large part of her time in a pink cardigan, and looked as if she'd worn the same one for many years.

But my physical difference was nothing compared with my emotional one – the one those in authority couldn't so easily see, which is perhaps why no one ever picked up on it. Had I turned up in rags, perhaps they would have. As it was, internally, whatever the clothes I was in, I was not at all like any of the other children at school. I was very withdrawn – today, the word 'depressed' might be used – and terrified of saying anything wrong in case it ended in a situation where I wouldn't be able to stick up for myself and so end up getting hurt. I also feared people would either laugh at or ignore me, which they often did, both at school and home. After all, what could I have to say that anyone would want to listen to?

I didn't have friends because I didn't know how to make any, and no one asked me, and I would have to make up things when we were all asked to share our news, and everyone else talked of days out and holidays – things that were completely alien.

They also talked of parties – another alien concept – and the girls in my class seemed to have them all the time. As a party date drew near, they'd talk excitedly about what they would wear and what present they were getting and I'd long to be included, to be noticed. To be accepted by someone. To be *seen*. I'd stand there, thinking sadly, 'What about me?' and wish and wish my real family were not my family – that I belonged to a family who were happy and had parties, and one day I'd wake up and my life had all been a dream. That I was really a little girl from a happy, loving family, who'd let me have parties and invite all my friends.

So ignorant was I in such matters I didn't even understand how being invited worked. One day, in the playground, when I was older – about nine – I saw a girl called Joan, who was in my class, discard an envelope. I gave it back to her, unsure if she'd really meant to drop it, and she explained she didn't want it because it was an invitation to a birthday party from a girl she no longer liked. She told me I could have it, and I couldn't believe my luck because I couldn't understand anyone ever throwing away a party invitation.

I carefully filled in the section where you had to say if you could go and gave it to Jenny, the girl whose party it was. She looked puzzled, and just stared at me, so I explained what had happened, and that Joan had said I could go in her place. Looking back, I feel such sorrow for my nine-year-old self, but at the time I'd no sense this wasn't how things worked. Of course, Jenny, and her mother, probably stunned by my lack of social grace, agreed I could go to the party. Which meant I had something to look forward to, like all the other girls, but also that I failed to learn anything of use. I subsequently didn't understand that that *wasn't* how things happened, and remember following another girl's mother (she worked there) around the school, letting her know I could go to her daughter Linda's party. I only understood after Linda's friends kept on telling me that no, I *couldn't go*, because I hadn't been invited. This hadn't registered with me at all. Not, that was, until Linda's mother approached me, and explained gently that Linda didn't want me at her party, which meant she was sorry, but I couldn't go. Not going was obviously upsetting, but knowing I wasn't welcome was so much more so.

But in some ways, looking back, it wasn't such a bad thing. There was one girl, Anne, to whom I'll always be grateful, who, alone among her friends, invited me to her party, all through primary school. This once-a-year event was both a pleasure and a torture, so much so that sometimes I was sick and couldn't go. I was socially inept, paralysed by anxiety, and so overwhelmed by being in a home so unlike mine, that seeing their laughter and friendliness actually made me want to cry. Looking back, I was a wreck; so distressed and sad, always just sitting, watching, unable to join in. I wonder now if anyone noticed my distress, or did I just about pull it off? I'll never know.

What I did know was the shadow that hung over being invited to Anne's birthday parties was that I'd never be able to reciprocate and invite her to mine. No one was welcome in our house.

CHAPTER 5

No one, that was, except more babies. Since starting school, and feeling so alone, I'd become particularly sensitive to my mother's disappearances. When she went away for long periods, I became desperate – walking from room to room, looking for her, as if she would miraculously appear if I looked for long enough. I couldn't understand where she was when she went away, because she used to just disappear without explanation. I'd go to sleep, or to school, and she'd be there, and then I'd wake, or come home, and she'd be gone. I'd then spend long periods, day and night (I couldn't sleep), sitting in my bed with my back against the wall, just staring, completely still and silent.

The thought of being in the house with just my father was unbearable, even with an aunt coming to look after us while he was at work. And though my mother not being there meant a brief respite from Grandpops, I would rather have endured that than not see her. When home from school, I counted every minute my mother was away and every minute felt like an hour, but when she eventually returned, generally with lots of commotion, she didn't acknowledge me in any way.

A few months after I started school, and my mother returned from yet another disappearance, she was brought in on a stretcher by some ambulance men. By now I'd come to realize that her longer disappearances often ended with her bringing home a baby. She had one with her now, and she was laughing and joking with the men who were carrying the stretcher. I watched them come in, and all I could think of was how much I hated the baby, for stealing her away from me. Adam was born just after my fifth birthday, two years after my brother Jack. My mother's sixth pregnancy had been particularly awful, and when my new brother came along, it was clear he had suffered as well. He was born physically damaged, with one badly deformed leg, which apparently would never, ever grow.

My mother talked more about Adam's disability than I'd ever known her talk about anything. It was almost as if it made her feel important, and she'd sit him in his huge pram in the centre of the living room as if he was a circus attraction. He was all at once the centre of attention and even more neglected than the rest of us. Though on permanent display, strapped in, immobile, he was, for most of the time, ignored by her. He would put his hand in his nappy and eat his own poo, and laugh, and I couldn't understand why he'd do that. Was it because he was hungry or because he was bored? And why did my mother always laugh when he did it and then just leave him and his pram smeared in poo?

She always referred to him as 'Adam who is crippled', and seemed to have decided because of his physical disability he'd never be able to achieve anything. She'd laugh at him as if he had something wrong with his brain too, even though nobody knew that. Once Adam was born the rest of us got even less attention than before. In order to get some, I'd make it my business to deal with his endless dirty nappies. I hated doing it all the time, but it was better than doing nothing; at least it made me feel I was useful.

My mother would never let me help her with Adam in any other way, and secretly I was relieved. Deep down, I didn't like him and wished him dead. I was frightened of him and only too happy to leave her to it; because nothing had ever been explained about what was wrong with him, I was terrified to touch him, because I thought I might catch whatever it was he had, and end up a spectacle, like he was. Even so, there was a part of me that envied him, because though the 'attention' she gave him was mostly talking about him to other people and laughing, it was attention even so, and I craved it. It didn't help that every day I was made to go to school. I was sure she'd soon forget me altogether.

My father, of course, was completely uninterested in Adam, just the same as he was about the rest of us. My nan, however, was incensed.

'Breeding like rabbits, the pair of you!' I remember her shouting at my mother one day. 'Couldn't stop, could you? Not until you'd brought a cripple into the family!'

Though she did have a point about that, she was wrong. My mother, my father, Grandpops, Daniel. Did I but know it, we were a crippled family already.

Not that anyone in the outside world knew. As well as my father's policy on visitors – no one was entertained by him willingly, *ever* – my mother, I realized, was as good at pretending to be a model mother and homemaker as she was bad at both activities behind closed doors.

Periodically, she'd take her growing brood out, and it was very stressful. Going out meant looking and acting our very best, so that everyone my mother knew could see how well she was doing. And my mother, having lived in the area all her life, knew lots of people.

She'd always dress up for these trips. Red lipstick, rouge, her long black hair carefully brushed. She'd also take great care over her children's appearance – particularly the girls. My sisters and I would be identically dressed – often, when we were small, in pink-and white-striped dresses with silver stars on them, and the matching pink cardigans that would almost become heirlooms. It felt strange being trussed up so neatly in this way – such a contrast to the squalor indoors. She'd take a flannel and then scrub all the bits that showed – our hands and our faces and our knees.

Once satisfied that we'd not embarrass her visually, at least, she'd warn us about our behaviour. She always said the same thing; if she had to speak to any of us more than once about anything, then as soon as we were home we'd be hit – hard.

We'd set off then, and my mother became someone else. People would regularly stop her on the street. 'Oh, Pamela,' they'd say, 'they all look so nice. I don't know how you do it. They are *so* well behaved!' And she'd laugh, her tone of voice very different from usual, brushing aside the compliments but obviously loving them. Inevitably, she'd have to reprimand one of us about something, and, once home, the charade would be over.

She'd then begin slapping and, much of the time, the main recipient was my poor younger sister. I was far too shy to do anything when out that would cause her to reprimand me. From when my sister was only about four my mother would slap her repeatedly, all over her bare arms and legs, only avoiding her head, as she always said hitting her head could cause brain damage. I could never bear to watch. I felt the slaps almost as if it were my own legs being hit, and wanted to scream at her to stop, but nothing ever came out of my mouth. My sister would go from happy and smiling to disbelief and misery in an instant. We'd then have to change back into our dirty, scruffy clothes while my mother went to make a cup of tea. She'd be humming to herself as she did so as well. As if the pain she'd just inflicted meant nothing. Almost as if it had never happened.

I hated going out of the house, full stop, but particularly going out with my mother. I was extremely timid and used to try to hide behind her but, for some reason, she always seemed to want to draw attention to me, pulling me out from behind her and pushing me in front, particularly in front of the men she used to talk to in the village. They'd be standing in their gardens and she'd always stop to chat, laughing and apparently enjoying all their banter and suggestive comments.

As I got older, I hated it even more. Particularly the men who bent down and put their faces close to mine, putting their fingers on my chin and saying: 'You're a little beauty. You'll break a few hearts when you're older, you will.'

I never understood my mother's behaviour around these men.

It felt all wrong. It made me feel horrible and upset. I found the men scary, intimidating, threatening.

I also hated that she used to make me lie. Where at home she mostly seemed not to register my existence, when we were out anywhere, or in company, or visiting relatives, she'd make me sit beside her and tell stories. She was insistent I tell everyone I'd seen Father Christmas, and explain in graphic detail what he'd looked like and said. I'd never seen Father Christmas and I knew everybody knew that, but she'd keep on and on. I could never understand why she'd do that. Up until the age of eleven she insisted he existed, and expected me to believe too – and the sad thing is, I did. I must have sounded so ridiculous.

She'd also tell everyone I had a friend who was a blue elephant, and make me describe him to people in great detail. Why would she do that? I couldn't understand it at all. Why did she want to make me feel and sound so stupid? Why did she want to be so unkind?

A long time later – *decades* later – I'd have an answer of sorts, but for many years I would find it completely unfathomable. It must have been me, I thought. It just must have been *me*.

CHAPTER 6

In the winter of 1961, when I was six, we moved to a larger house, a mile away. The new house was up a lane on the side of the main road. The move happened because my father's boss had been able to lease the house from the wealthy landowner, after a long lease to an old family had come to an end.

The move hadn't looked too auspicious to start with. When my parents first went to see the house it was undergoing modernization, and looked more like a building site than a home. But by the time we arrived all the work had been completed and it looked, to me – used to the squalor of our current house – like nothing I'd ever seen before.

It was a large semi, constructed out of sandy yellow stone, and set among fields at the bottom of hills. Situated at the end of the lane, on its own, it was next to an apple orchard with pigs in and a stream running through. There were cows and horses in the neighbouring fields and a farm and further cottages at the top of the lane.

Inside it was spacious, with three bedrooms instead of two, which meant one for me and my sisters, one for my brothers, and another for my parents and Adam. And though there was still no heating, it had a sitting-room fire, plus a Rayburn in the kitchen to heat water and keep us warm, and, best of all, it had a bathroom.

Looking back I suppose I had grand ideas about how my life would be from that point on. I think we all did – we were terribly excited, and when the day came to move we were all falling over ourselves to help, running up and down the tailboard of my father's lorry, bearing boxes. Even he seemed happy that day. Certainly, for once, he wasn't shouting.

Though some of the boxes my mother had mindlessly filled would be destined to remain in the loft for all time, I unpacked in a flurry of excitement, the lovely smell of fresh paint everywhere, our few possessions looking lost in the large empty rooms. Here, or so I thought, life would be different. All the mess and the stuff and filth was all gone – never, I hoped naively, to return.

But it was the bathroom that most equalled happiness. My mother, for a short time, would bathe my siblings and me in it and I loved it. The frequency of this activity soon diminished, however, and before long it only happened rarely. Usually I bathed myself, and had clean school clothes once a week, and the rest of the time the bath was left filthy, with spiders running around in it. If not empty, it was used mostly to soak dirty washing, which would sit there, cold and scummy, for days. The lone slimy flannel would be chucked over the side of the bath or the basin, reeking of my father's shaving cream. The same couple of towels used by everyone were so filthy and rank they were hard.

Our family now also started growing. My mother's big ginger

cat, called Winston, came with us, and straight after we moved in, given the big garden, my father began bringing other animals home. Rabbits, guinea pigs, chickens and a cockerel, which he picked up in the markets where he drove livestock.

Grandpops, too, visited regularly. He'd catch the bus from his house, often twice a week now, to go to the pub and the bookies and to pay us a visit, never forgetting, as well as bags of vegetables for my mother, to seek me out and 'tickle' me (and probably my sisters), just as long as my father wasn't around.

Indeed, our new home was soon every bit as unclean as the last one, and every bit as unhappy.

But even greater unhappiness loomed. Towards the end of that year Adam fell seriously ill with pneumonia. As the youngest of a poor family with six children, his start in life hadn't been promising. But with his disability and the fact that he'd been born into *our* family, he couldn't have had a worse start.

He was taken to the General Hospital, in the next town. When I came home from school one day he was gone and very soon I felt afraid. I'd hated Adam since his birth, for taking my mother away from me – despite the fact that she looked after him so poorly and erratically, he nevertheless got what little attention she could muster – and now I felt worried this might be my fault. What had she done to him? Why was he in hospital? Why was my mother spending all her time with him while I was sent to school 'out of the way'?

By the time he'd been in hospital for a couple of days, these thoughts were going round and round in my head. I was standing outside school one afternoon, waiting for the coach home, and all I could wonder was what had he *done* to make her be with him and not me all the time? I wandered over to the edge of the playground, preoccupied, and suddenly saw movement within the hedge. I instantly felt afraid and jumped backwards. Was it a snake? I was always thinking someone or something was going to get me and in my mind it was often a snake. Then I remembered the terrifying stories my mother used to tell me about snakes, and how, if you walked on the common without looking, you might be bitten and die. There was an element of truth in this. Adders were common in our part of the world, particularly *on* the common, which was sandy, and only five minutes from school.

I started picking up stones and throwing them into the hedge, and before I knew it I was shouting, 'I've just seen a snake! I've just seen a snake!' hoping someone would hear me. In my mind the snake was huge, and slithering towards me, and was going to jump out and bite me or curl around my leg, so tightly I wouldn't be able to get it off. I edged back further and stepped on a big unsteady stone, which unbalanced me and sent me tripping into the hedge, and made me fall onto another stone – one sharp enough to cut the skin on my shin. On inspection, it was red, with two distinct grazes. It had just started bleeding, and for a moment I thought a snake really had bitten me, and then a story took root in my head. I decided to pretend I'd been bitten by a snake so my mother would worry, come home from hospital, and bring Adam with her.

The coach arrived then and, my story now up and running, I limped towards it slowly, also making sure when I sat down I rested my injured leg, which was really hurting now, across the seat.

It was pouring with rain that day and, once we'd arrived in the village, the local farmer's wife, who'd driven to the coach stop to pick her sons up, offered to take me and my siblings as well – we could then walk on home from her farm. It was to her that I first ventured to announce what had 'happened', but she just said 'Oh, yes', unimpressed, and drove on. She'd later call round to apologize to my mother for not believing me, but for now it seemed my plan hadn't worked.

Nevertheless, I persisted, and when I got home and told my mother she reacted as if it was her worst nightmare. Which it probably was. She'd only just returned from seeing one sick child in hospital and now she'd another potentially fatally ill. She looked tired and sad but all I could think of was how angry I was at her for spending time with Adam, and not with me, and so I reasoned that it served her right.

She immediately called for an ambulance, which was dispatched from the local cottage hospital. I was amazed and frightened at how quickly things had started happening – I had no idea my mother would call for an ambulance, but now she had how could I tell the truth? I knew I'd be in real trouble. It seemed like only minutes before there was an ambulance lady standing over me, taking my pulse.

I was then rushed, with my mother, to the General Hospital, and put into a bed close to where Adam was sleeping under an oxygen tent in a little cubicle.

A snake bite in Britain, then as now, was a rare event, and the hospital had no supplies of serum. It was necessary therefore for them to have some sent down from the city, and this, being an emergency, was done by helicopter.

I wasn't feeling very guilty for fibbing about the bite now, because not only was my mother with me, but I thought I could see Adam as well. I was, however, frustrated at the time they were taking – how stupid were these adults to believe me? I just wanted them to go so I could go and see Adam. If I could just see him I was sure I could take both my mother and him home.

The doctors who examined me were convinced by my wound though, and pointed out where they thought the snake's fangs had gone in. As a consequence they were confused by my complete lack of symptoms. In the end they concluded this must have been because most of the venom had already come out. They decided, therefore, not to use the serum after all, but to keep me in for observation.

As a consequence I was in hospital for a couple of days, next to my little brother. I crept out of bed before I went to sleep, and as soon as I woke up in the morning, to check he was okay. I was very frightened the first time, as I walked slowly towards the cubicle; frightened of getting told off for being out of bed, frightened of being told off for looking at Adam and frightened of what I might see. One night I checked on him as usual, at bedtime, and was therefore shocked on arriving at his bedside the next morning to find the cubicle was empty.

Adam had in fact been moved to another hospital and this was the same hospital where he then died. All I knew for sure, however, was that he'd vanished from his bed, and I was completely distraught. I was convinced he had simply disappeared and nobody would know where he'd gone.

I was discharged the same day and his name wasn't mentioned, and I was too terrified to ask. By the time my mother told me he'd died, two days later, I was so hysterical and out of control I burst out laughing and couldn't seem to stop. When he was alive I'd watched my mother with him and wished him dead, and now he *was* dead, I believed I'd killed him. To feel I had such power was a very frightening thing, as was the guilt I felt for having slept through that night; had I stayed awake, I felt sure I could have saved him. I had a lot of anger for him too. How dare he escape from the family and leave me in it. *I* was the bad one. It should have been me.

My mother only made one comment: as Adam was crippled he 'would have spent all his life in a wheelchair anyway', and that was that. I was not asked if I wanted to attend the funeral.

After that, it was almost as if he'd never been alive. My mother and father never referred to him again in my hearing, and there were no tears, no discussions, no family conversations or recollections involving him. His toys and clothes just disappeared as if he'd never even lived with us, and no explanations were given to me about anything. There was nothing at all, either physical or emotional, to indicate he'd ever existed. I was not taken to see or put flowers on his grave, and I'd no idea the business of dying meant someone was no longer alive.

In the midst of this emotional abyss, I felt terrified. Was it me next? By now I was seven. When would *I* die? I also didn't understand the process of death and felt a powerful anxiety for my little brother. What would Adam eat and drink and who'd give it to him? He couldn't go and get it, because he had a bad leg, and couldn't walk. And, anyway, how would someone who was dead even know what it was he liked to eat and drink?

At school they'd said dead children went to heaven, to live with God, and that heaven was up in the sky. I looked up to see if I could see him in the sky, with God, but I couldn't. Was he going past, looking for us? In any case, how would he get into the sky when he was now lying in the ground? I decided my mother must have really hated him to have left him all alone and put dirt on top of him, so he couldn't breathe. He must be scared of the noise of the wind when it blew, and cold too, because he was buried outdoors. And what about his coat? Did he have his coat? And what if it rained? Would he get wet? Would he be afraid of the dark?

I couldn't stop wondering how he must have felt, being buried. Did he watch as the spadefuls of earth fell on top of him? Did he hold his breath, terrified, as everything disappeared from sight? I was desperate to run away; to go and see if I could find him, but at the same time I was too scared to actually do it, because I worried it might be that if I got too near to him, the same thing would happen to me.

I made a promise to him instead. *I will think of you every single day for the rest of my life and never forgive myself. Every time I eat or drink some will be for you, and I will not fall asleep again, ever.* I ended it by saying how sorry I was, how I never meant for this to happen, and how much I hoped he could forgive me.

Years later, when I was ten, I learned that every Christmas after Adam's death, my mother would go to the churchyard, where he's buried, in a grave next to her own mother's. Here she'd lay a wreath, but this act of remembrance wasn't shared with me. It was only at the Christmas before my eleventh birthday I plucked up the courage to go and see his grave, but I still couldn't accept he was never coming back. That he was truly gone, in the absence of anyone speaking to me about it, had become something I simply refused to face.

Did my mother wish to spare me? Exclude me from her grief? Have me just forget and move on? Whatever the reason, my brother's death was the endpoint, and – for me, anyway – a start. The start of the feeling that it should have been me and not him – a feeling that has persisted all my life.

CHAPTER 7

Just the same as any other young child, I never questioned why my family behaved as they did, or tried to work out what might drive them to do so. Though school had taught me we were different, and in a thousand depressing ways, it would be way into adulthood before the wretched truth dawned. As a child I just accepted that difference, and spent much more time dissecting the way it made me *feel*, as a consequence of having been born 'full of woe'.

That my life *was* full of woe was without doubt – even though I still didn't really understand why. Yes, it was clear that my father's violent temper was frightening, and also that my mother's indifference to me really hurt, but I had no understanding that Grandpops' horrible manhandling – endlessly, week after week, throughout my childhood – was wrong. And I didn't feel anything but gratitude towards Daniel, despite his 'love' for me involving me having to do such revolting things for him every single time he came to visit.

No wonder I had turned into such a sad, unhappy child.

But some things are universal among children, however grim

their lives, and the excitement of Christmas was one of them. Just like any other child, I grew excited in December, swept up by the air of festivity in school, the making of decorations, the singing of carols, the expectation of presents if we were good. Despite my continuing isolation and my awkward, unhappy state, even I couldn't help hoping for happiness at Christmas, despite experience so often telling me otherwise, particularly where my nan was concerned.

Nan was a powerful influence in my life, and her malevolence towards me was as unexplained as it was relentless. My father's mother was the polar opposite of my own; where my mother was neglectful, erratic and unstable, Nan was fiercely controlling, judgemental and strict. The only trait they seemed to share – apart from their mutual dislike – was that both, though complete opposites temperamentally, could be cruel.

With extremely short straight hair cut above her ears, Nan was small and stocky. She lived quite close to us throughout my childhood. And frightened me in the same way my father did, in some ways more, because she frightened *him* too, and my mother said he never made a decision about anything without first obtaining her say-so. The only decision, it seemed, he *had* made without her, was to marry my mother.

Nan was married to a man we all knew as Grandad, though my father, in fact, wasn't his son. He'd come into Nan's life when my father was two years old, the child of a man who, even on her deathbed, Nan never identified. All we eventually knew was that, when she was a teenager, she'd had a crush on an older, married, factory owner, who disowned her as soon as she fell pregnant with my father and was never seen again. The only reason my father knew Grandad wasn't his dad was because my nan's sister insisted, at the time of my father's fourteenth birthday, he needed to know, if not who his real father was, at least that he wasn't Grandad's biological son, in case he wanted to get a passport or get married, and needed his birth certificate.

There's little doubt Nan's difficult upbringing contributed to the woman she went on to become. Her mother died when she was about seven and her father, an alcoholic and a womanizer, quickly remarried and had more children. Her maternal grandmother, fearing for her granddaughter's welfare – she was apparently both disturbed and 'sickly' – took her to live with her in order to bring her up away from her siblings. This meant there was an even greater distance between them, and when she visited her father they teased her mercilessly. When the second wife died, her father married a third time, and Nan ended up in a large family of siblings and half-siblings. It's unsurprising she fell pregnant and wished to escape, or that in later life she became so controlling and fierce – the antithesis of the sickly little motherless girl, as well as the wayward teenager with an illegitimate child.

But whatever the reasons for her nature, all I knew was she frightened me and had done for as long as I could remember. Which wasn't surprising. Some of my earliest memories of her, sketchy though they are, are of her treating me with aggressive indifference. She looked after us for my mother on a regular basis, both coming to the house to help out – or take over – and at her own house, when my own mother couldn't look after us because she was ill or working, or having another baby.

Nan had her own ideas about how best to deal with toddlers

and babies, and would put me in a drawer to sleep. But not just in an open drawer, taken from a dresser – one that was still *in* there, which she would also close. It was a big old heavy chest and a big old heavy drawer, and the force required to close it meant it shut with a jolt, and sawdust would fall into my eyes and mouth, compounding my sense of panic and the terrifying realization I was trapped and might be shut in there for ages.

She also, when my mother was in hospital giving birth to my sister, took it upon herself to 'potty train' me – though no potties, it appears, were involved. I was seventeen months old, and this fact came to light only many years later, via letters I found – Nan had presumably written to her in hospital. It certainly added substance to the terrifying early memories I had of wetting myself on the path in her garden, and her yanking me across the concrete, marching me angrily to the outside toilet, and then shutting me in behind what felt like the most enormous wooden door. My screams fell on deaf ears, I couldn't reach the handle, and I didn't understand what I'd done wrong. I just felt this terrible sense of not knowing how to be a good girl, and sobbed, confused and upset.

Despite her rigorous attention to the goings-on in our house, she seemed, at the same time, not to like us. She did give me some positive experiences and parenting, yet, as I grew older, it always felt more a point-scoring exercise – to show how much better than my mother she was at mothering – than out of any feelings of love.

Indeed, apart from my older sister, her first grandchild – and a girl – it seemed that none of us meant anything to her, and especially not me or my younger sister. Indeed, most of the time, she seemed to view us with distaste, as the urchins of the bastard son she'd conceived by accident with a feckless man, and – to make matters worse – who'd grown up to marry a woman she considered unfit to be a mother. No wonder she thought the family to be in need of her aggressive interventions.

My mother would happily, for the most part, accept these. Only occasionally would she show any spark of anger or rebellion, like the occasion when my nan, looking after me one time, decided to cut off all my hair. My mother was incensed – a rare moment of maternal anger – because she thought, and said angrily, Nan had done it out of spite, to try to make me look like a boy. Nan had always wanted a little girl of her own, and to my mother's mind, she cut my hair because she was jealous of my mother having daughters.

I found this knowledge terribly upsetting. Nan would often come round and say to my mother, 'I'll take Faith home, out of your way.' I hated this feeling of being 'in the way' and didn't know what I could do so I would not be. My mother certainly acted as if I was in the way most of the time, and I'd rush around trying to be as helpful as I could so that I wouldn't be, and there'd be no reason for her to let Nan have me.

I'd often hide for ages when Nan came round, because I knew if she couldn't find me she'd have to leave without me or she'd miss her bus. Sometimes, however, I didn't have a choice, and would be packed off on the bus to stay with her.

Once there, the routine was always the same. I'd be run a warm bath with bubbles, to stop the bath getting dirty, and ordered to take off my clothes. These she'd kick into the corner of the bathroom, while she screwed up her face in revulsion. I

hated that she kicked my clothes in the corner like that, treating
them as if they were just filthy rubbish. She'd then scrub me
and scrub me, all the time telling me how dirty I was. She'd
do the same with my hair, shampooing it over and over, telling
me again how filthy my hair was, how filthy my mother was,
and how disgusting it was for her to have had so many children. She'd also pass comment on Grandpops' home, and my
other grandmother, who wasn't even alive still. 'Disgusting,'
she'd say. 'Never seen anything like it. And to think your dad
wanted to marry into that! He wasn't brought up like that, we
were different from that. I don't know what was wrong with
him.' By the time I was allowed to climb out, I was clean on the
outside, but felt dirty on the inside. Much dirtier and ashamed
than when I'd climbed in.

After scrubbing the bath to 'get rid of all the dirt', Nan would
don rubber gloves, pour disinfectant into the water and wash my
clothes. Once again, she'd talk to me throughout the operation,
commenting again on how filthy they were, and pointing out,
once she'd scrubbed them, her nose wrinkled up, 'No other
washing can go in *that* water.'

But staying at Nan's had its good aspects too. Bedtime was
lovely – the direct opposite of home – because the bed had
clean sheets, which were wonderful to sleep in, and I had a torch
under the pillow so I could see in the dark. Breakfast, too, was
like no breakfast I ever had at home. I'd sit and watch while she
buttered the end of a whole loaf, then cut a thick slice to go with
my boiled egg. Having breakfast made for me, served to me, *given*
to me, was such a novel thing to happen.

Yet for all the concern she seemed to show for my well-being,

Nan was really no different from either of my parents, in that she seemed to offer not the smallest shred of affection. No different from my parents in that she didn't hug or cuddle me; no different from my parents in that she almost always made me feel unwanted and unloved. And no more so did she do this than at Christmas.

Despite the squalor and unhappiness around me, the Christmases of my childhood probably differed little, in many small ways, from the Christmases in most homes at that time. Though rooms were full to bursting with rubbish, we still had lots of pretty paper garlands and balloons. We also had a tree, and it was usually enormous, causing my father to swear and swear as he carried it in and set it up. None of us was allowed to help with the decorations – if we so much as touched a bauble we'd be angrily chastised. It was his job, and his alone, and we were only allowed to watch.

But Christmas Day was also the one day in the year when my mother would put out bowls of sweets and nuts and fruit, and let us help ourselves. The point would usually arrive when my father thought we were being greedy, and start swearing, but for a brief time we could behave the way other families did and feel Christmassy and jolly and have fun.

The night before Christmas, on every year I could remember, my father would take all the bulbs out of the upstairs lights, in order that we wouldn't see Father Christmas arrive, or open our stockings (his old socks) until he said so. It was scary, but if we so much as squeaked, we were told, he'd fill up our stockings with coal.

As it was, come morning, I realized I'd obviously managed to drop off, because I could see he'd been and all would be well and we'd have a happy time on Christmas Day.

I'd open my stocking to find a great hoard: a packet of tissues, a toothbrush and some toothpaste – a truly wonderful treat – plus a pencil with a rubber on the end, a small diary, some chocolate coins, a satsuma and some nuts. My main present, when I was eight, I remember, was a blue toy typewriter, with its own ink and paper, which filled me with joy.

We were all so grateful for our presents, but just in case we weren't, our parents told us straight away they'd all been bought 'on tick' and now they must start over again, borrowing for next year's. As long as we looked grateful enough, my father wouldn't swear, and we'd all sit down to Christmas lunch happy.

Grandpops would be there, drinking port and lemon with my parents and, as at every other time, finding opportunities to seek me out and 'tickle' me (and, I suspect, my sisters). But though he'd corner me upstairs when he went to the bathroom, at least for periods in the day, the presence of my father meant I had some time mostly unmolested.

There'd be turkey, and a pork joint, and boiled potatoes and Brussels sprouts, and for afters we'd have jelly and fruit – not Christmas pudding, as my father didn't like it. I loved Christmas dinner, and looked forward to it greatly. I just wished we could all sit together round a table instead of having to eat it on our laps in different places, because every room and surface was so covered in junk – dirty clothes, ironing, knitting, ornaments, vases full of bits of paper, coins and smaller ornaments, stacked-up crockery, pictures, mirrors, newspapers, shoes, coats, toys and baby stuff.

After lunch, because this was the one day my father wasn't at work, he'd wash up – us children would dry – while my mother and Pops went and sat in the sitting room. We'd then all sit quietly while the grown-ups listened to the Queen's speech, and then Nan and Grandad would arrive, laden down with presents for us.

It was my father who, stationed on the floor, by the tree, always took charge of handing out presents. This, in itself, caused me anxiety. If you didn't show enough gratitude, or opened it too fast, or, worst of all, made eye contact with him having committed either sin, he'd quickly fly into a rage.

On one particular Christmas, when I was around eight, the present he passed me from Nan was long and quite heavy, and I felt a big surge of anticipation. I wanted to rip off the paper as fast as I could, but, aware of the rules, I peeled it slowly and carefully, to eventually reveal a box covered in brightly coloured crêpe paper. I remember feeling pleased that Nan had gone to so much trouble to even paper the lid of the box. I also real-ized it was a shoebox, and my excitement began to mount, as I wondered what type of shoes she might have chosen. I opened it – now anxious to get them out and try them on – to find a wodge of pink tissue inside. I began to part it, now concerned that there seemed to be nothing in there, but then spied some-thing in the corner and got my hand around it. And then I saw it. It was a small tin of prunes. I glanced at her then, and, as she caught my eye, she smiled. She said sweetly, 'I thought you'd like those.' Anxious not to cause a scene, and get into trouble, I began picking up bits of ripped wrapping paper, keeping my head down, to hide the tears that threatened. 'Thank you,' I said politely, as I knew I must. 'I do like them.' It was only later, when I felt it was safe to do so, that I left the room, to cry hot tears of distress.

Of all the things that have confused me, looking back on my young life, Nan's treatment of me at Christmas remains inexplicable. None of my siblings received prunes from her at Christmas, and no one, certainly not Nan herself, or either of my parents, passed comment that I should be singled out like this. I had had prunes from her before – I don't recall ever having had anything different – but, every year, probably up into my teens, I nursed the hope that this time it might be different. But, no – each year my tin of prunes came disguised as something else; apart from the odd occasion when a small tin of cream was given with them, it was only the boxes that varied. My nan gave me a tin of prunes for Christmas every single year, until her death in 1991.

CHAPTER 8

By the time I was ten, so stark was the contrast between my home life and that of the outside world, I was increasingly terrified to leave it. I'd been attending speech therapy classes in school for some time, and though one of my school reports of that time reads something like 'doing well, in spite of grave difficulties', all I knew, having read it much later, was that I – and my parents, come to that – must have been doing a good job of keeping the true squalor and dysfunctional nature of our home life from the attention of the authorities.

I still spoke very little, and was missing school almost as much as I was going. In my third school term in 1960, for example, I had forty-two absences recorded on my school report. It's still a wonder to me, looking back at my childhood, how no one noticed.

But not such a wonder, when I think about it. There were still only two people, in my young life, who really 'noticed' me. One was Pops, who continued to seek me out every weekend – sometimes also in the week – and whose 'tickles' continued to distress me so much, and the other was Daniel, whose visits, in contrast, I still longed for. And as I only saw him once every two months, when he *did* come it always began by feeling magical, despite the anxiety I couldn't quite explain. Daniel didn't just notice me, he actively adored me. He told me so, over and over.

At this time I had begun to feel more in control of my feelings around Daniel, so when he arrived one particular summer afternoon – his eyes already searching for me, seeking me out, even as he bent to peck my mother's cheek – I realized I felt calmer about my anxiety than I had when I was younger. I knew Daniel loved me, and that he didn't mean to frighten me. He cared for me, wanted to spend time with me alone, would give me the thrill of his undivided attention.

I was sitting on the corner of the sofa when he arrived, with my hand dangling down over the arm, half watching television and half watching him. I both dreaded and longed for his approach.

I didn't need to wait long. I heard him coming, but pretended I didn't know it was him and continued to stare at the TV. As ever, I felt too anxious to look, feeling panicky as he sat down so close beside me that he squashed me right into the sofa arm.

He immediately started stroking my hair and leaned his face into mine. 'Hello, little girl,' he whispered, close into my ear. 'What have you been up to? Aren't you going to look at me?'

I could feel his breath in my ear now. It was hot. He laughed softly, and I felt something wet, like his tongue, touching my ear and my neck. It sent shivers up my back and instinctively I moved, though, pinned as I was, I wasn't going anywhere. I tried to sit forwards, but as I did so he pulled me towards him, laughing again and kissing the side of my face. He picked up my hand then, and brushed it across his lips, before lifting me onto his lap and cradling me in his arms, as if I was a precious tiny baby.

'Look at me,' he urged, tickling my tummy. 'Come on, *look* at me, you little minx!'

As ever, I found it almost impossible to do this. 'Tell you what,' he said then. 'Shall we go and see the cows?'

The cows lived in the field just up the lane, behind the barns, where we children often went to play when the farmer wasn't around to tell us off. It had big bales of straw stacked in it, and in the middle of one of them was a big hole we'd created when jumping from stack to stack. I looked up at them now but didn't tell Daniel about it, because I never told Daniel anything ever. I still felt way too self-conscious and awkward to speak to him, and though he talked to *me*, he never seemed to mind when I didn't reply. He had his hand in mine, his fingers all laced through my own, which always made me feel funny inside.

There were some cows in the yard, and in the field with the horses, and Daniel leaned on the gate to stand and watch them, pointing and laughing. He kept looking down at me and then lifted me up and sat me down carefully on the gate. I leaned towards him because it felt as if I was going to fall off backwards. 'Don't worry,' he said gently. 'I won't let you fall.'

He hugged me then, tightly, my face in his jumper, and then his mouth was touching mine and then his teeth, and then his tongue – he started pushing it down my throat, and it choked me. 'We haven't got much time,' he said. 'Someone might come. And then we wouldn't be able to be together, would we?'

I said nothing. I was still trying to get my breath back. 'You know I love you,' he went on. 'Don't you?' And then he undid his trousers. 'Look,' he said, pulling out his enormous great thing. 'Look what you do to me, you little minx.'

I'd seen his thing many, many times before, but seeing it again never felt any less shocking. The feelings of badness welled up, unstoppably, inside me, and I felt like the worst girl in the world. But *why* did I feel like this? Daniel loved me so much. *Really* loved me. Thinking this, I felt guilty, as I always did once he'd got his thing out, because I wasn't sure if I wanted Daniel to *really* love me. Not like this.

He watched me all the time as he slowly touched his thing. He was touching it up and down, his breathing growing louder, his face going redder. I felt scared and muddled, mixed up. I didn't want to watch. I closed my eyes.

'Look at me! Come on!' he whispered, his voice all raggedy now. 'Look at me!' So I opened my eyes and he was staring straight at me. He stared at me all the time and, without looking down, I knew he was still touching his thing.

He lifted me off the gate then, all of a sudden, and I knew I would either have to touch his thing too, or, instead, he would put it in my mouth. I definitely didn't want it in my mouth, because of all the things he made me do I hated that the most. I began to feel nauseous and panicky. Just knowing what would happen made my legs start to tremble and I wanted to start running but my feet wouldn't move. Daniel was still watching my face – his eyes never once wavered – and he bent down, took my hand and placed it inside his own, on his thing, and started to move it up and down again. He started slowly, then he began moving both our hands really fast, and stuff came out of the end really quickly. It was warm, and it ran down the back of my hand, seeping all in between my fingers. I started crying then and, as ever, I couldn't stop.

'Don't cry,' Daniel said, stroking my hair. 'I *love* you. You mustn't cry, you hear me?' He put his thing away and linked his hand once again in mine. 'This is a happy time, and you're a *very* special girl.'

As ever, I felt sad, sick and very bad when Daniel left, and those feelings would persist for many days. But eventually they'd fade, and it wouldn't be too many weeks before I was once again longing for his return.

My day-to-day existence, however, had no such highs and lows. I clung to my mother at all times. Not only did I find it really hard to be separated from her, I also felt responsible for her. Not surprising, given what I now understand about her condition, but at the time it was more a direct, if unknowing, response to it. As I got older, her indifference, bizarre behaviour, and neglect, made my attempts to engage with her ever more desperate.

Though I was also, at all times, on guard with her, because I never knew what to expect. Her mood, always unpredictable, could turn in a heartbeat. My younger sister, for example, since she was tiny had always hated having her hair washed. By now she was eight, and would always protest loudly when beckoned to her turn at the kitchen sink. She'd start crying and, by the time my mother got hold of her, dragged her over and pushed her head under the tap, the crying would turn to screams. She'd scream all the time her hair was being washed, while my mother shouted: 'If you don't stop that bloody noise, I will give you something to cry about.' But one day, my mother was more canny. She called my sister, put an arm around her, bent down and whispered, 'I have a very special present for you, and if you are a good girl, and don't make a fuss when I wash your hair, you shall have it.'

I watched my little sister's anxious face turn to a smile, and how quietly and meekly she stood over the sink. Then, of course, as my mother towel-dried her hair, my sister wanted to know when she could have it. 'I've been a good girl,' she said. 'Haven't I?' To which my mother replied, 'Yes.' But then she spun her around – it all happened in the blink of an eye – and started hitting her really hard, all over her body – the backs of her legs, her arms and her bottom, all the while shouting: 'There you are, there's your present, you little cow! I'll bloody teach you to play me up! Don't you ever cry again when I'm washing your hair!'

I could hardly bear watching this, the shock left me bewildered. And then angry – such cruelty – I wished she was *dead* – and then guilt that I'd done nothing to help my sister.

By now, my mother had ruined our lovely home. It seemed to happen almost overnight. The chaos and filth had returned, and it felt just as it had at the other house, only worse, because there were now even more rooms disgusting and full of junk.

She just couldn't seem to stop collecting things. There were carrier bags and boxes of stuff *everywhere*. Bags hung on the door handles to every single room, stuff hung on the doors themselves, and all around them, leaving only a small walkway into each room. We could hardly ever use either the dining table or chairs as both would be covered in piles of magazines and junk.

There was no place that wasn't occupied by rubbish. In every room, under the beds, on the stairs, in every cupboard, on the landing, on the sofa, even piled high on every windowsill – her stuff was absolutely everywhere you looked. It was both terrifying and overwhelming; as if she'd spread herself everywhere, all around, in every corner, and there wasn't even a tiny space left for the rest of us.

Being older – and, in some ways, more frightened of her behaviour, because I could observe it with more clarity – I needed to find ways to cope. Every day, in the school holidays, and weekends, after school, and when I was absent, I'd try to clean parts of the house. Our house felt more and more like an extension of my mother, and, as such, I felt this great responsibility for it as well as her. I also hoped – vainly – if I could clear up, my father would be happier and get on better with my mother. As it was, he'd be constantly shouting at her, very often now, in response to her persistent questioning of him, and accusing him of seeing his 'whore'. 'You won't go to heaven,' she'd tell him. 'You'll end up in hell!' I'd started my own life under the shadow of one of his affairs; it was due to his affair with his boss's teenage daughter that he'd lost his job and we'd had to move in the first place. His affairs would continue for many years, but in truth they were just another aspect of the misery – the central unhappiness in my life, apart from being constantly interfered with by Pops and so messed up about my feelings for Daniel, was my mother, who was getting more strange every year.

My relationship with her left me with the same sort of anxiety I'd feel when very small, when I was either left and not fed, or when I *would* have her attention, but I wouldn't know what she might do, or how she'd be.

Washing and cleaning were my only way to ease my anxiety. I spent a lot of time washing and cleaning. My mother didn't very often wash any bedding. Our blankets, which were black army blankets, shiny with dirt, and itchy and smelly, were far too big and heavy for me to attempt to clean. But I could do our sheets, which were equally disgusting. My little brother Jack's, in particular, were horrible, covered in brown and black stains, and filthy from where he would habitually suck the corner. The kitchen sink was always overflowing with dirty crockery, so I'd take the bedclothes to the bathroom, put them in the bath, fill it, and then tread on them to squeeze what filth I could out of them, before taking them downstairs in a bowl and carrying them out to the garden and hanging them on the line.

The house smelled too. Winston, my mother's ginger cat, would go to the toilet anywhere he pleased, and no one would ever clear it up. His piles of dried faeces – particularly under the beds – remained there indefinitely and made me feel sick. I would try to clear them up, but they made me retch and retch. My mother had also acquired a dog. He was a Jack Russell, and was constantly tormented by my father. He spent most of his time tied to a chair leg in the kitchen, because if let loose he'd bite anyone who came to the house, start barking, and never stop.

My mother's menagerie outside had grown as well. The sheer quantity of animals in the garden was breathtaking. What had started with a little collection of small animals and birds had grown – as they were free to mingle with each other as they wanted – to a collection of over a hundred rabbits, a similar number of guinea pigs, many hens, and a cockerel. She seemed better at and more happy caring for these than her increasing offspring of human dependants.

The rabbits and guinea pigs were in two big cages, balanced on a wooden stand my father had made. It leaned against the side of the house, opposite a chicken house and run. When we walked home from school we picked dandelions, hogweed and other greenery for the rabbits and guinea pigs to eat. The chickens had scraps of food we left, plus grain from the cattle markets my father went to. My mother collected their eggs every day. I can't remember us children being allowed to. We were, however – and in particular my sister – expected to clear out the guinea pigs' and rabbits' poo. As my mother only dealt with it rarely, it'd pile up in big heaps in their cages.

My father sometimes brought home farm animals, too, to fatten up for market. Pigs, lambs, sheep, even a Shetland pony on one occasion – all of which shared space with the junk that was also out there: old cars, piles of wood, logs, old tin cans, discarded oil drums and an old pick-up truck, that became his workbench for sawing logs.

In the orchard next to the house there were a couple of sows (plus their piglets) who would chase us and bite us if they managed to catch up with us when we climbed over the fence to scrump apples. We'd often be stuck up the trees, sometimes for what seemed like hours, as they wouldn't move far enough to enable us to climb down again and run safely back to our garden.

The business of feeding her human family seemed more complicated for my mother. She cooked, but as with everything she seemed unable to grasp the nature of the whole. Nothing was ever cleaned. The cooker's top, sides and front were permanently covered in black grease, as were the walls around and the floor in front of the cooker, as well as the green Formica table that stood next to it. My mother fried food every day. Unless he was to be gone early, at say, four, she'd cook breakfast for my father – sausages, bacon, eggs, a boiled pork chop, tomatoes, bread and butter and tea. My mother said he needed the good food because he was out working, earning the money to keep us.

Once she'd fed him, and he'd gone, my mother would often take up her position on her chair in front of the Rayburn. She'd have the Rayburn door open and be reading a magazine, ripping bits out of it as she did so and dropping them onto the floor beside her. These bits of paper were the genesis of much of the chaos that spilled out into every room of the house. She'd be still in her dressing gown, unwashed, her hair messy, and would very often stay there till lunchtime. I found the sight of my mother at such times hard to bear. I wanted to scream at her: 'Why don't you *do* something?' but at the same time I felt desperately sorry for her too, and guilty for all the bad thoughts she'd make me have wondering why she couldn't be like other girls' mothers: laughing and kind, and just somehow more alive.

I'd start clearing up then, clearing the remains of my father's delicious breakfast, and wondering why he had food we didn't. And then I'd feel guilty again, because he did go to work, and he did earn all the money, and if he didn't then we'd probably all be dead.

But the filth in the kitchen didn't just come from his breakfasts; my mother cooked chips for us almost every night. We lived on chips most of the time, it seemed. Sometimes we'd have stews, made from scrag ends of meat, or mince, or liver my father got from the slaughterhouse for nothing, and sometimes a pie or toad in the hole. This, however, depended on how she was feeling. Sometimes too, in the school holidays, if she was feeling energetic, she'd make a jam pudding and custard and would actually sit down with us while we were eating. But then she'd start telling us her jokes about people weeing and pooing and 'blowing off'. She'd laugh so much there'd be tears rolling down her cheeks. It was one of the very few things that seemed to make her animated – slightly hysterical even – and, caught up in this, we'd laugh too.

She didn't often spend time washing up anything, and the two big metal chip pans made the whole kitchen smell horrible. She'd cook them in batches, and great bouts of smoke would billow around, seeping into every last corner of the house. She often had chip pan fires, which terrified me while she ran in a frenzy, trying to put them out. I'd sometimes attempt to clean the disgusting pans myself, carefully straining the fat from them through a tea strainer into a jug, and throwing away all the ancient black bits. I'd then attempt to scrub them, but it never worked. They stayed black and would never come clean.

I'd also try to wash up, but there was so much dirty crockery in the sink I couldn't even turn the taps on properly. And it was never just piled in the sink either. The kitchen table, the yellow cupboard and the red kitchen cabinet would almost always be covered in crockery and pans of congealed, rotting food, some of which would have green mildew up the sides. There would even be piles of dirty saucepans stacked on the floor, sometimes with remains I could clearly identify – the green beans, for example, Pops had brought the previous Saturday. He still brought my mother vegetables when he came, because if he didn't we'd hardly have any. The only other veg we ever seemed to have were the potatoes, cabbage and swedes my mother said my father used to pinch sometimes from where they were on sale on the trailer parked up the road.

My mother never seemed to notice the mess. She never fretted about it, or commented on it, and seldom said, 'I must tidy up.' It was almost as if she couldn't see it. By now she'd spend lots of her time just sitting. I couldn't understand why she'd want to sit where she sat, because much of the time she was parked only inches away from where she kept a pan of my father's dirty underwear boiling on the stove. It'd be there for days, and would keep boiling dry, but she never seemed to deal with it, or hang it to dry – she just topped up the water, again and again, for what seemed like for ever. Eventually, she'd tip the whole lot into the sink, where it would remain for a few more days, among the dirty dishes. She'd also often have another pan, of boiling chicken, on the go. She always bought 'boilers' as they were cheaper, and, as with the underwear, they'd boil away for days – until my father could tolerate the stench no longer, and then swear at her, and she'd put the stinking pan out in the yard. Mostly, she'd remove the boiled chicken before she did this, but the cooking water would remain in the pan, growing mildew, until the next time she wanted to use it.

And then she'd go back to her endless bouts of sitting, and tearing bits out of magazines, and humming. She hummed more and more, even when out shopping. She also, increasingly, had started twisting her thumbs. Passing them over one another, again and again, quickly, first one way and then the other. She had started tapping as well, clicking her long dirty nails, endlessly, on the wooden arm of her chair. Her tapping almost had a kind of tune – a clear rhythm. It went clickedy, clickedy – click, click, click – clickedy, clickedy – click, click, click – clickedy, clickedy – click, click, click – on and on, often for hours at a time. I hated her clicking. It made me feel irritable and angry. But I never said anything to her.

She looked so hopeless, I couldn't bear to upset her.

CHAPTER 9

Perhaps unsurprisingly, when the time came to leave primary school, I failed my end-of-year exam. Not that I really understood what the exam was about. All I knew was that I had to take a test, that my mind was blank, that I didn't know the answers, and that I panicked I would get them all wrong.

As a consequence, I did, and was duly assigned to join the infamous class 1, the dunces' class at the secondary modern. I could at least walk to this school, though, as it was only a couple of miles distant, up a hill and through the town centre. My mother told my older sister Susan she had to walk to school with me, but as she didn't want to be seen with me – ever – she and her friends would keep their distance behind, laughing and joking about things I couldn't share, while I, acutely embarrassed, walked ahead.

My sister was very naughty throughout school. She was in trouble a great deal, though when chastised she'd laugh openly in teachers' faces. She'd also, from time to time, hit them. In hindsight, it's remarkable she was never suspended or expelled, as she'd sometimes have the PE teacher in tears, and the headmaster on the phone to our mother.

From day one, it seemed, I was tarred with the same brush. 'Oh, you're *her* sister, are you?' they'd say to me, looking stern. It probably didn't help that I was placed in class 1, where I had to count oranges and apples and do dunces schoolwork. I hated it. It made me feel sick and headachey. As a consequence, I cried all the time and refused to go to school so, eventually, my mother called them. She told them how unhappy I was, and asked if I could go up a class. The school said that as my primary school test results had been borderline, they'd see if I could cope in class 2.

Though initially joining class 2 was daunting, the teacher, Mr John, was so kind and welcoming, and quick to silence the other children – who all knew where I'd come from, and taunted me – I felt that at last I could do better. But it was a double-edged sword: Mr John, like Daniel, seemed to really like me, and would single me out for special attention.

Mr John made me feel anxious whenever he came near me, in exactly the way Daniel had. It took me straight back to child-hood – to being bewildered yet quiescent. To being powerless and unable to tell anyone to go away. Every time he approached me I was always on full alert: fearful, without understanding why. Another girl might have told him to back off, but I couldn't. I experienced the same conflict that happened with Daniel, whose attention and interest I had always craved and needed, despite him making me do such revolting things.

By now, though Grandpops was still manhandling me regularly, the walks out with Daniel had stopped. At some point between my finishing primary school and going to secondary, Daniel had decided – it was not at my instigation or demand

– to stop taking me off for our 'walks'. Though still confused, and still craving the attention he gave me, I had become increasingly instinctive about avoiding his physical advances. Perhaps he understood better than I did at the time that it would not be safe or prudent to continue. He would still be all over me, bestowing kisses and cuddles, and whispering creepy things to me, and he still had – and would continue to have – power over me. But with hindsight, I believe there was something more too – what Daniel really liked was little girls.

Mr John's presence made me panicky in the same way Daniel had; so strong was the sensation whenever he came close to me that I felt if I opened my mouth to say 'Stop it', my reaction would be outside my control. I therefore just accepted it, and tried not to panic. Instead, I'd walk around school with a permanent pain in my tummy, and a tightness in my throat that wouldn't go away.

I was also becoming aware of my body. All the younger girls in school were expected to do PE wearing nothing but a T-shirt and pants. Stripping down to these – dissent was not permitted – made me feel terribly uneasy. It was made worse by the fact no one else seemed to care. They were all laughing and joking, and seemed completely at ease with their bodies, while I was almost paralysed with fear. What if someone looked at me, or peered in through the window? Or walked into the changing room and saw me? I was so anxious about my body – how it looked, how much I hated it – I thought I'd die of embarrassment.

I was not only concerned about my appearance, however. I was also extremely uncoordinated. I was, almost literally, crippled by my lack of confidence. Who knows what I might have achieved in different circumstances? As it was, I'd spent all my life being told I was stupid and silly by my mother, and now I believed that. I felt ungainly and hopeless, and doing sport – especially team sports – just reminded me I wasn't up to scratch, and I would let everyone else on the team down, look completely ridiculous and be hated.

I desperately wished I could be good at PE and gym and swimming, because if I was, perhaps the other girls would like me. As it was, I soon noticed I kept getting a rash, that seemed to get worse whenever I had to run. It wasn't a big deal, apparently; something inherited from my father, and the doctor, when my mother finally took me to see him, was very relaxed about it. My mother, on the other hand, probably sick of me begging her to do it, wrote to the PE department informing them I must take no further part in sport from then on.

Initially, this felt like a massive relief, but, ultimately, it made things worse. Already socially isolated, due to my feelings of low self-worth, I was now physically isolated too, standing in corners of the gym and on the touchlines, just watching, feeling useless, underlining my difference in the most obvious way.

By the time I'd completed my first year in secondary school, I was despondent, disheartened and miserable. Even before we broke up for summer, I was already worrying and anxious about having to go back in the autumn. I'd developed a strong sense of being on my own in the world, without the confidence or know-how to deal with it. I couldn't wait for the holidays to begin. Though home was a place of confusion and loneliness, where I felt powerless, bullied and totally without control, at least I wouldn't have to face the schoolgirls who bullied me as well. I was no safer at home, in reality, of course, but at least home felt familiar.

Plus there was also Phillip.

In a world where almost every male I encountered made me feel bad, my older brother Phillip always made me feel better. I felt closer to him than anyone else I'd ever known – young or old, male or female; he made me feel grounded, somehow. He had his own difficulties with life, just as I did, and part of my love for him was bound up with pity. He always seemed vulnerable and self-conscious about his looks. He had teenage spots, greasy hair, glasses, and was a little awkward, something I could easily relate to. I felt so bad in myself – both on the outside and inside – that I felt a strong connection when around him. He had the same challenges to deal with as I did, but he seemed so much stronger than me, with so much less self-loathing, and much more able to deal with things. He was quietly spoken and sensitive, and I admired him enormously. Where I'd become resigned to all the bad things that had been done being my fault – this being the only way I could process them; why else would they have happened? – Phillip seemed to have a determination about him, to do better, to make something of himself.

I always felt better and safer just knowing he was around, and when he went away I felt a huge sense of loss. It was almost as if I was lacking something necessary for my survival, and I'd think about him every day. I aspired to be like him, to the point I even wished I *were* him, despite also worrying about him trying to overcome all his difficulties.

I never felt afraid around Phillip. We'd sit and discuss things and laugh. I felt no tension or anxiety, and my tummy didn't hurt. With Phillip, what I felt was accepted.

It was a warm summer's day, towards the end of the holidays. Soon I'd have to go back and face school and the bullies but, for the moment, my time was mostly mine. Though most of it was spent cleaning the house, washing and hoovering, and listening to my mother's endless rounds of filthy stories, at least I wasn't in school, feeling hated.

Phillip's friend Derek had come round to see him. Derek lived in the next village and, although I didn't know him well, I quite liked him. He didn't have much of a family, was stocky, with dark hair, and always seemed fun. He certainly always seemed to be laughing. They were having a cup of tea in the kitchen with my mother, and I was really glad to see them.

It had been a particularly miserable couple of weeks, as I'd just had a horrible disappointment. I'd been asked by a girl in my class, Sandra, if she could come and stay with me for a couple of days. She lived in a children's home and it was because of that that my mother finally agreed she could come, because she announced she felt sorry for her. Also, my father had lately started not coming home some nights, so he wouldn't know. I was surprised – Sandra and I weren't friends because I didn't *have* friends; she was just another girl in my class. But at the same time I was flattered and excited, and I set to work making everything nice. I decided we'd sleep in the dining room, the upstairs being way too horrible. The dining room was horribly dirty and messy too, but there was a sofa bed in there we could sleep on together, so I did every scrap of ironing – it was piled, as always, to the ceiling – gave the room a thorough clean and moved all the rubbish.

But on the morning she was due, my mother had a call from the children's home, who were very angry, to say she wasn't coming after all. They'd found out it was all part of a plan she'd hatched so she could see a boy from school she'd been having a secret relationship with. Worse still was that Mrs Eaton, the owner of the home, thought Sandra and I had hatched it between us. I was not only disappointed, but felt let down. Yet again, it wasn't that someone wanted to see me. I had just been used.

Phillip and Derek had plans for the afternoon – they were going for a walk along the riverbank behind the field next to our house, to fish for minnows. There were lots of minnows in the river at that time of year, so they were relatively easy to catch. We'd take jam jars to catch them, but we'd always let them go.

I hung around for a bit, as it was better than doing nothing, hoping they might ask me to join them. Phillip did, and said they thought they'd head down to the island. It was a little piece of higher ground in the river, so called because it was in the middle of the water, and you had to wade across the river to get to it. Sometimes the water was too deep and fast to cross, but today was calm and the river was running low, and I was only too keen to go with them. They were both in their mid-teens and I was twelve, and pleased to be considered important enough to be asked.

We made our way down the front garden and across the orchard, dodging the pigs, then getting over the fence and straight into the river. We then walked through it under the bridge and through the field that ran alongside, and were soon across the water and on the island. The boys were wearing plimsolls, but I'd put on my wellies, as the stones on the riverbed were sharp. I had to cross to the island very slowly, holding my skirt up to keep it dry, but before long we'd all started kicking water at one another, so by the time we were across it was soaked anyway. We all fished for a bit, then the boys both bent over the water, calling 'Here! there's some here!' and we all plunged in our jars.

We caught our minnows and proceeded to spend some time inspecting them, and once done, we tipped them carefully back. It was a warm afternoon and, now tired with the fishing, we went back on to the island to sit down. Once on the grass, Phillip pulled a pack of playing cards from his pocket, and suggested we have a game. It was a new game, he explained to me. One I hadn't played before. He told me it was called 'Strip Poker'. He was laughing as he said this, and glanced at Derek too. 'It's new,' he said again. 'It's usually just us boys that play. What d'you think? Shall we start and you can see if you like it?'

He went on to explain that if I got dealt certain cards, I'd have to take off an item of clothing. This didn't worry me unduly because I thought I'd ensure I got rid of those cards, the way you did in other games, like rummy. I trusted him anyway. I didn't think we'd be taking any clothes off, not really. We'd get rid of the bad cards and it would be okay.

But we began playing and for some reason I wasn't having any luck. I obviously hadn't thought it through. I'd been so pleased to be asked, I hadn't really thought about what 'taking our clothes off' meant. It hadn't occurred to me I'd actually be put in the position of becoming half naked.

But I seemed to be dealt the wrong cards every hand, and while the boys had only removed plimsolls and socks, I was already down to my pants. I'd removed everything I could: my skirt, my blouse, both wellies, one after another, plus my hairband, the last thing I had left.

I lost the next hand, and with nothing else to remove I told him I wasn't going to take my pants off. 'That's okay,' he said, laughing again. 'Never mind about that.' Then he explained that it was okay if I didn't want to remove them – the way the game worked was that if I didn't want to do that, I'd instead have to let him touch me 'down there'.

I stood up immediately, feeling uneasy. I was so taken aback by his suggestion I couldn't seem to think straight. Had I misheard him? Surely he hadn't said that, had he? I looked at him, to see what his expression might tell me, but as I did so, he stood too and stepped towards me. Without waiting for my answer he pushed his hand down my pants, and I stiffened at the feel of his rough, dirty fingernails. I knew they'd be dirty – boys' fingernails always were. I could feel him moving his fingers now, trying to push them inside me, which hurt. He then shoved them hard into me and moved them around and then immediately withdrew them, half turning now to Derek, who was standing, hands in pockets, looking awkward.

'D'you want a go?' he asked him. I was stunned when I heard this, and also very worried he'd say yes. Derek looked at the ground, and then at my face. He shook his head. 'No,' he said to Phillip. 'No, I don't.'

I stood there staring at Phillip till I could hold his gaze no longer, then looked down, not knowing what to do next.

I couldn't believe what had just happened. There was silence, then. Nothing moved, no one spoke. I could feel this terrible upset rising inside me. Why had Phillip done that? Why would he *want* to do that? Had he planned it all along? I was so shocked, and I hadn't a clue what to say or do. I simply couldn't understand what had happened, or why. This was *Phillip*. What was happening here? Because *he'd* done it, did that mean it was okay?

Phillip turned on his heel then, and Derek quickly followed.

'Come on, we're going back now,' Phillip said. I didn't answer. I stood there, not moving, watching their retreating backs and not knowing what to think.

Then I followed, at a distance – neither boy looked back – and, once home, I went straight up the stairs to the bathroom. I had spent lots of time cleaning – had been doing it all my life. Not just pots and pans and crockery and filthy sheets, either. I had spent lots of time scrubbing Daniel's 'stuff' off my hands over the years. Or off my chin, or my wrists, or where it had dripped down and dried on my dresses. But this was new. Here I set about scrubbing myself . . .

CHAPTER 10

The incident with Phillip affected me greatly. As I approached my teens, I became obsessed with my own death and thought about when and how it would happen. Everything around me felt dark; I felt ugly, dirty, disgusting and useless, that I didn't belong anywhere, and that I didn't know what to do.

Terrified by the strength of the dark feelings I'd been having, I made an appointment to see the GP. What I wanted, I suppose, was to talk to someone about them, but I found it impossible to articulate what had happened with Phillip and the GP ended up, I think, barking up the wrong tree. I was offered a course of antidepressants, together with the instructions to 'discover myself'. Have a nice warm bath, think, touch my body all over, and try to establish 'what I liked'. I left feeling more sick about myself than when I started, and I didn't take the antidepressants for long, as they made me feel even more desperate.

Instead, I withdrew into trying to work myself out. I couldn't understand why this should be happening to me, and not, on the face of it, to anyone else. Why was I so different? Why so unhappy and afraid? My elder sister, now almost fifteen, seemed

happy. She'd come back from outings and talk about all the fun
she'd had when she was out, as she often was, with her friends.

My mother did intimate that it hadn't always been so. She
told me things about my sister that had happened to her when
she was thirteen, and I wondered if thirteen was just a difficult
age, and the reason I felt so strange and depressed. Perhaps it
would get better. I so wanted to believe that. I didn't want to
have to take antidepressants. Perhaps the solution was to be more
like my sister, to do what she did, to try to go out and have fun.
Perhaps then, I reasoned, I'd make friends and be happy and not
worry quite so much about dying.

I had been saving a little of the money I'd earned potato
picking before Christmas; the bit I didn't spend on buying
presents. I also had a little Christmas money of my own, plus a
small amount from my thirteenth birthday. I decided I'd spend
this on something nice to wear, and eventually chose a smart
cream military-style dress, with long sleeves and brass buttons on
the shoulders, cuffs and front. I really liked it, not least because
I'd bought it myself, and it was new. I had something of my own
to go out in, something that hadn't been worn by anybody else.

I didn't have anywhere to wear it, of course, but in a mood of
determination, inspired by my purchase, I put it on and walked
into town. It was a Saturday afternoon, which meant that, hopefully, my sister wouldn't be around, which was important because
I knew if she saw me she'd taunt me. She was in town all the
time, but never usually on a Saturday during the day, because she
had a job at a local farm.

I had little in the way of a plan. The only thing I knew about
town and what you did was that there was a place called the

Honey Globe, a cafe where everyone hung out. From what my sister said, it sounded exciting. There was a jukebox, and everyone sat listening to music and smoking, and sometimes a crowd of teenagers would gather at the cafe before going on outings together.

I was far too self-conscious to go in on my own, but just as I was standing leaning against the wall I spotted Ellie in the distance, a girl from school.

'What are you up to?' she asked, as she approached me.

'I was just going up to the Honey Globe,' I lied.

'Me too,' she answered, and we fell into step. As we walked, I could hardly believe what I was doing. I was walking through town, in the company of another girl, and we were going to the Honey Globe together. When we got there, I could see she'd been there before. She strode in, full of confidence, and led the way across the room, then down some stairs that led to another room in the basement. There was a pool table, and lots of yellow-topped tables and yellow chairs, and there were groups of mainly boys, sitting around them, all with cups of tea or coffee, or cans of Coke. Quite a few were smoking, and the song on the jukebox was 'Everlasting Love'. It was quite loud.

One of the older boys, who was sitting on the edge of a table with his legs casually thrown over the back of a chair, looked over as we entered, spotted me, smiled and said, 'Well, hello.' I felt horribly self-conscious. I hardly ever talked to girls, let alone boys.

Ellie again led the way and we went over to the counter to buy Cokes. While we were over there she told me the boy's name was Colin and he lived in the next village. She told me she thought he fancied me. I admitted to her that I thought he was good-looking too, and we went back to his table and sat down. She was very relaxed with him – they both talked and laughed together – but when he asked me a question, I couldn't seem to think of a single thing to say. Ellie told him who my sister was and he smiled and nodded. 'Ah,' he said, 'I see. I know your sister pretty well.' His voice was warm and friendly, and I was pleased at the way he said it. He obviously liked her, and it was also clear he quite liked me too.

We all chatted some more – I was feeling a little more relaxed now – and when Ellie announced, at teatime, she had to be getting home, Colin asked me if I'd like to go for a walk with him. He suggested we might walk up on the downs.

This was new and stressful territory. Up to now I'd never thought about the concept of boyfriends; just had the vague notion of how nice it would be to be taken care of by someone, especially someone like Colin, who was friendly and good-looking and – to my shock – seemed to want to spend time with me.

However, this was so outside of my experience I felt terribly tongue-tied, inexperienced and young. He was so much older than me, so much more worldly-wise, and not knowing what he wanted – not knowing what *I* wanted – I felt completely out of my depth.

But at the same time, I'd no idea how to say no to him. I had no sense of being allowed to say 'no', to anyone about anything, least of all a male who wanted something from me. Saying 'no' to someone was to reject them, and I didn't want to do that – my upbringing had taught me other people's feelings always, always came before mine.

I therefore said yes, and before long, we were walking together towards the downs. As we headed out of town, bathed in spring sunshine, Colin reached across and took my hand. I felt a bit afraid, and in my stomach there were the first flutterings of panic, but at the same time, I didn't want to pull my hand away. This was scary but it also felt grown-up and special – like I was out walking with *my* boyfriend.

We eventually got to the path, and crossed the stile that led to the downs, and some way along the path that formed a ridge along them, Colin suggested we sit down on a nearby bench. He put his arm around my shoulders, turned towards me and kissed me, which made me panic, and I started mumbling about getting home.

He tried gently to coax me to stay. 'Come on,' he said, laughing, 'we've only just got here!' and, presumably taking my silence for assent, continued to kiss me as before.

But panic was rising in my chest. Any fond thoughts I'd had about him being my boyfriend were expunged in an instant by a physical sense of dread. I felt frightened and, at the same time, so angry at myself. He'd been so kind, so attentive, so *interested* in me, yet it was all as nothing compared to my overwhelming fear about what might happen next. He'd clearly thought I was up for something I really, really wasn't, and in letting him bring me to this bench I'd misled him – and now I was in trouble.

He obviously couldn't sense my distress either, as the next thing he did was place his free hand on my knee. Now I really panicked. I jumped up and immediately started running, my heart thumping, desperate to get away.

I could hear him coming after me. 'What's wrong with you?' he shouted. 'What's the *matter* with you?'

Without thinking, I bent down, snatched up a stone and threw it at him, then doubled my efforts to run as fast as I could. I didn't know if it had hit him or not, but he was still following and shouting. 'What's your *problem*?' he was yelling. 'You mad or something?'

I clambered over the stile, and fled towards the hill and home, tears of anger and exasperation at myself streaming down my face. Now everyone, *everyone*, would know what I was like. Colin would probably tell everyone how useless and stupid I was. That I got all dressed up in nice clothes and wore make-up but actually, when you came down to it, I was dead inside.

And he was right, wasn't he? Because there wasn't any 'I'. I had no likes or dislikes, no personality. The only way I could cope was to master the business of making everyone around me feel happy. My only need was to make sure I considered others' feelings. My own feelings about anything were of absolutely no consequence – all that mattered was that I didn't upset anyone.

Yet more and more I was discovering doing so was hard. That encounters with boys and men would be intolerable in themselves, because they would – it seemed – always mean them touching me. That Colin just wanted to 'get his leg over' seemed clear. How stupid of me to think he liked me as a person. And even if he had, being 'liked' by a boy clearly involved doing things that distressed me. But *why* did it? Why was it so frightening to me and so all right with every other girl? There seemed nothing I could do to make my affliction go away. Being a Wednesday's child was going to be my destiny.

Unless I could conquer my fear. Stop feeling so afraid and let boys do what they wanted. Kiss me and touch me and every-thing else. What I needed to do was to try to like it. Maybe trying to like it was the answer.

When I got home, I took off my lovely new dress, and care-fully hung it in my wardrobe, unable to imagine when I'd ever wear it again. A few days later, however, I found it screwed up and dirty in a pile of washing strewn on the bedroom floor. My older sister had taken it and worn it without asking, then just chucked it on the floor among her own filthy clothes. It was the sort of horrible thing she did all the time.

CHAPTER 11

My father's boss, Mr White – the only boss I'd ever known my father have – was, according to what many people said, very much like my father temperamentally. Like my father, he spent a lot of time shouting and swearing, and he also smoked roll-ups while he was out driving his haulage lorry. He was a lot older than my father, short and stocky, in contrast to my father's tall, imposing frame, and he always seemed to wear a long brown coat, of the type worn by butchers and men in hardware stores. In its pockets would often be warm melting Mars bars, which he'd offer to me whenever I went with my mother to help her clean his dark, scary house.

We used to do this because Mr White was now terminally ill. He became ill shortly after we moved, and with his condition worsening all the time we lived there, he eventually asked my parents to help him run his business, with the promise they'd have first refusal to take it over and run it themselves when he died. More importantly, he also promised that they could move into his house, which was directly across the road from his lorry yard.

His death upset my father greatly. Despite their shouting and swearing, they were evidently close, playing the father–son roles for each other that neither man had in real life. After his death, however, it transpired, via his solicitor, that he'd sold the business to a Welsh couple called Mr and Mrs Wilson. The Wilsons knew nothing about livestock haulage, and were keen from the start to enlist my father's help to show them how things should be done. My father couldn't bear this. Livid about having been cheated out of what he'd thought would be his, he hated the Wilsons, and lost his temper frequently, shouting obscenities and ranting, and generally behaving unpleasantly and patronizingly towards them, even though he did the work and ran the business. Eventually Mr Wilson brought his son Simon into the company and put him through HGV training. In this way, my father became superfluous to the business, and in the summer of 1968 he was told by the Wilsons he was no longer needed and, as a consequence, would lose both job and house.

Furious, my parents decided to go to court – with the length of their tenancy they could be classed as sitting tenants – but the court ruled against them and ordered the family to vacate the house within three months. Naturally, the council were required to step in, as it would soon have an unemployed father and his homeless children on its hands. They offered us a small three-bedroomed end-of-terrace house on a council estate in the village, very close to where Nan lived.

I'd felt anxious about moving from the moment we were told – particularly about being so close now to Nan – and the move, when it came, was horrendous. All the animals – hundreds of them – had to be taken to market. The cat had died, so only the dog came with us. My mother seemed not in the least upset about losing her menagerie, however – and far too busy stressing about what was going to happen to all her rubbish.

Eventually we were finally installed or, rather, my mother's junk, in its mind-boggling quantity, was installed, and we all had to move in around it.

My nan was horrified and very cross with my father for inflicting us on her. She made no secret of the fact that she wasn't happy about having this unkempt rabble of children, relatives or otherwise, moving in so close to where she lived. She wasted no time in rushing around the village, making sure everyone was in possession of the facts: why we were all like we were (my mother's input, obviously), what had happened with the business (her son was blameless, clearly) and how she did so much to help us out, and how it simply wasn't right to squeeze such a big family into such a tiny house and how we'd have been much better off staying where we were (i.e. well away from *her*).

The house, which would be our last, and the one in which my father, now aged seventy-nine, still lives, did feel tiny after our last one. It was completely unmodernized and had just three tiny bedrooms, a small old-fashioned bathroom, and a small lounge with an open fire. The kitchen again was tiny, but at least it did have a small scullery tacked onto the back.

As it was the end of the terrace, it was situated on a corner – in this case, a chilly windswept one, lashed by the wind and rain. When we moved in the decor was startling. Everywhere had been painted in bright primary colours – the sort of colours that hadn't been seen in either of our previous gloomy homes. Even so, it wasn't cheerful – it looked horrible. This prompted my mother to make the decision to repaint the lounge ceiling and kitchen walls in gloss paint, in order to facilitate better cleaning. I was completely bemused by this idea. Her track record for cleaning was essentially non-existent. When exactly did she think this would happen?

We'd be lucky to see any walls anyway. My mother's junk, which had already taken over the whole of our previous house, completely overwhelmed all these tiny new rooms. The garden too, which was narrow, but at least of a good length, was filled up with her overflow of rubbish straight away. Any space left was soon taken by my father's mass of belongings: gates from his lorry, planks of wood to repair sections of the tailboard, and the large partitions he used inside it to separate the animals. In short we soon proved to be exactly the sort of household my nan had warned the neighbours about.

But suddenly we did *have* neighbours, not just the one or two we'd had in the past. My father seemed to take little time exploiting that fact. Always a womanizer, he had often not been where he was supposed to be when out moving livestock. But now he had many more women to choose from. My mother, who by now was having rows with him constantly, told me the binoculars he kept on their bedroom windowsill were so he could see into our female neighbours' bedrooms. I was shocked. Even though she lived in a dream world I felt certain she was telling the truth.

For me, though, the move was a very big step. It felt like I'd suddenly been transported into the real world, with all its families and happenings and so much going on. Perhaps now that I wasn't living in the middle of nowhere I'd feel less isolated and out of things. Perhaps I could pluck up the courage to make friends. Even put behind me all the horrible recollections I still had about what had happened with Colin.

But as it turned out I wasn't prepared. It was more like suddenly being given access to unlimited ice cream and, having never experienced the sensation before, not recognizing the point where you should stop eating.

It would be a while before I learned that lesson, however. In the short term I felt the first stirrings of optimism that I'd ever felt. There was a youth club in the village hall my brother had started going to and you had to be thirteen to join. Being eligible, my plan was to walk down to the village hall, join, and try to make some friends.

I was standing looking out of the kitchen window that afternoon, aware of a rare and pleasing feeling of real excitement. Grandpops had called round for his usual visit, and he and my mother were out in the back garden. I could tell he was discussing with her what changes she could make (but probably wouldn't ever) to the garden.

They came back indoors, my mother to make a pot of tea, and Grandpops to sit in his usual armchair, now stationed in our new sitting room. The chair was next to the sitting-room door, which opened to the staircase and hall. My mother had recently bought a second-hand bureau, in which to keep, among other things, all the paperwork and ledgers for the new rival haulage business she and my father had decided to set up. Opposite this there was the usual collection of her belongings, stacked in a big heap the other side of the doorway. So in order to go upstairs and start getting ready, I had to walk very close to Pops to get past.

I had, over the last couple of years, grown increasingly adept at keeping my distance from him, as he continued to grab me and 'tickle' me whenever he visited. Though the foul things he did were still a part of my life – a weekly torture – I'd no means of knowing what he did wasn't normal. I thought it must be simply what grandads did to granddaughters everywhere, whether they liked it or not. As with boys, I didn't know whether other girls liked it. All I did know, and I felt this more strongly all the time, was that I didn't like it, didn't want it, and would avoid him whenever possible, today being no exception.

Him lunging at me, laughing, as I tried to slip past him was therefore nothing I hadn't expected. However, I was preoccupied today with going to the youth club, and thinking about what I'd wear that would make me look good. When he then grabbed me and pulled me tight against him, onto his lap, it now felt like a real invasion, in a way it never had before. It might have been to do with my hormones – by now I'd just entered puberty – or it might have been because it reminded me of what had happened with Colin.

I didn't know; all I knew was I hated what he was doing and felt a huge surge of disgust. I had my back to him – unsurprisingly, he'd grabbed me from behind – and my hair immediately became tangled in the pocket watch in his breast pocket, snagging as I tried to move my head away. His arms were tight around mine – they were pinned to my sides now – and he immediately began making the familiar noise with his teeth. He moved one of his arms, securing me more tightly with the other, while he began moving his free hand very fast over my torso, seemingly intent on making contact with my breasts. He had my legs pinned, in exactly the same way he always did, with his own legs crossed tightly around them. He got his hands beneath my top, and then my thin cotton bra, and was now grabbing each breast in turn, clasping them both roughly and making a new sound as he did so – a sort of 'wah' sound he made in time with his groping – and pulling on each nipple, very hard.

It really hurt. But I couldn't get away; he was too strong. I felt so embarrassed, so ashamed and so totally violated – aware something new and horrendous was going on, and it sickened me. I struggled and struggled, rendered speechless with shock, but also too busy fighting him off, and eventually, almost casually, he released his grip and let me go.

As I fled up the stairs, I could hear him laughing. Laughing, as if what he had just done to his own granddaughter was nothing but an amusing bit of horseplay. I threw myself on my bed, holding my breasts in my hands. They'd let me down – that's what they'd done; they'd let me down. And I hated, really *hated* them for it. I started crying and couldn't stop. What was *wrong* with me? And why didn't somebody do something to help me? But who? What could anyone *do*?

It would be a very long time before the scales fell from my eyes and I'd come to accept the foul ordeals I'd suffered at the hands of my own grandad for what they really were – sexual abuse. But this one encounter made a serious impression. On me, because I knew I'd never let him near me again, and on him, because it was soon clear he knew that. He had reached a stage or, more correctly, I'd reached an age, where his casual masturbation with me as a sex toy was becoming untenable. I don't know whether he worried I'd tell someone (who?) or whether he just had a sixth sense he had to stop it – who knew? I even wondered if the real reason Grandpops stopped was because what he most enjoyed was the fear in a powerless little girl's eyes, and I was little and powerless no longer. But whatever the reason, he never touched me again from that day. Not that he needed to, I remember reflecting later. He could now turn his attention to my young sister Karen.

I abandoned my plans to go to the youth club that evening. I curled up into a ball on my bed and went to sleep. At least that way I could blot out the shame and humiliation.

CHAPTER 12

My new freedom from the attentions of Grandpops was a profound relief. But another big challenge was looming. I was due to go back to school almost as soon as we moved in. Doing so was getting more difficult with every year, and my growing insight into my problems made it worse. I'd run away from school nearly every day, either at the start of the day or at lunchtime.

When I was in school, my behaviour was by now being noticed. I started dressing inappropriately, rolling up my school skirt in a provocative manner, and accessorizing our rigorously enforced uniform with brightly coloured chiffon scarves, in an attempt to be rebellious and so have some chance of fitting in.

In reality, I began spending most of my time in a state of anxiety, and often hid in the domestic science store cupboard. I would also take the opportunity to steal food for my mother while I was in there, because she seemed to be so sad and hopeless, and I desperately wanted to make her better. It also relieved the feelings of guilt that racked me, for hating her so much at the same time. Also, perhaps if she felt better she'd clean the house, come to open days, care about my work, and become more like other girls' mums.

Bunking off, too, presented opportunities for stealing. A lot of the time all I'd do was sit in a bus shelter, sad, cold and hungry, ducking if a car or a person came by that might ask what I was up to. But sometimes I'd get a bus into town. There I'd steal clothes for myself and my mother, mostly by walking into dress shops, choosing something, trying it on under my own clothes in the fitting room, then marching straight out.

I was absolutely terrified of getting caught. If I had been I knew I'd feel even worse, but then I'd go back and do it again anyway. There was a part of me that felt elated by the sensation and, just as would happen later when I would drink too much, each time I stole I craved that excitement again.

When I was still thirteen I found a job. My father had been ranting about keeping us 'fucking kids', and how it was time we all got 'fucking jobs', so I looked around and got a Saturday job, working in the local grocery store. This afforded yet more opportunities for stealing. I already spent most of my earnings on food for my mother, but stole a few extras too. I'd steal things like tins of processed peas and mince and sometimes – it being her favourite dessert – a treacle tart and a tin of cream.

I felt, and still feel, hugely guilty about this. My employers were an elderly couple, and while he used to send me up ladders, and then stand under them, she was caring and lovely and very motherly. Though the three women who also worked there were rather snobbish and often unkind (one even pointed out to me how she'd hate it if her daughter 'grew up like' me) the lady owner was always friendly. I could easily have gone home for lunch when I worked there, but she'd prepare me thinly sliced bread and butter, with a small pork pie, tomato and a freshly brewed pot of tea. This small act of kindness always made me feel special, as did the feeling of satisfaction – something I didn't experience anywhere else – that I was good at what I did, both quick and efficient, and that I knew exactly what I was doing.

But even as she went next door to her house to make my lunch, I would help myself to things for my mother. Such a terrible breach of trust, and one that still haunts me, made worse by the fact that I was sure they always knew and, for whatever reason (awareness of my circumstances?) they chose to ignore it.

Back in school my behaviour was becoming increasingly extreme. I had started writing anonymous letters to the head teacher. 'Faith Scott,' I'd write, 'is taking pills all the time and she desperately needs help.' With the help of a handwriting expert, the school eventually traced these to me, with the result that at last my cries for help had been heard and I was sent to a child psychiatrist.

My relief was immense. Finally, someone would be interested enough to try to help me stop being so stupid and feeling bad and full of woe.

The psychiatrist seemed nice, and certainly listened, but as always I was unable to say much. Even had I been able to explain what I was feeling, I could never find the strength to get the words from my mouth. As a consequence, I spent most of the time just sitting there, feeling awkward, and wishing he'd either try to help me to speak or, if he didn't want to, just tell me to go.

Anything would be better than just sitting there feeling his eyes looking at me.

After some weeks of this, my mother, who I knew had been taking pills (Valium, and if she ran out of those, Librium and lately several medicinal glasses of brandy, every night), casually informed me she'd been speaking to the psychiatrist and he'd told her the few things I *had* said, and she'd had to let him know the 'real' truth. My mother's 'truth' was not surprising. I apparently told lies and made up stories all the time, and had been doing both all my life. He shouldn't, according to her, have been worrying. I'd always been a particularly difficult child and all my siblings were fine.

Armed with this knowledge of both adults' complicity, and given that at this point I knew nothing of my mother's fragile state, I'd no choice but to conclude, yet again, the problem lay with *me*. I realized the meetings with the psychiatrist were futile, and where I'd previously spoken little, I now didn't speak at all. I'd spend the entire hour with him sitting staring at my feet.

It was decided, as a consequence, there was no point in my continuing to see him, and I was put on another course of anti-depressants. These I did take because now I'd become really afraid there was something seriously wrong with me.

I gave up again soon after starting, however, because once again they made me feel so strange. I also felt like a nutcase – someone bad and also *mad* now – as well as hopeless and alone.

Ironically, given that the domestic science cupboard was my one place of sanctuary in school, it was during a domestic science lesson I decided I would, instead, take all my pills in one go and, hopefully, never wake up. I did initially consider doing it in the girls' toilet, but I didn't want to die in a toilet on my own.

By now I was really feeling lost – far, far away from every-thing and everyone, as if I was falling down a deep black tunnel, with nothing under my feet to hold me. I clutched on to the sink in my domestic science kitchen cubicle, to stop myself from falling, and pulled the bottle of pills from my cardigan pocket; I'd stashed them there expressly for the purpose. My fingers couldn't seem to grip the bottle cap to undo it, but eventually I managed, and started tipping pills into my palm and popping them into my mouth. Amanda, my classmate, had been watching. 'What are you *doing*?' she asked, alarmed.

I explained my intention to swallow as many as I could, which made her laugh. But then, presumably seeing my determined expression, she called the teacher over. By the time she arrived I'd swallowed a few more, and Amanda explained what I was up to. Which made the teacher shout.

'What on *earth* do you think you're doing?' she demanded. 'What's the matter with you, for goodness' sake!'

Her ticking-off done, she took me off to the sick room, where she laid me on the bed and called an ambulance. I was fully conscious but even so she didn't address me directly. 'How many pills has she taken?' she asked Amanda, as if she'd know much better than me. My teacher's decision not to talk to me directly reinforced my own decision to end my life. Correctly or otherwise, it seemed pretty plain to me my presence on the earth didn't matter in the least and my decision to die had been a sound one.

Two ambulance men arrived in the sick room and hauled me to my feet. I was then marched through the school, a paramedic at each elbow, while the pupils we passed stood and stared. I'd no idea – because nobody spoke to me at any point – the brisk walking was to keep me awake.

I was rushed to Casualty, feeling by now very drowsy, and trolleyed into a room full of doctors and nurses and equipment. Now someone did address me, if only very briefly, to let me know they must pump out my stomach. My wrists and legs were then strapped to a bed, which two nurses, taking hold of the tops of my arms, tipped so that my head hung down over the end. Instructing me to swallow, they began pushing a thick orange tube down my throat. It made me retch straight away and then I couldn't stop retching, grasping the sheet frantically, my eyes and nose running, gasping for breath, feeling as if I was choking. One of the nurses started gently stroking my hair and saying, 'It's okay, it's okay,' over and over. It wasn't okay though. Not at all. Why was she saying such nice things, but doing something so horrible at the same time?

Eventually, however, I managed to stop retching for short periods and they began pouring liquid down the tube. I could feel it in my stomach and as it began its return journey the retching started up for a second time. It seemed like an age before they finally pulled the tube out, by which time I was completely exhausted.

When I awoke I was on a ward, with my mother and uncle (who'd driven her to hospital as my father was working) sitting next to my bed. They were talking to the psychiatrist I'd been seeing and he was suggesting I might be better off in care.

I burst into tears as soon as I heard this. I couldn't bear lying there listening to them talk about me as if I wasn't there. Nobody seemed to care what *I* wanted. I felt a failure – I should have known the pills wouldn't work – and was terrified I'd now be sent away. I mostly couldn't bear the thought of being separated from my mother, and wanted to be as far away from hospitals and psychiatrists as I could get.

Despite my intention to make death the answer to my problems, now all I wanted in the world was to go home.

CHAPTER 13

I did make it to the youth club eventually.

Three months after my overdose, I decided to take a different sort of action. I was seeing the child psychiatrist again, but it seemed as pointless as ever. I felt dreadful, and confused, and at odds with myself, so nothing of consequence had changed. I had, however, reached the inescapable conclusion, in order to cope, I would need to present a different face to the world.

In most areas of my life I was still a mess. He didn't know it, but I still felt betrayed by the psychiatrist, for colluding with my mother. School, too, was still a nightmare. Consequently I played truant most of the time. My mother didn't care. In fact, I think it pleased her. If I didn't go to school I could play mother to her instead.

Looking back, it seems strange that at no point did anyone suggest she was mentally ill, and probably had been for the whole of her children's lives. How different might things have been had I grasped this one simple truth – that she wasn't well? That she had been abused herself? That she was sick? As it was, I just continued to blame myself for everything, casting about for

reasons why I felt the way I felt – a non-person, with no existence except in relation to her.

But the youth club, I decided, might provide sanctuary. In a
place where no one knew me, I could pretend to be someone
else. My older brother Phillip went to it, and had done for some
time, and I finally plucked up the courage and asked to go with
him, the incident by the river now long despatched to a hidden
corner of my mind. It was held in the village hall, in the room
behind the stage, and to get to it you had to walk past the other
youth club members. On my first night some were playing
badminton, I remember. I felt horribly self-conscious, just as I
had at the Honey Globe, but right away I was greeted warmly,
both by the youth leader and her husband. I was also relieved
to see, as my eyes scanned the room, none of the young people
there went to my school so knew nothing about my overdose.
Here, at last, perhaps I might be able to make friends. Most were
older, however, particularly the boys, a lot of whom had cars
and motorbikes, and who seemed very keen to get to know me.

After my experience with Colin, I found this attention difficult to deal with. All I knew was being with boys always seemed
to involve doing things that made me feel uncomfortable. But I
so wanted to be like other girls. They seemed to like all that stuff.
Why couldn't I?

On my first night I was walked home by Paul, 'walking home'
being the thing boys always wanted to do. Paul seemed nice. He
was smartly dressed, friendly, and seemed popular. Despite my
memory of what had happened with Colin, I agreed, because
though older he felt safe to be with.

As soon as we reached my house, however, he started kissing

and caressing me, which I hadn't expected. We'd only walked home, for goodness' sake! But this time I didn't panic. I just stood there and let him. I felt absolutely nothing, nothing at all, but so desperately wanted to; what was wrong with me? *Why* didn't I like what he was doing? And more to the point, did other girls really like it or were they all pretending? And why did being with boys always have to involve all this touching and kissing anyway? Somewhere deep inside there was another feeling too. One of wanting, just as used to happen with Pops and Daniel when they started making odd noises and acting strangely, to burst into hysterical laughter.

In the end, I said I had to go in, and that was the last I had to do with him romantically. I was now anxious around him and happy to avoid him, and he seemed just as happy to avoid me.

Over the following few weeks I was walked home a lot. By Ian, Ron or Rob, by Keith, Chris or Steve, and the routine never, ever varied. The kissing would start, and then the touching and stroking, and with most of the older boys (who scared me, as they were so insistent) there was their obvious desire to 'go all the way'. I'd convince myself the best thing would be to pretend I liked it, while at the same time trying to find excuses not to 'do it', which soon meant I earned a reputation. One of the boys, Chris, made this very clear one night, when he called me a 'prick teaser' in front of everyone.

With the benefit of many years of hindsight, it's so sad to look back at the girl I once was and remember that my principal response to being the subject of everyone's derision wasn't just the obvious one – embarrassment for myself – but also worry that I'd embarrassed my older brother, especially given what he did to me!

But my difficulties with boys, distressing though they were, would turn out to be far less of a challenge than the trauma I was soon to experience with grown men. They were, I already knew unconsciously, an infinitely more scary prospect.

When the time came for choosing roles in the end-of-year school play, I didn't even have to audition. Perhaps sensing I wouldn't put myself forward, and possibly because of his feelings about me, Mr John, who still taught me music, offered me a very small part, as a belly dancer, along with a group of other girls. The play, *The King and I*, was the first organized school activity I ever got involved in and, as it turned out, also the last.

Our costumes were decidedly risqué. We wore yashmaks over our faces, see-through muslin trousers and shimmery tops. It was nerve-racking performing, but positive too. We were a group, and when the girls laughed, I was able to laugh with them. For that brief time on stage, when rehearsing or performing, I felt something new — that I belonged. I also had my face half-hidden, which made it easier, and I felt proud to be a part of it, and did my best.

My parents didn't come to see me. I asked my mother, but she said they had too much to do. This shouldn't have disappointed me, because they never came to the school for anything, but even so it really upset me. I felt such sadness, such a strong sense of being of no consequence, especially when looking into the audience as we danced, and seeing all the other parents watching *their* children — how they threw their heads back, and laughed, and clapped. They all looked so interested and happy; not sad, angry and preoccupied, like mine were.

The performance was in the evening, and it had already been arranged that I'd be included in a lift from the father of Maria, one of the other girls. He'd obviously come to watch her and would take us all home in his van.

Despite the absence of my parents, I felt happy being with the other girls. It was late on a Friday night, which, at thirteen and a half, felt very grown up, and having to pile into the van added to the fun. Maria's father, however, had other ideas. He suggested that I ride up in the front with him, as I was the girl with the longest legs. This was true – I was tall for my age – though in no sense an asset; it just made me feel more visible than the others, when what I desperately wanted was to blend in. I didn't want to be in the front – I wanted to be in the back with the others, but I didn't argue – how could I?

We set off up the road, and a few minutes later, we began approaching the area where I lived. I was turned around at the time, trying to laugh with the others, when I realized we'd just passed the turning to my house. I was too shy to say anything – was Maria's dad going another way? – and then felt confused as we pulled up outside Maria's house, and her dad insisted he drop her off next. She argued, but he insisted and eventually she got out. Once again we set off, but once again we passed my road. I already knew what was going to happen this time, as the van was travelling way too fast to stop there. My confusion turned to fear. What was going on? Why hadn't he dropped me off *that* time? As each of the other girls was dropped off, one by one, I could feel a choking sensation rising in my throat. Why me? I kept asking myself. Why not one of the others? What, I wanted to scream now, was *wrong* with me?

When the last girl got out, he turned the van around slowly, and finally began driving towards my house. I'd begun praying the van would move faster and get me home, when, without a word, he began stroking my thigh. Still silent, he then moved his hand up between my legs. Terrified and speechless, I hardly dared breathe, as he pulled the van up outside my house. He then picked up my hand, held it tightly in his own, and put my fingers round his enormous erect penis, which had appeared in his lap seemingly from nowhere. I felt violently sick as he used it to bring himself to orgasm, still without saying a single word. I was repulsed and bewildered, unable to believe what had just happened. Why me, I thought unhappily, why *me*? He let go of my hand then, and I scrambled from the van, and ran as fast as I could towards our gate. I was breathing so hard I thought I might explode.

When I got indoors, my parents were watching the news on TV. I wanted to shout at them, tell them exactly what had been happening while they'd been sitting watching the bloody news! But I didn't. I was only thirteen, but I already understood. What on *earth* would be the point in doing that? My father would start shouting, my mother would make excuses for him, saying I must be mistaken, and what did I do to cause it? All in all, I just knew there'd be a big scene and, ultimately, I'd end up feeling worse. There was no point in them knowing because I knew they wouldn't defend me. They never had before. They wouldn't now.

When I returned to school the following Monday, I felt changed in a new and awful way. Previously awkward around the other girls in my class and my year, I now felt worlds away from them. I didn't know what to say to any of them now, particularly Maria. What was there *to* say?

I felt dreadful, like a traitor with a secret, that I was a bad person and that this was all my fault. It was made worse by the fact that the family lived close by and my parents knew both him and his wife. She was a leader in the Guides, and he was well respected locally . . . who would believe what he had done to me? I used to wonder what Maria would say if she knew, and felt sure she'd call me a liar. I used to watch her and think to myself 'If only you knew . . .'

But what I mostly felt was the grim realization that I was utterly on my own, and that I didn't really matter to anyone. That a man I hardly knew – a man who knew my *parents* – felt he could get away with doing such things to me made me sure there was something *in* me that made bad things happen. It was an awful thought and it seriously depressed me. To add to this, the girls no longer seemed to like me now that the play was over, and it made me feel angry at myself for believing I could be one of them. Everywhere I went in school now, I felt hated. Beth would slap me around the face and push me at break time. Gaynor would deliberately walk into me, knocking my head against the corridor wall, or push my tummy against the handrail if we passed on the school stairs. Vera frightened me particularly – she was so big and threatening – coming right up to my face and calling me a stupid little cow. She'd then barge me, saying: 'Get out of my way, bitch, and stay out of it.' And everyone, inexplicably, found this funny. They'd all laugh and then walk off laughing more.

I didn't know how to deal with this. I didn't even know why they were doing it. Except for the obvious reason – I was worthless and different. I was the stupid, silly girl my mother always called me. The one all the horrible men liked. The one who couldn't tell them to go away. The one who felt so afraid all the time. I'd learn, much later, that Maria's father chose *me*, as opposed to any of the other girls he knew, because men like that often have a keen eye for a target; they know not to choose the confident girls, from loving homes. They choose vulnerable girls who are too afraid to fight them off or speak out. Girls who wouldn't be believed. And I was one of them. I'd been conditioned from such a young age to think everything was my fault, that by now I didn't know any different. And as no one had ever encouraged me to say what I felt or to choose what I wanted, I no longer even knew what that was. I was just a receptacle for others to abuse. An empty vessel. Everything *was* my fault.

A couple of months later, I started my periods.

Presumably because I'd missed so much school I'd learned nothing about what was going to happen, and the sight of the blood terrified me. I was so shocked I started screaming, and then shouting to my mother – who was downstairs – completely in a panic about what was happening.

She came upstairs and started talking in a stage whisper. 'Shut up!' she hissed. 'What do you think you're doing, you disgusting thing! Your brothers and dad are downstairs!' She looked cross and I couldn't fathom why. She pointed her finger then. 'Do you want them to *know*?'

She went into her bedroom and returned with a dirty-looking, twisted, pale-pink thing, which I'd later find out was called a sanitary belt. She then threw some enormous sanitary towels at me, which again I later realized must have been the type used following a pregnancy. 'Put that on,' she said, gesturing to the pink thing in my hand. 'And if you need some more towels, they're in my wardrobe.'

I sat in the bathroom for a while, unable to stop crying, then finally forced myself to put the disgusting sanitary belt round my waist. I felt awful, ashamed, even more of a bad person. All this disgusting paraphernalia revolted me, just as much as it all clearly revolted my mother. And as a consequence, I now felt revolting too. Worse still, this seemed proof I was going to end up *like* my mother, which traumatized me even more. I went straight to bed and cried myself to sleep.

Nothing further concerning periods was ever mentioned by my mother again. Even so, blood was a constant in our house. My mother had always been either pregnant or bleeding, and now I understood the reason why. Her reticence about discussing periods was not unexpected, given she never discussed anything with me. But her apparent dislike of female matters being broad-cast around the house was a little strange given her own habits.

She had, over a long period of time – all of my life – amassed a stack of used sanitary towels in her bedroom. They formed a pile nearly to the ceiling, beside her wardrobe. She'd regularly bring smaller piles of these downstairs, to make new stacks of used sanitary towels beside her chair. She'd intermittently grab towels from this pile and throw them on the fire while she sat and read her magazines. The smell as they burned was beyond description, and one I'd never forget.

Why she did it, I had no idea. She seemed oblivious to the stench, which was incredible, and oblivious to how anyone in the room with her might feel. I didn't have a clue what I should do with my used towels, but there was no way on earth I was doing *that*. I used to wrap them carefully, take them to school and put them in the disposal bin.

I couldn't bear the thought that one day I would be a woman too, and spent several months following the beginning of my periods desperately trying to pretend I was a boy.

The used sanitary towels weren't the only foul thing around the house. My mother had had whooping cough as a child and, as a consequence, had severe and chronic asthma. She'd cough a great deal and repeatedly spit phlegm into pieces of toilet roll. Once done, she'd stuff the resultant ball either down the side of her chair or into the bucket beside it. They invariably remained there for days. It was revolting enough listening to the constant coughing and throat-clearing, but to have to clear the tissues from the chair sides, empty the bucket and, worst of all, collect up all the tissues that had missed it, was truly disgusting, and made me retch.

That my mother's behaviour was unusual was becoming more apparent with every year, even if I'd no notion of what was usual. As I entered my mid-teens she became obsessed with the occult, and was convinced she'd lived a previous life and had returned in a different body. She believed she'd been a soldier in the war, but because she got killed before she could learn everything she should, she had to come back now to learn it.

She told me she had a spirit guide who lived on her shoulder. He was a little male Indian, called Henry, and she had to ask him if it was safe before doing anything that meant leaving the house. The house itself was apparently full of ghosts, and because she was brought up by witches (she said all the women in her family were witches, some of whom were burned at the stake), she had a relationship with them; they were people who'd 'gone to the other side'.

She collected books about reincarnation, and now began going to strange meetings. Sometimes she'd go alone, and sometimes with other family members. They'd return with stories of dead people being spoken to, and of having had their palms read.

Only once was I persuaded to go – I found the whole idea very frightening – and it was every bit as gruesome as I'd feared. There were people walking around in long black gowns, with hoods so big they could pull them almost right over their faces, giving the impression they were faceless. They walked with a stoop, which made them seem even more ghoulish, and didn't look up or speak at any point.

My mother was very excited – I could tell that straight away. She'd bought herself a box of chocolate peanuts and raisins, called Poppets, and was humming and tapping on the box ever more quickly while she waited for the meeting to start.

But then, suddenly, a small light pierced the gloom, illuminating three people on the stage. There were two of the shrouded figures flanking a little old lady, who immediately raised her hands and called: 'Is there anybody there?' My mother was galvanized by this and pulled out a little red book from her handbag, into which she started scribbling all the names the old lady was calling out.

When I asked her why she did that she told me it was so she

could think about the names later, to see if she could identify any of them. She seemed desperate to have something to contribute to the list of dead people; trying to think of everyone dead she'd ever known so she could shout out that she knew them too. It was unsettling to see her like this; so agitated yet so excited by all this scary stuff.

Worse, she seemed to have half the family believing it too, even though it seemed so obvious to me it was all make-believe and self-deception. It made it feel even harder to establish what was false and what was real; she had so little grasp on the real people around her, yet, as with her animals when we'd lived at our last house, she seemed to find dead people so much easier to care about.

CHAPTER 14

Perhaps as a subconscious protest against my mother's obsession with the occult, when I was around fourteen, I joined a local church.

I'd all but given up on youth club. Aside from the reputation I seemed to have acquired, I'd grown increasingly fearful of some girls there. One in particular, who wore knuckledusters, had started threatening me; I wasn't exactly sure what the reasons were – probably just because I was younger and new to the village and had drawn so much negative attention to myself. And I certainly wasn't about to take her on.

So when I saw a poster outside the Free Church advertising a youth group meeting, I decided to try it. I'd had little experience of either church or churchgoers, but had gone with Nan when I was younger and always liked the sombre nature and silence of a church.

I didn't know what I expected, but the decision turned out to be the right one. As soon as I met the pastor who ran the youth group I fell immediately in love. It didn't matter that he was old enough to be my father. It didn't matter that he was married

– his wife was lovely too – and it didn't matter that he had a child and another baby on the way. It wasn't a love I planned to do anything about. I just wanted to be included in his world. He was so kind to me he made me cry. It was as if he was the fantasy father I'd never had; he exuded goodness and gentleness and interest in me. I began going to church twice every Sunday.

The pastor was a wonderful man. And despite his physical presence not being that of a heart-throb, I'm sure, looking back, he was used to being the subject of adoration for many a teenage girl in need of friendship and support. He treated me so kindly, and with such respect and concern, that he immediately became my parents' worst enemy.

My mother, in particular, was furious. She told me to stay away from 'that church', as it was dangerous, and the kind of people who went there were all odd and needed help. She told me there were lots of stories about the sort of people who went to 'free churches', and my father, whose contribution was as articulate as ever, was to simply warn me to 'fucking stay away'.

My mother also added that once people like that 'got me', I'd never get away. They'd alter my mind and make me believe all sorts of evil rubbish and, anyway, as I'd been confirmed in the Church of England, if I went to any church, it had to be that one, so I'd end up with Jesus in heaven. Despite the fact neither she nor my father went to church (in fact my father told me he couldn't go because he was too wicked) my mother had been telling me all my life about the importance of this; that it was only because she had bothered to christen me that I wouldn't be going straight to hell. Except now I might still go to hell in any case, because people who went to *that* sort of church were definitely not welcome in heaven.

In a rare burst of defiance, I ignored her. I continued to go to church, albeit in secret, because everyone who went there was so kind and friendly – and I'd hardly ever known such a thing. It was also much better than being in my house with all the anger and swearing and arguments and filth. By now my mother had produced two further children – a girl called Mary and a boy called Mark – and there seemed to be more blood and mess than ever. She'd leave her bedsheets pulled back and her bedroom door open, and the sheet would be covered in drying blood.

I kept going to the free church for several months, having at last found a place where I mattered. My nan found this annoying too. These days I avoided her as much as possible, but on the odd occasion I did see her it seemed to make her really angry, and my going to church clearly made her even more wild. 'Who do you think you are?' I remember her saying to me one day. 'You come into this village and now you think you own the place.'

Eventually, and entirely without my knowing it, the pastor made a visit to my parents' house and asked if he might adopt me. My father's response was unequivocal. 'Don't you ever come near this fucking house again,' he warned him, 'you fucking daft cunt.'

My mother gave me chapter and verse on all this some months after it happened, and I was deeply moved when I found out. The pastor never spoke to me about it personally, but I found out he'd been concerned about my welfare, and was only reassured when a lady at the church, who'd been at school with my father, convinced him all was okay.

I don't doubt both he and she believed this. As with everyone who only knew the face my father presented to the outside world, she'd have known nothing of what went on behind the facade. And this was compounded by the fact that her son and my brother were close friends.

I continued my relationship with the church even so and began increasingly getting involved. I started going to rallies with the pastor that Cliff Richard sang at, and would often take boys from both school and the church along too. One boy, called Ted, I liked very much and we began seeing each other as girlfriend and boyfriend – my first ever proper teenage boy–girl relationship; he was the first boy I'd spent time with who didn't touch me.

I'd met him at the youth group and I really fancied him, even though on the surface he was an unlikely boy for me to like. He was confident, big-headed even, older than me, and a carpenter. I couldn't believe it when he asked if he could walk me home and didn't touch me – only very gently kissed me.

His parents were dead and he'd moved to the area from the south-west, in order to live with his sister and her husband, who owned a pub a few miles away. I felt so special when I was with him – once again, I genuinely seemed to matter – and we began seeing one another regularly. Often, on Sundays, when my father was out working, he'd come to the house and spend the afternoon with me, which was wonderful, but also made me anxious. I was always terrified my father would arrive home before he left, and start shouting and swearing and being vile; he hated anyone being in the house, but especially someone male, and would have taunted me into saying something so he'd have an excuse to be really aggressive.

But I couldn't cope even with Ted. Much as I liked him, I couldn't seem to accept that he liked me too. In fact, I was increasingly scared, as I got to know him, that the more he got to know me, the sooner he'd realize what I was really like, and then he wouldn't like me any more. I couldn't bear this. I couldn't bear the thought of the hurt I knew I'd feel. So before that could happen, I decided to finish with him. He was so upset, and when we parted I was all over the place, but somewhere in my fourteen-year-old, desperately unhappy mind, I felt convinced it was all for the best.

Better, I decided, to stick with what I knew; that I was ugly and uninteresting and useless, not worthy of the attentions of a nice boy. Better to stick with the sort of boys who only wanted me for one thing, boys who were definitely not too good for me. Boys who were able to reinforce my feelings of self-loathing, by insisting evenings out always ended the same way.

I decided I could cope with this better. Better to give them what they wanted sexually, than to panic and run away and feel even worse. Better than having someone make me question myself, like Ted had done when he'd bought me a beautiful suede handbag for Christmas, that I knew someone useless like me didn't deserve.

So I was grateful, mostly, for the sexual attention. It was simpler, less anxiety-inducing and it was familiar. Because by now, even though I didn't consciously know it, I was already on the edge – full to bursting – with all the horrible secrets I was keeping.

★   ★   ★

But if I'd written off the idea of being worthy of a boyfriend, I was still lonely and desperate for a friend. So I was thrilled when Ellie, who'd taken me to the Honey Globe cafe eighteen months back, started spending time with me at school. I worked hard at this friendship, because it was one of the few I'd ever had, and being Ellie's friend mattered greatly. I stopped going to church, because she said it was boring and old-fashioned, I took care not to upset her, and I always tried to please her – if I crossed her, she'd tell all the other girls and then I was bullied again.

Ellie was fun to be with, though – full of confidence and always laughing. She taught me how to smoke Embassy cigarettes, down the bank, in the school grounds, which made me cough, and reminded me horribly of my mother, but I persevered because smoking seemed to help me fit in.

Ellie was also a bit wild. She was the daughter of a chauffeur who worked for a local aristocrat, and they lived in a huge old tied house. Her bedroom was massive, and it was always a treat if we went somewhere and I was allowed to stay at hers. Always, that was, except when she wanted to bring a boy back; on one occasion, she managed to sneak one upstairs. I was made to sleep underneath her bed, where I had to lie there and listen to them doing it. Though nothing to do with me, it made me feel dreadful. Dirty, for some reason. Ashamed.

Ellie also stole £10 notes from her father's wallet, which horrified me even more. It was something I'd never dare do myself, *ever*, yet I felt sure, from the way Ellie's mum used to look at me, she thought it wouldn't be happening if not for me. I was a bad influence, because I came from a rough family. I'd say things to Ellie – suggest she shouldn't do it. But she'd just laugh and carry on regardless.

One day, Ellie asked me if I'd like to go to a disco with her. It was held in the village near to where Grandpops lived, so, though close to where she lived, it was a long way for me. I knew I could sleep over at her house afterwards, but I wasn't sure how I could get there.

'Simple,' she told me. 'You just thumb a lift.'

I'd never done anything like that before, and wasn't even sure how you did. So she showed me and, on and off, I spent the rest of the day practising. I squashed all the feelings of anxiety that kept surfacing as I made my way, on that first cold, dark January evening, to the main road, to wait for a car. I'd heard a lot of stories about hitchhiking, and was pretending a boldness I really didn't feel. But I was determined to do it.

As it turned out, hitchhiking was to be the least of my troubles. Yes, it was invariably a man who picked me up and, yes, it was always scary; I already knew more about certain types of men than I'd have liked, and no amount of perfectly unthreatening experiences made my relief any less when I got out of a car. But at the same time it was exciting. I was fifteen years old now, and I was going off to discos with a friend.

Ellie and I went to the disco a lot at the weekends in the spring and summer of 1970. It was called *Flames* and was at the edge of the village, behind the pub, and was always dark and mysterious and throbbing with young people. You'd have to get a stamp on your hand when you first arrived so they'd know, if you went out, you'd paid. They played all the music that was popular at the time: 'In the Summertime' by Mungo Jerry, 'I Want You Back' by the Jackson Five, and 'All Right Now' by Free. Everyone drank alcohol and ID didn't exist. If you looked old enough you got served, and everyone did. I didn't like alcohol much – and still don't – but I did enjoy Babycham, and sometimes had gin, though I needed lots of Coke to hide the taste. The boys always seemed to drink lager.

It was where boys and girls danced and 'got off with' one another and the atmosphere was always exciting; dark, very smoky, full of people. Boys would come, boys would go – we'd sometimes accept the offers of one or two that looked nice – but mostly Ellie and I would put our handbags on the dance floor and happily dance round them all evening.

I'd invariably sleep at Ellie's afterwards, and get the bus home in the morning. But one night, in October, she suggested something else – that we go and stay the night at a hotel. I felt immediately uneasy, and said so. I explained I'd never stayed at a hotel before, *ever*, had no money, and besides, how would we get there?

Which made Ellie cross. 'God!' she said, irritably, 'why do you have to be so boring and old-fashioned?' It turned out this boy – who she'd been dancing with all night, and who she'd been after for weeks – had come by car with his friend so could give us a lift.

Now I felt even more anxious. I hadn't spoken to this friend – I hadn't even seen him – but, as ever, I felt I had to go along with what Ellie wanted. So we climbed into the back and drove off to the hotel. Once there, I felt even more mortified. I had on a long green and white maxi dress, but no coat and, crucially, no shoes.

Looking back, it seems almost inconceivable that in October I'd go out without shoes. But I'd actually do it regularly, and had done all summer, because I always felt too tall (I *was* tall) when I had my shoes on, and was as sensitive to Ellie's jibes about my height as I was to her jibes about my weight.

I was also not expecting to be walking any distance. I danced barefoot at the disco anyway, so it wasn't an issue, and the only outdoor walking, or so my logic went, would be from the pavement to whichever car picked me up when I hitchhiked.

Now I realized this only compounded my problem. I didn't, by any stretch of the imagination, look like someone who'd stay at a hotel. I also now realized I'd got things all wrong. The boys weren't just dropping us off at the hotel. They intended to stay there as well. I tried to keep calm and reason with myself: *Why shouldn't they stay? They have driven all this way. What difference will it make to me and Ellie?*

But then we were taken upstairs and shown to two rooms, and the full extent of my naivety dawned. The first was a big double, which Ellie immediately claimed. 'This one is our one!' she whooped. I went to follow her, and she placed a hand on my chest. 'Not you,' she said, 'you're not staying in this room. This one,' she said, taking the boy's hand, 'is for me and Ben.'

I just stood there, agog, while she closed the door behind them, and then realized the porter was holding a fire door open for us further down the corridor. Not knowing what else to do now, I turned and followed him, Ben's friend behind me, my heart now banging against my chest. We passed through another two fire doors and more corridors – the upstairs of the hotel was like a maze – and by the time he finally unlocked a door and ushered us inside, I didn't have a clue where we were. I was relieved to see it was a twin, and not a double, like Ellie's, but even so I felt almost as if I was having one of my mother's asthma attacks; I was struggling to find breath.

For the first time that evening I looked properly at Ben's friend, and could see he was older than the rest of us. He had thick black hair and a dark shadow of facial hair too, and I imagined he must be well into his twenties. Neither of us spoke for a long, long moment, and I almost felt relieved. Was he as embarrassed as I was? But my hope was short-lived. He'd obviously had quite a lot to drink, and didn't seem embarrassed in the slightest.

'Oh, well,' I said, laughing nervously and gesturing to the nearest bed. 'I'll sleep in this one.' I then got in, fully clothed.

I lay there for a bit, my face close to the wall, listening to what I assumed were the sounds of him undressing, and then, to my horror, I was aware of the covers being pulled back, and felt him getting into my bed behind me.

I held my breath, feeling a sick panic rising in my stomach, and almost gagging at the feeling of his body up against me, and the obvious erection he had pushing against my lower back. He grabbed my shoulder then and started trying to yank my dress up and pulled at my pants, attempting to force himself inside me from the back.

I grappled desperately with him, trying to keep him away from me, but he kept trying to push his penis in me from behind. My arms hurt from the pinching of his fingernails and I could feel his hot breath in my ear. It seemed a long time before he finally gave up and got out again. I heard him climb onto the other bed.

I lay rigid in my own bed, then curled tight against the wall, like a foetus, hardly daring to breathe, wide awake, afraid.

The room fell silent and finally I risked turning over, finding being able to hear him but not see him too scary. But what I then saw was him once again advancing towards me, fully naked, his erect penis out in front of him.

We struggled again and, despite the alcohol I could smell on his breath, he was slim and fit, and clearly very strong. He seemed determined to pull me over onto my back so he could force his erection between my legs, and I had to use every ounce of strength to stop him.

Out of breath, momentarily, he then gave up, flopping heavily on his back on the bed beside me, alcohol fumes coming from his mouth. Not a word passed between us at any point.

I should scream, I thought. Cry for help. *Scream*, get some *help*! But even as I thought it, no sound came out. All I could think of was how much trouble I'd be in. I didn't know where I was, didn't know where Ellie was. Didn't know anything of any help at *all* – just how much trouble I'd be in. This was my fault. I'd made this happen by letting myself be brought here. Had let it happen because I hadn't said 'No' at the start. I was on my own with a man who was drunk and determined to have sex with me, and it was obviously all my fault.

Perhaps sensing that I wasn't going to shout the house down, he roused himself for another attempt to overpower me. This time he took hold of my arms and tried to pin them to the bed, while again trying to throw me over onto my back. In response, I immediately rolled back onto my side, pulling my legs as tightly as I could towards my chest, but he then straddled me and, clearly not concerned where he was jabbing, started trying to ram his penis into my bottom.

Now I lashed out and hit him, rolling back over as I did so and, still wordless but now, at last, apparently discouraged, he climbed off and went back to the other bed.

My relief, once again, was short-lived. He persisted for the rest of the night, his attempts only interrupted by him going into the en suite bathroom and urinating noisily with the door open. And though I was mostly able to wrestle him off me, at no point, except to lie there and pant and get his breath back, did he ever completely give up.

At some point near dawn I must have finally dozed off, because I awoke relieved to see it was finally morning, but also in a state of disbelief. Yet we walked down to breakfast as if nothing had happened. Almost as if he hadn't spent the entire night attacking me, but we'd simply climbed into our beds and gone to sleep. Ellie and Ben were already at a table, eating a hearty cooked breakfast and laughing.

I crossed the room, my bare feet sinking into the thick carpet, and my heart sinking at the thought of the sight I must have looked. I whispered to Ellie – how on earth were we going to pay? But she smiled and told me I mustn't worry. Ben and his friend were going to pay for the rooms, and she'd already agreed she'd pay them back. The men both left soon after, and I knew she never would pay them and, inexplicably, given the night I'd been through, this knowledge made me feel even worse.

And we still had no way of getting home. 'Oh, don't worry,' Ellie said. 'I'll ring this boy I know. He really fancies me. He'll come and get us.'

As we waited, I was entirely lost for words. She didn't ask and I certainly didn't want to tell her what had happened – besides, she was too busy telling me all about Ben, and what a lovely night they'd spent together.

Then the boy came and got us and, as promised, drove us home. I sat in the back, listening as they chatted, all the time with her hand firmly on his knee. What made me incredulous was that she didn't just *not* fancy him. She didn't even *like* him. She just used him.

I couldn't get my mind around that at all.

CHAPTER 15

I was no stranger to feeling worthless and dirty, or to feeling cross and remorseful about myself either. But the incident at the hotel was a watershed. As the days turned into weeks the feelings persisted; I began feeling dangerously angry at myself. I had such intense feelings of self-loathing by now, it was as if I needed to try to destroy my very being. I began binge-eating, or not eating, and taking laxatives and diuretics, all of which made me feel awful. I hated myself on the inside *and* the outside. Hated my ugly face, my horrible hair, my height, the size of my feet. I hated the sound of my voice and how stupid I was – hated every last thing that made up Faith Scott, and came very close to trying to take my life again.

Why hadn't I acted more boldly? Yes, I'd fought him, with every ounce of strength I had, yet why hadn't I summoned help? Why hadn't I simply fled? Or hit him even harder? Even killed him? And why, once it was over, had I not reported him? Gone to the police and shopped him for being the rapist that he was?

Because, at that point in my life, I didn't even *see* it as rape. I saw it as the natural culmination of the damning fact that I'd never said 'No'.

I thought a lot about Ellie, too. Ellie liked sex. She told me. She seemed to *do* it all the time, so she clearly wasn't lying. Crucially, too, she didn't *just* do sex. Boys who had sex with Ellie still wanted to be around Ellie. Still pursued her, flirted with her, wanted to spend time with her. Ellie was proof that having sex with boys was normal. It was obviously *me* who had the problem.

Yes, I was angry with her. How could I not be? I couldn't ever imagine setting her up with a stranger and just expecting them to get on with it. That said, if I had, she probably wouldn't have minded. She loved boys. She loved sex. The problem of hating it was mine alone. So, in the end, it was easy to internalize everything. Hope the nightmares – in which he was usually faceless; just a menacing form, often just an erect penis – would eventually lessen and go away. And to accept that because there was something so wrong with me, I really needed Ellie in my life.

And I needed to think more like Ellie. As the year drew to a close I started going out even more. I decided I'd blot out the horrible memories by making new ones. I took up drinking and smoking and dancing with boys with an almost religious fervour because, temporarily, it helped blot out the pain.

It was at the same disco – *Flames* – that we'd gone to that fateful night, I first laid eyes on Robert. Robert was older than me. He was in his early thirties, while I was still not quite sixteen. He was really good-looking, and I liked him immediately, and it seemed he was keen on me too.

He'd drive round to my house (though never coming in, obviously) to pick me up, and take me to the pub. We'd talk and have fun and I gradually began to feel there was hope for me after all. Robert wanted to have sex with me every single time we went out but I managed to hold him off. By now my fear of the consequences if I *did* let him have sex was greater than my need to acquiesce. But he was patient, too – I think he was confident that, eventually, I would cave in.

In short, I knew it couldn't last. Didn't normal girls eventually consent to having sex with their boyfriends? And if I didn't, how long was he going to stick around? Yet if I let him have sex with me, what then? I already felt bad enough about myself as it was because, deep down, I knew I didn't really ever want *any* man to touch me, even one I really liked. Which was all wrong, surely? I *should* like it.

And if we did have sex, it seemed clear what would happen. He'd no longer be interested in me, because I wasn't interesting. My refusal to have sex was the one hold I did have, but its grip was becoming increasingly tenuous.

I asked him, after much soul-searching, one evening: 'If I agree to have sex with you, will you still want to go out with me afterwards?'

'Of *course* I will!' he answered, sounding like he meant it. 'Of course! I'll want to be with you even more!'

So that night I consented, for the first time in my life, to having sex with a man. We climbed into the back of his car and had sex and I hated every single traumatic, painful moment. He clearly enjoyed it but I felt nothing. I felt hollowed out, empty, disappointed and sad. Why would anybody do this willingly?

He took me home then, his manner playful, jokey and reassuring. When I got in, still anxious about what had taken place, my mother was sitting in her chair. She had a skein of wool over the arm and was humming as she wound it into a ball. She looked up as I entered but said nothing.

I stood and watched her for a bit and when she'd finished she stood up, then went and picked out this horrible, disgusting, goldy-coloured jumper from one of the heaps of stuff around the room. 'Hmm,' she said. 'Now this. What shall I do with this? Hmm. I shall unpick it and make a bobble hat, I think.'

I continued to stare at her, thinking *why*? Who'd want a bobble hat? Who'd want a hat in that disgusting colour – even if she finished it, which I knew she never would. And then I just blurted it out. I felt bad and I needed to tell someone. I needed some reassurance because the thing I'd just done felt not so different to the things that had been done by men *to* me, and which I'd hated so much, and which haunted me. Was I now *like* them? One of them? It was all so horribly, wretchedly confusing. 'I've had sex,' I told her. 'I've had sex with a man.'

She stood straighter, her expression suddenly changing. 'You've *what*?!' she shouted, immediately very angry. 'You stupid bloody girl! You silly, *stupid* bloody girl! Don't you understand? Now they'll *all* want it! *All* of them! You stupid, bloody, silly, bloody girl!'

I stared at her, not knowing what to say. She'd confirmed, not just by her words, but by her response, I'd been right to feel bad and alone. That I'd been born a Wednesday's child and that my destiny was fixed. It would surely lead me to failure, to getting everything wrong and to unhappiness, and there was nothing I could do about it.

I went to bed even more upset than when we'd done it, but at least, I consoled myself, I had Robert. My mother *had* to be wrong. And I had Robert, who loved me. I didn't care about anyone else.

But Robert didn't turn up to take me to the pub the next evening, even though that's what we'd arranged. He didn't show up the following night either, and when I eventually plucked up the courage to phone him, he told me he was going on holiday and would telephone me when he returned. I waited patiently, but I knew what was going to happen, and it did. I never heard from him again.

I don't know what I learned from my experience with Robert. What seems obvious seen through so much older, wiser eyes would appear to have been painfully absent. Because from then on, a pattern emerged. I'd go out, I'd dance, I'd 'get off' with older men, I'd consent to having sex – in the backs of cars, mostly – I'd hate it, and just pray for it to end and when, as they always did, they'd ask me how it'd been for me, I'd invariably answer: 'Mmmm, okay, nice . . .'

The truth, of course, was that sex was loathsome. Just as loathsome as it had been every single time Daniel had pulled those faces, made those noises, made me touch his rigid thing, squirted his warm pungent stuff in my mouth – choking me – or all over my hands and clothes. It was loathsome; as loathsome as Grandpops' tickles, and I knew I'd hate it for the rest of my life. Though how long that would be was uncertain at the time as I honestly believed I might do away with myself before I consciously realized what I was doing.

I could not, however, hate men. My fear, dread and loathing about the things men sometimes did was obviously because I was such a bad person.

But I'd now become adept at creating an exterior, so I could pretend I was normal, which did allow me some sort of life. At least I went out, and at least I still had Ellie. But what I didn't have was any sort of plan for the rest of my life.

I was told I was allowed to leave school at fifteen, which I was only too happy to do. By the time I'd endured the assault in the hotel, I was essentially drifting, with no idea what sort of job I might do. I was still working in the grocers, but by now, almost two and a half years after I'd begun, my position felt more and more precarious. I was still stealing food for my mother. I couldn't stop myself – it was the only way I could ease my guilt about not being able to change her. If I couldn't make her better, at least I could give her something nice, and food – even with all its scary associations with my childhood – was something that seemed would do that. Some days, I was the only one allowed to use the till, and I knew they were watching me and, though I'd never stolen money from them – only food – I felt sure that soon they'd confront me.

I needed to leave anyway, and get a full-time job. My father was becoming angry and shouting all the time about how long he'd 'fucking kept us'.

My mother's input, as ever, was minimal. 'Your role is to get married,' she kept reminding me. 'To have babies and look after your husband. Careers are not important for women.'

This felt terribly depressing. My mother had spent her whole life, one way and another, as a slave to men. First her father, Grandpops, who I'd eventually learn abused her both emotionally and sexually, and then to my own father, who treated her appallingly, was cruel to her, kept giving her baby after baby, and spent what free time he had with other women. My mother was pathetic in the real sense of the word, and the thought I might become like her was horrifying.

It was my mother, however, who found me a job. A start in a local hairdressers who were looking for an apprentice. I was so painfully shy that I couldn't think of a single thing to say to the customers.

After two weeks at the hairdressers I got my first wage packet and brought it home. It was only £3.50 – an apprentice's pay – so my mother decided that my keep should be set at £1.50 a week.

My father went berserk at this, jumping up from his armchair and rounding on her, as if she'd committed some heinous crime.

'I've been fucking well keeping her for years!' he started shouting. 'And I'm not fucking doing it any longer! I'm not fucking keeping her' – he jabbed a finger in my direction – 'while she fucks around doing fucking hairdressing, earning next to nothing – she can do a proper fucking job like everyone else. In full-time service I was, when I was fourteen – fourteen! – let alone her fucking age! And her fucking brother too – fucking staying on at school, when he should be fucking out working! I'm fucked if I know,' he finished, while my mother stood there looking completely defeated. 'What is the *fucking* world coming to?'

I made a decision that day, about my father. My father who resented me so much. Who seemed to feel anger at my very existence. I'd stood there and listened to him ranting at my mother, about me – not *to* me, just *about* me, as ever – and I decided if there was one thing I was set on, it would be to never want or have anything from him *ever* again.

I left the hairdressers the next day, and went to work in an electronics factory. At least I'd earn a 'proper' wage, as he put it, pay my keep, and become independent. My determination, however, was short-lived. It took me only till lunchtime to realize that I could not spend my entire life putting screws into plugs.

The reality hit on the way home. I'd no proper job, no money and no boyfriend. I hated my father. Hated that his terrifying outbursts were becoming more and more frequent, and now creeping beyond the miserable four walls of our house, to neighbours, to Nan, to anyone, really, who dared get in his way. I hated being part of my so-called 'family' more than I could ever find words for.

I was still seeing the psychiatrist, not because I trusted him, or found it helpful, but simply because it'd been part of being allowed to go home after my overdose. But now I decided I'd stop. Why not? It'd been two and a half years after all. What could they do to me if I didn't turn up?

And so I drifted. I babysat for neighbours, and I did cleaning work in an old people's home, and I had just about enough money; enough, at least, to allow me to go out at the weekends with Ellie, to dance and meet boys, and try to forget about the mess I was in. I rushed from man to man, never allowing myself to think about why, because it was just too overwhelming. *Everything* about my life felt too overwhelming, and all I could do, in my head at least, was to keep running from it, as fast as I could.

That I was in a downward spiral was clear. Except it was difficult to conceive of any aspect of my life that could be any worse. That it could even be *different* felt like a ridiculous dream. But it was about to become different in almost *every* way. From the moment, in *Flames*, when I met Joe.

CHAPTER 16

It wasn't that I liked Joe. Not initially. It was a Saturday night in June 1971, and I was at the disco, with Ellie. The DJ was playing 'Brown Sugar' by The Rolling Stones, which I'd later find out Joe loved as well; we'd often sing along to it together.

But I wasn't really concentrating on the music. Also at the disco was a girl I knew slightly, who was apparently engaged to a boy I knew better; I'd gone out with him several times and also had sex with him, not knowing he even *had* a girlfriend, let alone that she was his fiancée. Yet she was, and she was scary, and was out to get me. She was there with another girl, and both were trying to corner me, and I was frightened and didn't know what to do.

I was just trying to work out a plan, when I saw Joe standing at the bar. I recognized him, having seen him at the disco before, and decided to go up and chat to him. I had no particular interest in getting to know him better but if I was with someone, they couldn't hurt me, and it would also show them I wasn't interested in her fiancé.

He was tanned, and had shoulder-length, dark, untidy hair,

and dressed scruffily in jeans, boots, and an open-necked shirt, which I still remember today as being turquoise. He was leaning against the bar and he watched me approach.

'Hi,' I said, acting a lot bolder than I felt, leaning in so he could hear me above the music. There was a strange sweetish smell that seemed to cling to him.

'Hello,' he replied, smiling.

'Hi!' I shouted a second time. 'I think I know you, don't I? I'm sure we've spoken, but I can't remember your name.'

We hadn't spoken at all, as he probably knew, but he smiled again and said, 'Joe. D'you wanna dance?'

I nodded, he downed his pint and we walked to the dance floor, where we bobbed around, and he shouted conversation at me, none of which I could make out. It didn't matter. I just nodded and smiled where appropriate, glad to feel protected from the furious fiancée.

By the end of the evening, I still wasn't sure if I liked him, but he certainly seemed to like me. He had his friend drive me home in his flash E-Type Jaguar, and I could tell he'd arranged it to impress me. It didn't – the car, though big on the outside, was really cramped on the inside and, as it was a two-seater, I spent the journey crammed on Joe's lap, bent double as the roof was so low.

But there was something about Joe that made him different. He wasn't pushy, or forward, and genuinely seemed to like just being with me. He often commented I was too good for him; was even humble, which was something entirely new. And because I, in contrast, wasn't sure about my feelings, there was no pressure, no sense of urgency. We just drifted together and he was happy to be patient, in the hopes that I'd come to feel as he did. Sex with Joe would come later and would come naturally. Joe, in fact, would become the only man in my life I would ever enjoy sex with.

He was eighteen and, for all his gentleness around me, Joe was as uncouth as my father. He swore all the time, and seemed to speak to anyone and everyone without a care in the world about how he came across. This made him slightly frightening to be around, as there was always this potential for something to flare up and, on more than one occasion, it did. It was as if he was perpetually ready to take issue with the world – not aggressively, particularly, just entirely without concern for how others perceived him. He also had a side to him that disturbed me. One day, in a garden centre (where he used to steal stuff to sell) he pulled down his jeans, squatted, and did a poo in a large flowerpot, then, laughing, stood up and walked on.

He worked as a bricklayer's labourer, though as that job was dependent on the weather he also made money by other means, one of them being his regular small-hours outings, with his brother-in-law, to a neighbouring farmer's field. Here they'd dig up and fill sacks with potatoes, carrots and whatever vegetables were in season, which they'd sell to the neighbours the next day.

Yet despite all this, there was something I liked about Joe. He was good-looking (and never short of female attention) and seemed afraid of nothing and no one. Most importantly, though, was that he was never, ever mean to me. He was kind to me, accepted me exactly as I was, and never asked anything of me. Plus we'd talk about anything and everything. And though I didn't fancy him at first, I did enjoy the frisson of the danger I felt when in his company – never towards me, just the aura of it. But most important was that, with Joe, I was part of a couple, which meant I wasn't so alone.

By the time I'd been seeing Joe for a few weeks, life at home had become unbearable. I still hadn't found a proper job, and my father would constantly shout and swear at my mother about it. It was after I had recounted one such heated exchange between my parents about me that Joe suggested I go and live with him.

I jumped at the chance to escape. It was in the autumn – three months before my seventeenth birthday, and terribly young to be leaving home. But not having a family, in the sense of a loving, caring family, I felt I had nothing to stay for. It wasn't what I wanted, exactly, because I did feel so young, but though I was sad, I felt I had no option. I knew my father would be pleased to see me gone.

It soon became clear Joe's family was as dysfunctional as mine. His birth father lived some miles away, having won lots of money on the pools. After buying a swimming pool and some fast cars, he'd left Joe's mother for a much younger girl. He now had a new family of four sad little children, who were bullied by him, just as Joe had been. I used to visit them with Joe, and would see his violence in action. He was a terrible, truly scary man.

But it wasn't just violence that crippled Joe's family. Almost all of them – his mother, father, stepfather (his mother's new husband) and siblings all included – seemed to be drunk all the time. Every weekend was spent in an alcoholic haze and weekday evenings, providing anyone had any money, were no different. Christmas Day 1971, for example, saw us all sitting round a table not groaning under the weight of a turkey, but instead under the weight of all the bottles of booze that served as the family's festive lunch. No one seemed remotely bothered about food.

Being sober in the midst of this was strange and unsettling, and the world they'd created completely alien. I thought I'd escaped a house that couldn't be worse yet, in some respects – particularly in material terms – this *was* worse. They lived like people half a century before – surviving on scraps, like characters out of a Dickens novel. Their home, an old unmodernized council property, was barren – real bottom of the barrel stuff – and the life Joe's father lived could not have been a greater contrast. They survived with only the basics in terms of food, furniture, clothing and money, and the house was freezing all the time. I shared Joe's little bedroom – dark purple walls and carpet – and we slept together in his broken single bed.

Joe's older sister was severely epileptic and had fits all the time. She would eventually get married and have no further contact with her family, but back then her fits were frequent and scary. Despite this, and the pressing need for fuel and food, the whole family, whenever any money was in evidence, would sit for hours round the table, playing cards for money. I found the way they behaved towards one another when doing this very upsetting. Often, there'd be a whole week's wages at stake, yet one sibling seemed to have no compunction about winning and pocketing the lot, leaving the loser with nothing. Consequently, there was often – quite literally – nothing to eat, especially when it got close to the end of the week and Joe's mother had spent what little she did have buying ridiculously expensive freeze-dried Vesta meals – curries and risottos and the like – on the Friday before, when she got paid. She seemed a gambler through and through. If she lost most of what she had – to her husband, or a son – she'd invariably invest what little remained playing cards again, in the belief she could win it back.

But for all the privations – and the fact that I felt as out of place here as I'd felt unloved at home – it was calmer at Joe's house because nobody shouted, and apart from their strange attitude towards the pooling of money, they all seemed to genuinely get on. Joe's mother, in particular, for all her drink problems, was kind to me, always, and treated me as if I was a part of her family, and made me feel valued and welcome.

Apart from a brief stint in a posh boutique (where I was tongue-tied and hopeless), I still hadn't found any permanent work. But Joe, with his labouring and stealing veg and so on, was happy and able to support me. I mostly stayed at home, helping his mother with the shopping and housework. I was also a teenager, and here I could sleep like one.

It felt embarrassing to be sleeping with Joe in his parents' house – my father would never have allowed it – and even more so to sometimes get up and find it was lunchtime; something that would not have happened at my house in a million years – all the shouting and swearing would see to that. We lived life at a very leisurely pace, going to the local working men's club, or the pub, at the weekend and most nights staying in watching TV with the family, Joe and I curled up together in one armchair.

It felt so strange living this way – but I did feel comfortable around Joe, who'd look after me, turning on the water heater for me, running me a bath, and often buying me chocolates and flowers.

But the tentacles of what I'd eventually realize was my mother's illness were reaching out, desperate to pull me back.

One day, early in 1972, my father turned up at Joe's house, demanding I return home. This was not about Joe – my parents knew almost nothing about him – but the fact that while I was with him (their home was quite a way away) I couldn't be at my own house, caring for my mother, and she was becoming ever more agitated.

At seventeen, I had enough insight to understand what was happening, and why such pressure was being applied – as our mother–child roles had been reversed for most of my life. She had never mothered me. Hadn't ever cuddled me, sung or read to me, told me she loved me, kissed me better, made me feel cherished. Most importantly, though I still didn't understand it as such, neither had she protected me from the men who sexually abused me – indeed she reared me to believe I hadn't even *been* abused. She passed no comment – bar laughter – about Pops' constant manhandling of me, and at no point did she ever seem concerned in the least that Daniel would take me off on our 'walks' much less express interest in why or what we'd done. It was simply not discussed, and nor would it ever be. How else could I process what had been done to me, therefore, as anything but normal and right? Even so – and I now know how profoundly she has damaged me – I felt a huge responsibility for her. I didn't know she was ill, not really. Just that she needed me, and it was my duty to go home and look after her. She was apparently becoming ill with the worry of my not being there, at her side.

It was also the only life I knew. And though I liked being with Joe, I'd never really felt properly at home in his house; at least my house, if not a 'home', was familiar. I agreed that, as long as I could keep seeing Joe, I'd return.

Once there, however, I became more clear-sighted. Away from such close proximity, I could see how strange Joe's behaviour often was. One day, for example, after we'd just been out and bought some clothes, he had cut all of them up into little tiny squares. There was a reason for this, and for many of his other strange behaviours, but this was the seventies and I was young and naive, and didn't know about drugs. I'd certainly never been informed enough to identify that strange, sweetish smell around him. It was only years later that I realized he was addicted to various drugs, the principal ones being speed and marijuana – it was obviously that which I'd smelled when we first met. It also wasn't long before something else became clear. That I didn't really want to be with him. I'd probably gone to live with him for all the wrong reasons – to escape my life, not because I really loved him. By the end of the month I'd finished with him.

Back at home, things with my mother had got worse. She now spent every weekend going to jumble sales, tabletop sales, any sort of sale – just as long as there was junk to be had. She'd come home, her arms straining under the weight of carrier bags filled with second-hand books, pot plants, crockery and ornaments, which she'd wrap in newspaper and stuff into cardboard boxes, to be stashed in the loft and the shed. The house was as disgusting as ever but she didn't clean it. There was still dirty crockery on every surface, and the pedal bin reeked from its overflowing contents, which sat there and mouldered for days. There was dust everywhere, the beds were filthy and unmade, and my youngest brother and sister, now four and six, were completely undisciplined and neglected.

In the midst of all this, my mother would sit humming, cutting endless bits of paper out of endless magazines, or going clickedy-clickedy-click with her fingers.

My father was absent more than he was home, so it was little wonder he needed me back there. My older sister had left home now, and on at least three nights every week my father didn't return home either. Though my mother did tell me he was staying with another woman, she seemed little interested in doing anything about it. It was just a given, like the filth and the chaos.

By now I had at last found myself a permanent job, working as a cleaner in the old people's home I'd done casual work for. With cleaning being something I'd done all my life, I was very good at it and, strangely, enjoyed it. I'd probably have enjoyed anything that got me out of the house but, again, it was marred by my inability to hold normal conversations with the people I worked with. I'd been comfortable around Joe, but I still felt useless and out of my depth with almost everyone else, and older women made me particularly anxious. I now understand this was all about my relationship with my mother, but then it just felt like yet another handicap of being me.

As a consequence, for all that I did it willingly, I realized soon after moving back home that I was slipping back to the depressive feelings that had only lifted briefly when I'd gone to live with Joe. My life once more began to feel utterly without meaning. I returned to the doctor and was put back on anti-depressants, which once again made me feel desperate. It was perhaps this that was largely responsible for what I found myself deciding that spring.

I hadn't seen anything of Joe for three months when I spotted him in town with a girl on his arm who I thought looked uncannily like my mother. For reasons it would take me many years to unravel, this distressed me. I felt a great rage towards my mother, but at that time without any real understanding of why. All I knew was that I couldn't stop thinking about Joe's relationship and realizing it was making me wild. I wasn't thinking straight – how could I have been? But on impulse I resolved to get in touch with him, even though I no longer cared for him. This was because I'd decided (again, without logic or reason) I must spite my mother by having a baby with him. I didn't know who I most wanted to punish – her or me – only that it felt like a compulsion.

Despite his new relationship, Joe seemed keen to see me and as soon as we met I felt an almost overwhelming sense of sadness descend on me. And as we walked and talked it felt like there was something really bad inside my head; that I was being controlled by an emotion so strong that it couldn't possibly be me. We walked to the common and, despite how bad I now felt, I instigated sex anyway. Joe being Joe, he didn't argue. We spoke little, and certainly his girlfriend wasn't mentioned, but I'd expected that; with Joe almost everything in life was greeted by his cheerful 'easy come easy go' mentality.

When it was over I felt sick and ashamed. We didn't agree to meet again and nor would we for a few months. I said I'd ring him, and he answered with his characteristic 'see you around', and then we went our separate ways. My principal feeling, as usual, was sadness. I knew I wouldn't ring him. I'd brought him there to use him – though what I'd hoped to achieve I'd no idea. I carried on as before, feeling numb about it all, trying to blot out the whole incident – it now seemed like the utter impulsive madness it had been.

I was still working at the old people's home, cleaning, but now feeling sick all the time. My periods had stopped too, and when I started fainting I decided I'd better see a doctor. Incredibly, my conscious mind wouldn't let me consider the obvious answer to my symptoms.

At the doctors I explained my symptoms and had a urine test and, to my embarrassment, the doctor examined me and it was then he delivered his verdict – 'You are,' he told me, 'roughly three months pregnant.'

I stared at him in shock and left the surgery soon after. Only out on the pavement did the pressure inside release. I started laughing hysterically and couldn't stop.

CHAPTER 17

As I stood on the pavement outside the surgery, trying to regain control, I reconsidered. Perhaps the doctor was wrong. I couldn't possibly be pregnant. I hadn't *meant* to have a baby. Not a *real* baby. It had just been a strange, random thought, not for real. I couldn't think what to do. Should I go back inside and ask him to repeat what he'd said? Perhaps I'd heard wrong. He couldn't have said what I'd thought he'd said, could he? How on earth was I going to tell my mother? And what about my father? My blood ran cold. He'd kill me. He must never, ever know.

I held my hands against my tummy. A baby was growing in there, apparently, and its existence inside me felt terrifying. It was just like when I'd wished Adam dead, and then he *had* died. I had decided I wanted a baby and now I had one. Well, would have, in six months. Just like that. It frightened me so much to realize what I could make happen just by wishing it so.

I caught the bus back to the village in a daze. I couldn't think what I was going to do, or how I'd ever find the courage to tell my mother. She was sitting in her armchair when I got indoors, surrounded by her usual pile of carrier bags of stuff, and a big stack of slimming magazines. Slimming magazines were her current obsession.

'Do you know,' she commented as she glanced up, 'there are as many calories in a banana as a slice of white bread? Depending on the thickness of the bread, of course, and the size of the banana – about seventy.'

She picked up her mug of tea from the floor and drank from it, then scribbled this fact down in her little notebook. I could see there was a long list of calorific values already carefully noted down. I just stared at her, feeling the hopelessness of everything. What was I going to *do*?

I sat down opposite her, and a new thought suddenly hit me. What about *Joe*? Why hadn't I thought about Joe before now? I'd have to tell him. I'll telephone him, I thought. He'd know what to do. I went into the hall to make the call out of earshot. My mother didn't even look up.

Luckily, Joe answered the phone straight away. I blurted it all out to him in a panicky rush.

'Slow down,' he said. I couldn't hear any worry in his voice. 'Slow down and say all that again.'

I did so, and then he burst out laughing. 'I don't believe it!' he said. 'I don't believe it! I'm going to be a daddy! Don't worry,' he finished. 'I'll come round as soon as I can.'

When he arrived the next day, I was still in a complete daze, the intervening twenty-four hours having passed in a fog of anxiety. We didn't stop and discuss anything. We just both went into the living room, where my mother was again stationed, and I took a deep breath and said, 'I'm pregnant'.

She said nothing for a moment. Just stared and shrugged. 'Then you'll have to get married.' She looked at the little writing pad she had beside her again. 'It'll be all right,' she said, nodding towards it. 'I'll start making a list. Of all the guests that will need inviting, what needs doing and so on. I can make some cakes and we'll have to get some wedding invitations, we can book the village hall for the reception and—'

'Get married?' I spluttered. 'Me and Joe get *married*?'

'Of course,' she answered, carrying on writing things down. 'Your father will need to be told of course . . . hmmm.' She paused. 'I don't know how he's going to take it. Perhaps Joe should go home while we tell him . . . yes . . . Yes, that would probably be a good idea.'

I felt numb. I turned to Joe. 'Do you want to get married?'

He shrugged. 'Dunno. Yeah, why not?'

By now my mother was so busy scribbling down the names of everyone she'd invite and the food we'd be having she barely looked up as Joe left.

My father arrived home at his usual time and my mother told him straight away. She was clearly anxious now, but betrayed little emotion as she dropped her bombshell on my behalf; quickly adding that she'd begun arranging the wedding, as if, in doing so, she'd already got rid of the problem, rendering any further discussion unnecessary.

Predictably, his response was very different from hers.

'Fucking hell!' he shouted. 'We're not having another fucking baby in this house. You'd better find somewhere else to fucking live, and quick.' He then added, just in case either of us were in any doubt about his feelings, 'Fucking kids, I'm fucked if I know! What the fucking hell!'

His attitude towards the situation was as expected. He could barely tolerate having me in the house, let alone a new baby. Even so, it brought home to me just how scary the whole thing really was. I walked around in a cloud of misery, and kept bursting into tears, still unable to believe I had a baby inside me.

A few days later, my mother announced she'd booked the church. 'And arranged for the bells to be rung when you leave – that'll be nice, won't it?' she added happily, the whole business of this unmitigated disaster seeming to fill her with uncharacteristic energy.

Yet I couldn't imagine getting married, least of all to Joe. I hardly knew him, not really, and I certainly didn't love him, but what choice did I have? And hadn't my mother always said that I'd leave school and get married and have babies? Well, it seemed she'd been right. Now I was.

And it was becoming more real by the day. My father arrived home from work a few days later, with the news he'd found Joe a different job; one that came with a house we could live in.

'But he already has a job,' I said.

'Well, he'll have to fucking well leave it then, won't he? Fucking *hell*,' he answered. 'Give it up and go to this one, fucking ungrateful sod.' He turned to my mother with his habitual furious expression. 'That one should fucking think herself lucky!'

The house my father had found for us was on a farm in the middle of nowhere. Joe would apparently be able to work on the estate side of the farm, sawing and delivering logs and repairing fencing. The first time I saw it I was immediately struck by how isolated it was. It was situated a long way down a winding narrow road, which seemed to go on for ever, before turning into a lane. The house was up the hill, right at the top. Neither Joe nor I could drive, and the thought of living there – just the two of us and our baby – filled me with anxiety.

It wasn't small though. In fact, for just the two of us, it seemed huge. It was a large three-bed semi with a lounge and separate dining room, as well as a kitchen with a Rayburn. It seemed inconceivable this place would become my home, but there was no time for it to sink in. Joe had to start working for the farmer in three weeks and my mother was racing ahead with wedding preparations.

My father, too, seemed to be on a mission. As had happened to his own mother when she'd been in my condition, the priority was clearly to get me out as soon as possible. The only difference, it seemed to me, was that unlike my great-grand-father, my father couldn't be seen to just throw me out on the street, and risk the neighbours saying bad things about him.

Much to my mother's obvious excitement, he came home one evening with the news that an old lady he was doing a removal for (one of his business sidelines) was moving from a large house into a smaller one and had said we could have some of her unwanted furniture. There was a green sofa and matching armchair, a table and chairs, a huge old double bed and a small fridge. She was also throwing out her wedding dress, and my mother insisted it would be perfect. It was a white brocade affair, heavily embossed, with a huge train and veil, and smelled musty. It was too big, but my mother thought that was good because it would hide my bump; by now I was four and a half months pregnant.

I'd hardly seen Joe since we'd agreed to get married, and we'd not spoken at all about our feelings. We'd not discussed what we wanted; just been swept along, our assent to all the plans being made for us simply assumed. But how could I argue anyway? It was me who'd caused it all to happen.

I was deeply ashamed of my pregnant status and, as the time went on, rarely went out. I was terrified of being pregnant and terrified of giving birth and tried to pretend it wasn't happening. At my antenatal appointments I couldn't hide it, however. I'd be called out as Mrs Wicks, which was Joe's surname, examined internally and asked questions about the conception. That this *was* real was in no doubt.

On the day before our wedding (I was now roughly five months pregnant) the kitchen was in a state of chaos even more extreme than usual. My mother had made lots of fairy cakes, and was now sitting at the table, icing them. She was also making buttonholes from a pile of carnations, and had set aside horrible dark brown, orange and white bridesmaids' dresses ready to be ironed. I'd not seen her so animated in my entire life. Yes, she'd always had these phases where she went into overdrive, during which she knitted obsessively or made mountains of cakes, but it was as if marrying me off so young, in such circumstances, wasn't tragic, but actually all she could have wished for. Though she never held back in telling everyone that I was pregnant, she behaved almost as if elated by it all.

In contrast, I was completely overwhelmed. I felt like a

spectator watching all this being organized around me, unable to comprehend what was going on, and feeling I had no more control over it all than I'd had over my 'decision' to try to make a baby.

That night, Joe and I had a meeting with the vicar, who told us that at this point it was customary for him to talk to us about what marriage meant. And also, he added, to discuss the fact that children often come along soon after. 'But in your case,' he said sternly, his disapproval plain, 'I believe it's not necessary. I understand you've done that bit already.' I sat there beside Joe feeling so ashamed.

The day of the wedding saw my mother up early and straight down to the village hall to start arranging all her food. I was sent to the hairdressers where I'd done my brief apprenticeship, where it was decided I should have all my hair scraped off my face, tight almost as a drum, with ringlets at the back. It made my face look really long, and was horribly severe, as if indicating what a big mistake all this was. Once finished, they sprayed it with clouds and clouds of hairspray, so that I felt I could barely move my head. I could hardly stand looking at my reflection. I looked so ugly – especially when I climbed into the heavy dress and veil. The latter was so thick you could hardly see my features, and I worried what on earth Joe would think when he lifted it in church and saw my face for the first time.

But if he was disappointed, then we were probably quits. He'd been kitted out in a double-breasted jacket and too-short trousers, and had so obviously made an effort, which did move me, but at some point the previous week he'd got into a fight, and was now missing one of his front teeth. All I could think, as my father marched me down the aisle towards him, was what had I done in that one moment of madness? What were the pair of us doing getting married and becoming parents? We were like two rabbits blinking in a car's headlights.

There was no going back though and, after the ceremony – and the bells having duly been rung – the reception passed in a blur. My only clear memory is of watching Joe and his little brother playing chase all round the stage. Just like two excitable children.

Joe and I were deposited at our new home that evening by my brother Phillip, who'd driven my father's car. He dutifully unloaded all the presents while I watched, and then drove off, leaving us alone.

I immediately burst into tears. Joe, as was his way, seemed completely bemused by this and suggested the best thing to do would be to go to bed.

The bed itself had been made honeymoon-ready, and was full of rice and other decorations, but I was too drained to even brush them aside, I just crawled into bed and lay on top of them. I then turned on my side, away from him, and cried myself to sleep.

I continued like this for several days. Where Joe knuckled down to it, I couldn't get used to any aspect of it. I was now Joe's wife. I was going to have a baby. I was supposed to just get on and accept it. Which was something I knew I had to – I'd caused this, after all. But unlike Joe, who seemed to treat marriage and impending fatherhood as 'just another thing', I didn't seem able to do it. In the space of six weeks, everything had changed so completely, and I was reeling from the sheer magnitude of it all.

I couldn't even cope with cooking dinner. I could cook it, and Joe would eat it – would tell me he enjoyed it – but it felt all wrong for me to be sitting eating food I was convinced my mother needed so much more. The guilt I felt about leaving her – not being there to take care of her – was completely overwhelming.

But eventually, little by very little, I adjusted and settled and grew calmer. I even began to admit there were things I quite liked about marriage. I kept the house clean and tidy and there was space, now, for me. I could light the fire and sit by the television, all cosy, and watch whatever programme I wanted. No one was swearing or shouting (either at me or about me) and my home felt like a place of peace and order.

And also solitude, of a pleasing, rather than oppressive, variety. Though we did have neighbours – another young couple with a baby – I saw very little of either of them. They were hippies and they were also a little strange. His hair hung right down to his waist, and he smoked pot all the time, and though Joe worked with him, they didn't get on. They seemed to be in permanent competition for the estate manager's affections. His wife wore bright-orange dresses and had a fringe that fell almost to her nose, and I used to hear her shouting at her baby daughter through the wall. I was quite happy she rarely spoke to me.

I was also working, three days a week, for a lady who lived close to where I'd lived previously. I cleaned for her and looked after her three children. She'd collect me in the mornings and drop me home at the end of the day, and in between, when she went out, she left my routine up to me. So I'd wash and clean and shop for her, play with the children and feed them, and found the work absorbing and enjoyable. I particularly liked looking after her children.

I realized also that I was beginning to look forward to the evenings and Joe's return home from work. I enjoyed our evenings sitting in front of the fire, watching the TV as the sky darkened outside. Getting to know him better now, I began to realize I did have feelings for him and knowing those feelings were reciprocated made everything feel fun and exciting and secure. I also found him attractive and for the first time in my life enjoyed and felt relaxed about sex.

The only time we'd see my parents was at the weekend, when we'd take a taxi to their house so we could go with them to the supermarket when they did their weekly shop. We'd always have to dash around with my mother at breakneck speed, because if we didn't, my father – who always waited in the car – started shouting and swearing about us taking so long.

It was always a relief to finally get dropped back home by my father, and for the first time in my life I really began to appreciate the sanctity of having my own home.

The only blot on my horizon was my ever-expanding bump, which reminded me, however much I tried not to think about it, of the upsetting memories of my mother's childbearing years. The visions in my head were all so horrible. Chief among them, and the one I couldn't shake from my mind, was of the baby she conceived two years after Adam died – the one she said she had to have to 'replace' him.

She'd been seven or eight months pregnant and it was just

after Christmas, when she accused my father of not only sleeping with the 'whore' in the local pub, but also of sleeping with the 'polo girls'. These were the female grooms that accompanied the ponies my father transported to polo matches. There was lots of swearing and shouting, and as the argument escalated my father became violent, grabbing stuff to throw at her – cushions, piles of magazines, random clothes and so on – and then he began pushing her around the sitting room. I'd watched – too terrified to move and draw attention to myself – as she finally decided to flee the room.

In her haste, she missed her footing on the first step of the staircase, and fell heavily. She screamed immediately she hit the hall floor and clutched at her stomach, and I watched as a clear liquid began running down her legs and pooling on the tiles. Still weeping, she pulled herself unsteadily to her feet and climbed the stairs, my father following behind her.

I heard their bedroom door shut and then the house fell silent. I got up and walked with dread towards the liquid, which at first sight looked like water, but I could now see also contained blood. What had happened? Was she now going to die? It was then I remembered about the blood when she had babies. All the congealed pools of it, in her bed. All the mess and the gore and the smell.

Some instinct that night had me fetch a cloth and bucket, so I could clear the wide pool of liquid from the hall floor. As my hands touched it – it was slimy, not like water at all – I felt repulsed at the idea of touching something so intimate; something that had come from inside her. I retched continually as I cleared it up. I'd just finished when my father came down and told me, in tones that were very subdued, that my mother was okay and was asleep. When I woke the next morning my mother had gone. She gave birth to my sister Mary the same day.

I touched my own bump now, appalled at my inescapable fate. Like it or not, I was soon to do the same.

CHAPTER 18

In the last weeks leading up to the birth, I began having night-mares. In these, I found myself alone in the house, and the baby just dropping out of me without warning.

So vivid were these visions I was beside myself, and in an attempt to make the hospital do something to get the baby out of me, I lied about my original dates. I also kept turning up at the hospital, believing I was in labour, only to be examined and sent home again. It's because of this, I think, they decided to induce me; I lived, after all, in a very isolated place, and perhaps they thought my nightmares might come true.

To be induced, I had to arrive the day before and when I got there I was so terrified I couldn't stop being sick, but I couldn't now tell them the truth. If I did, they might decide not to induce me after all, and the thought of that was even more scary. So I rushed back and forth to the bathroom, pretending all was well, and awaited my fate the next morning.

I was taken to the labour suite after breakfast. They'd given me a boiled egg, which I'd been unable to eat, and I felt weak from the lack of food and repeated vomiting. I'd also begun to shake – by now uncontrollably.

The nurse put my legs into stirrups and told me that the next thing would be that I'd feel a sharp pain, when she went in to 'hook the bag'. I then felt something pulling and a pain in my stomach, and she told me my waters had broken. It was a horrible sensation which really upset me and I wished I'd properly understood what 'being induced' meant, for if I had I'd never have tried to make it happen.

An hour or so passed, with nothing happening. I asked the nurse, who was occasionally popping in and out, whether my baby would be coming soon. She looked a little shocked, but examined me again, and then told me, no, it wouldn't. I was only one centimetre dilated, apparently, and I needed to be at least eight.

A similar number of hours then elapsed, during which I remained mostly alone, with the nurse popping in and out to check on me. By the time Joe arrived, having finished work, my contractions had started to become stronger, and he seemed to find the sight of me rolling around, breathless with pain, a highly amusing spectacle. In hindsight, he was probably not so much amused as trying to make light of it, perhaps because he couldn't cope with seeing me in pain. It was as if we were still children, neither of us adult enough to deal with the terribly adult thing we were facing. In any event, he was flicking through a magazine from my bedside cabinet, resting it against my back as if he hadn't a care in the world.

Eight hours later, shocked and exhausted, I finally gave birth to our 6lb 2oz three weeks premature son. When they passed him to me I promptly threw up. Joe was really excited, however, and took him readily, then went off to find a telephone to tell everyone.

Back on the ward, a depression that had come almost out of nowhere grew deeper and darker, and increasingly impenetrable, and all I could do was curl up into a ball feeling weak and pathetic and hopeless. I spent my ten days in hospital feeling like an automaton, being shown how to feed and dress and change my baby, and in between would just lie on my bed facing the wall. I was the only mother on the ward who didn't attend the twenty-first birthday party of another mum. Not even when she came over to my bed to persuade me could I rouse myself to go and join in.

Today, my condition would be so obvious to everyone, and steps taken to alleviate its severity, but back then post-natal depression was, like so many other unpalatable truths, not widely or routinely diagnosed. 'The baby blues', as it was so gently described, was something you just 'shook yourself' out of.

But I couldn't. My baby terrified me, made me feel guilty, and he was such a beautiful baby, so fragile and innocent. I felt too young and inadequate to be a mother. I was afraid of him, afraid he had needs I couldn't even understand, let alone meet. I could barely look at him, let alone name him. Much as I enjoyed looking after my employers' children, this tiny thing was so different – so overwhelming. He was mine, and mine alone, my sole responsibility. It didn't occur to me he was Joe's responsibility too. I was also scared I would hurt him – not surprising, given my own babyhood – that I would abuse him, or even try to kill him. In the midst of this, Joe, who still seemed so excited about being a father, was popping in to see us both, genuinely happy, and then popping off again to 'wet the baby's head' with his friends.

When I was discharged I took the baby round to my mother's, because some instinct must have taken over, and all I really understood was that if *I* couldn't cope with him, then at least my mother could do better. In that sense, it seems obvious to me today I was still desperate for a mummy of my own. And despite everything I'd seen and experienced, I consciously believed that to be true. I didn't then believe she was a 'bad' mother generally – I thought it was *my* fault she'd been so with me.

She took over straight away. 'Here,' she said immediately, taking him from me. 'Give him to me.' She then swaddled him tightly in a cloth. I felt panicky watching her. It was a feeling I couldn't articulate, and yet was so strong. Here was my baby and what was she doing to him? I felt once again overwhelmed.

Breastfeeding had never been an option, not only because I'd felt so dreadful post-natally, but also, despite my positive experiences with Joe, because I still associated my breasts with what Grandpops had done to them, and as a consequence they felt 'bad'. The idea also felt difficult, like another type of assault, and the knowledge that I never got to – or indeed, will, ever – breastfeed my own children is something that still saddens me greatly, even today.

My mother, who I'd never seen breastfeed, immediately pushed the baby's bottle into his mouth and started telling my aunt, who was visiting, what a useless mother I was, how I never wanted to be a mother – was never going to have any

children – and now look at me! They both seemed to find this
very funny. In the midst of this I couldn't take my eyes off my
baby. Why wasn't she watching what she was doing while she
was feeding him? While she was laughing he could be choking.

Yet what could I do about her taking over in this way? I *had*
said those things, and she was right – so far I *had* been a useless
mother.

This set a pattern that never ever seemed to vary. I'd go to
her house, she'd grab my baby, say 'give him to me', and then
swaddle him and feed him. And it was her confidence that was
key. I felt so hopeless, it was a relief to hand him over. Deep
down I cared deeply for the baby I'd borne, but my conscious
mind was all too ready to agree. So I just had to put up with
the fact that, if anyone was there to listen, she'd repeat the same
thing to them – that, unlike her, I was completely useless as a
mother.

We eventually named our baby Alfie and, as the weeks passed,
we settled into a routine. My mother's principal advice to me
was that if he cried I should ignore him, except to feed and
change him, because, if I didn't, he'd end up a spoilt, demanding
and unpleasant child. So I didn't tell her that once I started
getting used to him, and feeling less fearful, I'd break this rule,
often, in the privacy of my own home. Though sometimes I'd
just want to sit and look at him, I started propping him up on
the sofa beside me, and played with him and laughed at all the
noises he'd make. He sometimes sounded, to me, a little bit like
a dolphin, but I didn't share this with my mother or she'd know
I was spoiling him.

When Alfie was three weeks old, I went back to work for the same lady, and took him with me. I'd felt guilty about not contributing to the finances, but going back to work was equally distressing. When I was working I was anxious all the time about Alfie, worried he'd wake and start crying and need feeding and my employer would be cross about things not getting done. She never suggested this was the case, but if I stopped working for even a minute to tend to him I felt enormously guilty. It was almost as if I'd been so conditioned to never have needs of my own, that everyone would be cross with me for illustrating that *he* did, as if such things simply weren't allowed. All of which was ridiculous thinking anyway, as I'd already insisted on taking a cut in pay, as I felt it only fair now I was bringing along a baby.

I seemed to live with guilt all the time. Guilt that I couldn't spend time with Alfie when I was working, and guilt for getting paid for doing work I wasn't doing because I was feeding him or changing him or getting him off to sleep.

On Saturdays, however, our time was our own, and we'd often wrap Alfie up and put him in his pram and walk the six miles to my parent's house so we could still go food shopping with them. I felt increasingly strange about the things my mother did with Alfie. Though to some people they might have seemed nothing out of the ordinary, I used to hate it that she was always so keen to take off his nappy, chattering all the time about 'his little willy' and finding it so funny that he'd wee, which he often did. She'd laugh and laugh about this, just as she'd laughed throughout my childhood about anything to do with willies, in all likelihood because of what she'd suffered sexually. That aspect of her personality I'd become used to, by this time, but in relation to my baby it felt horrible.

When Alfie was about seven months old, we were out shopping one day and bumped into Maria, the girl from school who I'd been in the play with and whose father had used my hand to masturbate with.

She seemed keen to meet up. She said she and her boyfriend had nowhere to go much, bar the pub, and they'd love to come and see our house. I felt embarrassed – had done around her since the incident – but unable to say, 'Did you know your father assaulted me?' Instead I said, 'Yes, that would be nice.'

Maria and her boyfriend started coming twice a week, and on Sundays, because they began coming ever earlier, I even started doing dinner, which we really couldn't afford.

Worse, though, was that Maria kept insisting I must go round and show Alfie to her parents. She apparently talked to them about him all the time, and she said they were really looking forward to seeing him. As usual, unable to be either assertive or find excuses, I was eventually persuaded and we all trooped round. Maria's father was obviously very agitated. While her mother cooed and fussed around Alfie, he looked anxious and wouldn't meet my eye. Eventually, after some forced laughter and a few noises made at Alfie, he went out, mumbling about going to cut the grass.

I hated it, but after that first visit Maria was keen to include us in all her family gatherings. And as Joe knew nothing about the past, and got on well with Maria's boyfriend, I felt unable to do anything but endure it. I was an adult now, but the feelings of duplicity remained strong. I felt as uncomfortable around her father as he so clearly did with me, as much responsible for the terrible things he'd done as he was doubtless terrified I might spill the beans.

But freedom from the rest of the world beckoned, because when Alfie was a year old Joe passed his driving test. So we bought a little car, and were independent at last. It was only an old banger but we loved it. Loved that we could take Alfie out anywhere we wanted, loved that we could go shopping on our own, instead of trailing round with my mother. Loved going to the beach, where we'd lay on a blanket in the sunshine, or to have picnics in the countryside, just the three of us.

It was the first properly happy time I'd ever had in my life, and I couldn't imagine being anywhere else now. As winter closed in we'd cut up logs together, for the fire, which we'd store in our little shed to keep dry. I loved our clean, quiet home, and though I was still struggling with Alfie emotionally, I loved that I could now meet his needs physically. Joe was always really nice to me, caring and gentle, and I'd started to tell him I loved him, because I did, and could imagine us being together always.

But then, when Alfie was eighteen months old, Joe came home from work one day and delivered a bombshell. He was bored and wanted to look for a new job. I was devastated. For the first time in my life I felt stable and secure, and if he left his job we'd also lose our home.

CHAPTER 19

Joe didn't seem to care. He was determined to move on, and gave his four weeks' notice anyway.

My father was livid. 'I found you that fucking job!' he shouted. 'That farmer trusted me! I have a fucking relationship with these people! You stupid bastard!' But Joe was adamant. Nothing my father said made the slightest difference. He was leaving. So now we had nowhere to go.

I contacted the council to see if they'd help, but all they could offer us was a bed and breakfast place in town, coincidentally close to the Honey Globe cafe. We had no choice but to take it, even though it was completely unsuitable; Joe had got a new job as a labourer, in a nearby town, and would now be away every weekday from six in the morning to six at night – sometimes later, if he had to work late to finish a job – and the days now seemed interminable. I'd got used to him popping home for lunch when on the estate, and now he was gone for twelve hours at a time and when he was home he seemed distant and preoccupied.

I was only doing my old cleaning job two mornings a week

now, as the lady's children were all in school, so I had a lot of time on my hands. But, uncomfortable hanging around someone else's house all day, I'd wrap Alfie up and we'd spend our time mooching round the streets or visiting my mother, or my elder sister. Yet I felt in the way at my mother's house now, so would spend my time engaged in the largely pointless task of cleaning up the mess, clearing out and scrubbing. Since living in my own home, it always struck me anew how alien and chaotic her house was.

Once again, I felt sad and lonely, and the depression I'd had since Alfie's birth, that for a time had almost lifted, now returned with a vengeance. I knew I had to do something or else plunge even deeper into the abyss, so I contacted social services to see if we could be moved from the bed and breakfast. What we needed was a place of our own again. Perhaps then we'd get back on track.

All they had to offer was a live-in job for me, looking after a family of six children, whose mother was due to have an emergency hysterectomy. Joe and Alfie and I would apparently have our own 'very large bedroom', and would share the rest of their 'nice house in the country'.

I took it − a rash and impulsive decision − and the three of us moved in straight away. Unfortunately, however, what they hadn't told me was that not only would the children's father be there, but also that the nice house was actually in the middle of nowhere and our bedroom was dingy, cold and damp. They were a poor working-class family, living in very poor conditions, in a house tied to a farm. Looking after all those children, plus Alfie, who was by now almost two, was exhausting, as was cooking for ten people every night. Joe was also now working much longer hours for hardly any more money, and even though I knew he'd brought this on himself, I still felt desperately sorry for him. Yet he told me he'd no choice but to stay late most nights; the firm were making people redundant, and if he didn't do the overtime, he might lose his job.

The father of the children I was looking after was a very strange man. He seemed unable, or unwilling, to make conversation, and mostly just stood or sat, watching me work, in silence, especially at lunchtimes, when we were on our own apart from Alfie, as his own children were all at school.

It turned out I was right to be wary. One lunchtime, when I was standing at the stove cooking sausages, and he'd been silently watching me for some time, he crossed the kitchen, put his arms around my waist and tried to kiss me. I pulled away sharply, disgusted and appalled, and though he immediately realized he'd done wrong and apologized, I knew I couldn't bear to stay there any more.

I'd planned to phone social services on the Monday to see if they could find us somewhere else. The mother was due home, in any case, and until then they'd just have to cope. But when I woke the next morning I felt terrible. I'd been up all night suffering from sickness and diarrhoea and now I literally couldn't get out of bed. I had a raging temperature too, and had no choice but to lie there while Joe, it being a Saturday, tried to look after me. Eventually I suggested I ought to see a doctor. By now, I felt sure there was something seriously wrong.

The doctor came and examined my stomach. He felt it was a

virus and that further bed rest was needed – I'd probably begin to recover the next day.

I didn't feel better the next day – in fact, I felt worse, could now barely stagger to the toilet and I couldn't pass any urine when I got there. By the Monday, really worried now, I asked Joe to drive me to the surgery, where we were told he must drive me immediately to hospital, and they'd telephone and let them know to expect us.

I felt even worse, hearing this. The next day was Alfie's second birthday, and now we had to stop off and drop him at my mother's; I knew this wasn't something that would be sorted out this evening, and I felt wretched watching Joe take him into the house. I was too ill to even get out of the car. Even worse was watching him hand her the Tonka truck we'd bought him, knowing I wouldn't be there tomorrow to give it to him.

Once in Casualty I was processed very quickly and given an anal examination. It was excruciatingly painful, but even worse was the news that I was going to have to have an emergency operation, because they could see something inside me had ruptured. The very air around me seemed full of apprehension that night. Was this it now? Was this how I was going to die?

I came round from my operation to find Joe and both my mother and father around my bed. They'd apparently been summoned there immediately after the operation as it was considered fairly likely I might die. The surgeon had apparently opened me up to find my insides in a terrible state. He had likened it to there having been some sort of explosion, and told me I'd been very lucky. Various nerve endings, my bowel, and my bladder, were all gangrenous, due to some sort of burst cyst. They'd also removed my appendix, which had been very close to bursting itself. Had it done so, I knew I might not have survived. I had a tube in place, draining the pus from my stomach, as well as a catheter and drip.

Once it was clear I *had* survived the initial trauma, I was told that I'd need to stay in for three weeks, and only if we had somewhere suitable to live could I go home. It was here that fate decided to be kind. Because the hospital so badly needed my bed, social services offered us a large, brand-new, centrally heated house, in the town next to the one where I grew up. Suddenly everything had changed for the better, and I felt positive about my little family's future at last. We stayed at my sister's while they fitted new carpets, and my father brought our furniture from his garage, where it'd been stored. I didn't like that our house was on a large estate, full of people, because I'd grown so used to the safe little world we'd created out in the countryside, just me, Alfie and Joe. But apart from that it felt brilliant. How wonderful to think we'd be back on our own as a family and could get back to the way things had been before.

Joe's behaviour though, once again, was worrying. He'd long since stopped behaving in the ways he had when I'd first met him, and he'd become increasingly distant with me. It was making me feel terribly anxious. I realized my own behaviour was becoming odd too. I started moving ornaments and moving them again, and couldn't seem to get them quite straight. I was actively having to avoid looking at them or else I'd feel compelled to keep touching them. I was also getting up earlier and earlier each day, in order to get through my housework. I'd become obsessive about cleaning; I'd scrub and scrub, anxious about anyone getting an infection. I had taken on more cleaning jobs to earn extra money, so if I didn't make sure our own house was completely spick and span, I'd not have time to do it in the evening. But at least we were in a home of our own again, and things would have a chance to settle down. I thought perhaps Joe was feeling the strain as much as I was and that, in time, it would sort itself out.

But perhaps I should have listened to my instincts, because I was wrong. One night, only a few weeks after we moved in, Joe came home and told me he was leaving me and Alfie. Then he got into his car and drove off.

CHAPTER 20

I kept thinking Joe would come back. I told myself he'd just had a bad day, and needed some space. The last few months had been incredibly stressful, what with his job and then my illness and the move and everything. Maybe everything had just got on top of him. It had to be that. He'd be back.

But he didn't come back. Not that day, or the next day, or the one after that, and I didn't know quite what to do.

I was still suffering the after-effects of my operation. Though I was working again, my bladder and bowel weren't working properly, and I'd get home exhausted and in pain. My bladder was very slow, taking for ever to work, and I'd spend ages, taps running, trying to concentrate, to persuade it to empty at all. My bowel, too, was sluggish and I felt sick and bloated; all in all I was completely drained physically.

Emotionally, however, I was like a cat on hot coals. How could he *do* that? How could he just leave me and Alfie without telling us where he was going or what was wrong?

By the time a week had passed, I plucked up the courage to call his work, but I was told he no longer worked there. So I called his mother, but she wouldn't even come to the phone. This upset me greatly, as I'd thought we were friends, not to mention me being her daughter-in-law, and Alfie being her grandson. How could she show such little concern for us? I began to suspect he might be there.

I kept trying to contact him, over the following days and weeks, but never succeeded, and felt increasingly lost and betrayed. I'd trusted him more than I had any person, ever, and couldn't bear the new thoughts that began forming in my head; that he was with another woman, just like my father, and that I was, as a consequence, the thing I'd been so terrified of becoming – just another version of my mother.

And then I remembered Joe had once taken me to meet a group of people who lived and worked at the riding stables near where he'd worked, as they'd had a dog for sale that we might like. It had been a strange business because as soon as we'd arrived at the place, he'd wanted to leave again, and couldn't get me out of there fast enough. At the time, though it had addled me, I had no explanation, and had eventually put it out of my mind. But now something about it jarred and I called his ex-employers again, and then the stables, and was able, through the various comments people made, to piece together an idea of what might be going on.

It seemed he hadn't been working long hours at all – far from it – but was instead spending a great deal of time at the stables, with one of the female grooms there, called Meg. I was distraught, but also angry. All that time I'd believed him about his employers having laid people off, when the truth was he'd been spending his days with another woman. I was so furious that one day, when Alfie was at playschool, I took a bus down to the stables and hid behind a phonebox so I could watch all the comings and goings, and try to ascertain which one was Meg.

But for all that, I couldn't bear to tell anyone. I felt such a failure, and so hurt, I couldn't bear anyone knowing. Life without him felt meaningless and, on a practical level, was becoming scary. With only the income from my meagrely paid cleaning jobs coming in, we'd almost no money to live on, and the bills were piling up. As a consequence, my relationship with Alfie began to deteriorate. I was finding it harder and harder to relate to him. He was clearly anxious too, even though he never actually asked about his father, and we were now back spending hours walking the streets, as I couldn't bear the silence indoors.

When Joe had been gone a couple of months, Maria and her boyfriend, Alan, turned up, and were very shocked to hear Joe had left us. So much so that, without telling me what they planned to do, they drove straight round to Joe's mother's house, and wouldn't leave till he'd returned home and they could confront him.

Following this, they got in touch and told me I must meet him; and that Joe had agreed we should talk. They then arranged for the four of us to meet at a local pub, and when we did I was shocked at how he'd changed. He'd lost a lot of weight, and had that funny sweet smell about him again. He was almost twenty-two now (I was nineteen) but it was as if, since he'd left, he had regressed to being the eighteen-year-old I'd first met; swearing and being aggressive and embarrassing – not to me, but to everyone else – telling a man who'd politely asked about a free chair to 'piss off'.

He then came home with me to talk further and eventually, though not, as far as I could see, enthusiastically, he agreed to come home. But that was Joe. It was the way he was and he'd probably never change. And if that meant we had him back, then that was good enough for now. Once he was home, I could try to make things better.

It was difficult at first, because I was so tentative and anxious around him, constantly waiting for the next time he'd leave us. It had happened once, so why wouldn't it happen again? This was compounded by my own turbulent feelings. Did I really still want to be with him, feeling like this? And it all must have been my fault, I reasoned, not *un*reasonably. Must have been something about me that made him leave. So strong was my conviction that it was my fault, I didn't even feel he owed me an explanation.

So when he suggested we have another baby – that it might help us – I felt a profound sense of relief. He wanted another baby, which meant he *did* want to stay. Which meant we *were* supposed to be together, and it would all work out. Somehow, I just knew he would never leave again.

I fell pregnant almost immediately. And, more relaxed now, I felt my anxiety slip away. But more trauma was just around the corner. I was still working for the family whose children I'd always looked after, and with Alfie now growing older, he'd come along and play happily with them. It was here, when I was about eleven weeks pregnant, that I started bleeding. I went to the toilet to investigate and became very, very frightened, as the blood simply wouldn't stop. The toilet wouldn't flush, and I realized it was broken, making it even more obvious how much

I was losing, and adding to my panic by making me feel dreadful about leaving my employers this horrible bloody toilet to clean up.

I tried to call my employer, but couldn't get hold of her and, not wanting to wake the children's father – who'd worked all night and was sleeping – I decided to telephone my mother. She'd just passed her driving test, so perhaps she could come. But it seemed she couldn't. 'Call an ambulance,' she said. 'I'm at work. It's really busy.' I was distressed by now and asked her to please come and get me, and she eventually agreed, though warned that she'd only be able to spare a short time. She'd recently got a new job, working for a car-repair workshop, and was adamant she'd have to hurry back.

By the time she arrived I was very relieved to see her, because I was terrified to even stand. When I did, I could feel the blood still dripping out of me. I still hadn't woken the father of the house, as I'd felt awful about disturbing him, but with no choice now, and my mother very agitated about the time, I told the eldest of the children to go and wake him if they needed him, to explain I hadn't been able to contact their mummy. Then, feeling horribly guilty, I gathered up Alfie and took him out to my mother's car.

She drove Alfie and me home at great speed. Her driving was a terrifying spectacle at the best of times, but today she was even more frightening. Once home she instructed me to get undressed and into bed, and then told me she must now get back to work. 'Should I call the doctor?' I asked, terrified that she was now going to leave me. 'Yes, do that,' she answered, and was gone.

In retrospect, I cannot understand how anyone could leave her own daughter bleeding and alone with her three-year-old child, whatever the circumstances. At the time, though, I had no choice but to deal with it. I went to bed and called the doctor and asked him to come, with Alfie sitting beside me on the pillow.

He arrived promptly – it was the same doctor who, when I was thirteen, had told me to lie in a hot bath and try to 'find' myself. He had no such creative advice today. Having examined me, and noting the amount of blood I was losing, he told me it would be a miracle if I hung on to this baby. 'You are going to miscarry,' he said. 'You are just going to have to let it happen. Call me again, of course, if you are worried about anything.' He also told me I'd have to attend hospital afterwards, so they could make sure everything had gone.

When he left, I just lay there, shaking with fear. I had severe stomach cramps and I knew I was still bleeding, and now I just wanted it to happen. But what *would* happen? I had absolutely no idea what to expect and I had no one to ask. What happened when you had a miscarriage? Would I go to the toilet and suddenly a whole tiny baby would fall out? Would I have to scoop it out of the toilet and wrap it in a cloth? It made me think of the kittens being drowned when I was little, being put in a sack and then drowned. And what if the bleeding didn't stop and I bled to death in front of Alfie?

But, frightened as I was, I couldn't bring myself to be a nuisance and telephone Joe. He was back working at his old job, as a bricklayer's labourer, and I really didn't want to disturb him, so I just continued to lie there, Alfie beside me, waiting for him to come home.

When he did I felt much better, and calmer, and when the doctor rang to see how I was I was resigned to hearing it would definitely happen soon. Yet it didn't. Not that day, or the next, or the next. And on the third day I was taken by ambulance to hospital, so they could give me a proper examination and see if the baby was still there. I stayed in overnight and had my answer very quickly. It appeared that this baby was hanging on.

It was an interminable, tedious, depressing pregnancy. I bled almost throughout, and was constantly in and out of hospital, and even when allowed home I was mostly confined to bed. I also suffered from repeated urinary infections, which tracked up to my kidneys and were excruciatingly painful.

Social services, concerned, arranged some home help for us. Someone came in for an hour and a half a day, to pick up Alfie from play school, and do some shopping and housework. However, the rest of Alfie's days were spent on or near my bed. He'd sit there beside me, playing quietly with his cars, making *brrm brrm* noises as he tracked them up and down the pillow.

It was to be another truncated pregnancy. One evening, at 10.30, when I was just eight months pregnant, my waters broke and we had to call an ambulance. Joe had to stay with Alfie, so I travelled to hospital alone and once there became the subject of a great deal of rushing around. Unlike my first birth, which seemed to go on for ever with nothing happening, this one was already causing concern.

They soon established that my baby was in the breech position and were also fearful that because my blood loss was significant, there may also be damage to its brain. Several times they tried to turn it – and, this being a teaching hospital, there were about fifteen junior doctors present – before deciding it wasn't possible and that they needed to deliver it straight away.

It was the sort of birth that today would have been done by caesarean; the pain was so intense that I kept losing consciousness, and required several injections, forceps, and to be cut to get the baby out.

But come out the baby did – I had a daughter. And though they rushed her off immediately, concerned about brain damage, something inside me told me I didn't need to worry. That when they finally gave her to me, she'd be okay.

The nightmare pregnancy was over, and I couldn't wait for Joe to see her. She was perfect, my little girl. Just perfect.

CHAPTER 21

She looked strange, my new baby, when they brought her back to me. Having been breech, and born so traumatically, her little legs were bent up so that her feet almost touched her neck, which made putting a nappy on her a bit difficult.

But in all other respects, she really did seem perfect, and when they wheeled me to the ward after they had stitched me back together, I just lay on my bed, her clear plastic hospital cot beside me, marvelling at the blue of her eyes and her perfect little fingers and fingernails, and the way she just lay there and seemed to gaze at me.

The difference between Alfie's birth and this one was immeasurable. I didn't feel that awful blackness descending, or that terrifying sense of being overwhelmed. I would be tested, of course, over the months that followed, but for the moment I could barely believe we had created something so beautiful.

Joe arrived at eight the next morning, and pronounced himself delighted with 'his little girl'. He thought she was beautiful too. He brought Alfie to the hospital later that day, and sat with him on the bed so that our little boy could hold his little sister. It was a perfect moment, and one I'd treasure for always. My joy, however, wasn't to last long.

In retrospect, the signs had been there all along. Right back when Joe and I moved into our first marital home, there would be women, from time to time, turning up on the doorstep, asking me questions about him and our relationship. With hindsight, it had been odd for them to do that, but at the time, though I was unable to work out why they'd come, I reasoned that as they were the wives and daughters of other employees of the estate, it was feasible that they might want to know more about us – after all, I'd never been in that sort of situation before. Also, I so wanted to be *able* to trust Joe that I could invent reasons for everything.

I had even found excuses for the business with the girl, Meg, from the stables. I knew it hadn't really happened, because he simply wouldn't *do* that. I knew he wouldn't go with another woman. He'd just been at a low ebb, and I'd been very ill – there had just been too much strain on our marriage. No, I'd decided, whatever had gone wrong in the past, I trusted my husband completely.

The early weeks with our daughter, who we called Jennifer Lee, were difficult and draining. Despite the difference in the circumstances of her birth compared with Alfie's, I was soon repeating my previous ways of thinking, and also accepting (a feeling endorsed by my mother) that I wasn't any good as a mum.

However, as the weeks turned into months I began, even though I still found it difficult emotionally, to feel more confident about looking after the physical needs of my children. The only problem was that money was so tight, and I had to work longer and longer hours. Juggling childcare was becoming difficult, and when I took a new evening job, at another residential home, when Jennifer was three months old, I had to arrange for my neighbour, Sue, to look after them every day till Joe finished work and could collect them. I'd become very close to Sue, who was older, and like a mum to me. Unlike my own mother, she was always praising me, telling me I *was* a good mum. I'd always listen avidly to any advice she gave, and would take pride in trying to emulate her, as I had great respect for her; working hard at getting my washing really clean, and pegging it out first thing like she did.

But Joe and I were seeing little of each other by this time, and I could feel my anxiety mounting as I sensed our relationship ebbing away. Even so, I still trusted him completely, and blindly, and always seemed to be able to find ways to ascribe odd goings-on to me just imagining things.

Even so, it was around this time that I had to concede situations that troubled me did so for a reason. We'd been invited to a party by a friend of my sister, and during this Joe disappeared. They lived next door to a pub, and it was here that I found him, in the car park, with my sister's friend. As soon as they saw me they sprang apart guiltily, and I remember a rare feeling, which lasted for one intense moment, of murderous rage.

It was at another gathering only a few weeks later that I was given more cause for concern when a girl who had spotted Joe came rushing towards us, arms outstretched, beaming. She was just about to fling her arms around him when he warned her off.

'This is *Faith*,' he said pointedly. She dropped both her arms and her smile, said a polite 'Hello' and backed away.

This time I plucked up courage to challenge him.

'Who was she?' I asked him. 'How do you know her?'

'From work,' he said, looking uncomfortable. 'I sometimes pick her up and drop her off at her work on the way to mine.'

I felt sick visualizing this. His guilt was so blindingly obvious. I didn't press him, because with Joe it was impossible to have a discussion if he didn't want to. He'd just refuse, and there was nothing I could do.

I was also afraid of what I might hear, and couldn't face it. I left the party on my own and went back to the car, and waited for him to follow. Two whole hours I waited, feeling powerless and insignificant. But the incident was never mentioned again.

Though we seemed to be getting on (however inaccurate my thoughts were on that score) he was becoming very unsettled at work. When Jennifer was two, and Alfie six, Joe left his job as a bricklayer's labourer and started working, as a labourer again, but for our neighbour. He was a wealthy businessman, and it wasn't long before his wife, who I knew to stop and talk to, was telling me how lazy Joe was and he'd been caught taking naps when he was supposed to be working.

Alarm bells were now ringing, as I feared once again that Joe – who had always been a law unto himself – would just decide to give up on work altogether and we'd be back penniless and homeless. By now I was working far more hours than he was, but I told myself it was important to support him, because he was clearly depressed. He would often spend whole days now just lying on the sofa, and he looked so down that when

I collected my wages I often gave him most of them to go and buy himself something to cheer him up. Unwittingly, I suppose I was acting as if I was his mother, and treating him like another of my children.

Then, out of the blue, Joe announced he had decided to become a taxi driver. Suddenly, instead of working barely any hours at all, he was working day and night six days a week. Then very soon after seven days a week, as he'd taken another job – a Sunday job, picking apples – to make up, he said, for having contributed so little for so long.

I felt grateful he was shouldering responsibility again, and also sorry for him, working such long hours.

I felt sorrier still to see how little money these endeavours were bringing in. But when I asked him why that was, his answer seemed obvious. Taxi drivers had to spend a great deal of time waiting for fares, and no fares meant no money being earned. It was a similar story with the apple-picking, apparently, which was at the whim of both the farmers and the weather. You had to be available if you wanted work, and if there were no apples that needed picking at the farm you waited with all the other apple-pickers for work at other farms. If there was work, you'd then be driven to where it was needed, but if not you'd had a wasted day. But you dare not go home, because the farmer would tell you not to bother coming back. There were always plenty of others desperate for the work.

Poor Joe, I remember thinking. With no qualifications and no particular skill, he would always be at the mercy of employers like this. No wonder he found life depressing.

As the Christmas of 1978 approached, I was beginning to

feel very low myself. So when Joe told me about the Christmas apple-pickers' party, I was pleased to have something nice to look forward to, and I'd finally get to meet all the other people he spent his Sundays with.

'What sort of thing should I wear?' I asked him, excited.

He shook his head. 'Sorry, Faith,' he said. 'But you're not invited. It's a works do. Staff only. That's the rule.'

Joe didn't come home on the night of the party. He said he was staying over with one of the other apple-pickers, as they'd be drinking, and he wouldn't be able to drive. In fact, it wasn't to be too long before I found out that there hadn't even *been* a Christmas party.

Christmas Eve that year saw Alfie very excited. In fact, over-excited, as children tend to be when they know Father Christmas is imminent. But I was fretting. My family were coming to tea that afternoon and Joe wasn't yet home from work.

Having my family visiting caused me anxiety at the best of times, not because of my mother, who'd generally be subdued, but because of my father's unpredictability. On the one hand, I was always anxious about his swearing and aggression around my children (particularly around Alfie, because he seemed to hate all his grandsons), but the converse of that behaviour was very stressful too. If he wasn't swearing, he was invariably stony-faced, and would just sit in an armchair, ignoring everyone. In this mode, he was equally difficult to deal with, as I would fuss around him – I couldn't seem to help myself – trying to jolly him out of whatever had put him in a mood, in case he suddenly exploded about something. All in all, managing my anxiety around my father took up a ridiculous amount of my time.

The situation hadn't improved between my parents either; indeed, things had got worse. Though he was still out womanizing, he'd also entered into a long-term relationship with a woman he stayed with three nights a week. When he wasn't there, she'd telephone the house regularly, and he would chat to her, brazenly, while my mother sat in the other room, calling her his 'whore'. That she could do anything about this was never suggested, much less discussed. His temper and foul language had also got worse, and he seemed to care less and less who he abused. Being around him made me almost unbearably anxious; you never knew when the next torrent of threats and swearing would be triggered, and the waiting was almost as bad as the moment when he vented his spleen in my direction.

I still had the powerful need to take care of my increasingly distracted mother and it ate into what little time I had free. I'd leave for work ridiculously early some mornings so I could walk – or indeed run – the four miles to where they lived, with Jennifer in her pushchair and little Alfie running alongside, to clean up her junk-filled house.

Grandpops was still a regular there, and though he'd long since given up trying to approach me physically, I watched appalled at how he'd turned his attention to 'tickling' my much younger sister's friends. The terrible noise he made through his clenched teeth hadn't changed, and the speed with which he grabbed them and furiously 'tickled' them hadn't lessened one iota.

Watching my sister's reaction was fascinating. She'd stand

some distance away, as they would scream for him to let go, and watched intently, rubbing her hands together nervously, and laughing anxiously as she saw them wriggle free, saying: 'I'm not getting near *him* again!'

Her own apparent fascination about how her friends would react – which was the healthy one of resolving to keep away from him – appeared so depressingly similar to my own that I wondered how many times he'd caught her and, like me, she'd been unable to escape.

I was still a very long way from accepting that the 'tickling' was, for him, sexually arousing, but I found it impossible to either be touched by him myself, or watch him do what he'd done to me to others. He was my grandad so by definition he was someone I shouldn't feel upset by, but I was still wary around him and knew I always would be.

My nan hadn't improved with age either. Now I was an adult she didn't even try to hide her distaste for either my mother or myself. Unless I made a point of addressing her, she invariably ignored me, which left me – just as it had as a small child – wondering what I'd done to displease her. Yet she never felt able to leave without some parting shot being lobbed over her shoulder, either about my mothering skills, whenever I left my children with my mother, or to criticize me for thinking I was 'better than everyone else'. She also liked to point out that if she was unfortunate enough to end up in the old people's home I worked in, or had the misfortune of being unwell in her own home, that she wouldn't want me anywhere near her.

Ironically, if she was running my mother down, I was the first person she tried to persuade to join forces, looking at me as she spoke, wrinkling her nose, and making faces behind my mother's back. 'I always wash up my own cup and saucer here,' she'd tell me, 'so at least I know there'll be a clean one next time.'

Just as it was with my father, if ever Nan arrived when I was visiting my mother, I'd spend the rest of my time trying to please her while, at the same time, waiting anxiously for her to say something unkind. I never could work out why she was so chillingly cold and unkind to me. I spent my entire childhood and half my adult life – till she died – trying to work out quite what I'd done wrong.

When Joe still hadn't arrived home by mid-afternoon, I began to worry – I couldn't imagine what had happened to him. He'd done an overnight shift the night before and I'd expected him to be back before lunchtime.

I kept ringing the taxi firm trying to track him down, but the phone just rang and rang, and I wondered how a cab firm who didn't answer ever managed to make money.

Finally, at around four, he turned up, just before the family were due. He was holding a clutch of Christmas cards and, without speaking to me, or acknowledging the time, went over to the sideboard and stood them up in a little row.

'Who are all those from?' I asked him, in all innocence.

'Just girls I know,' he said, his manner offhand, and tired. 'Just regulars I pick up in my taxi.'

I picked up the first of the cards. Inside it said, 'To darling Joe, with hugs and kisses and much, much more XXXXXXX'.

I felt anger and jealousy rise like bile. And indignation, too. How could he be so blatant – just putting those cards there, for all to see? I plucked them up, one by one, took them out into the garden, and put them into the dustbin. Joe stalked after me immediately, uncharacteristically furious, and for the first time ever I was wary of his anger.

He pulled them back out of the bin, then went around to the front, unlocked his car and shoved them inside. With perfect timing, two cars were now coming up the road. In the first I could see my father, with Grandpops beside him and doubtless my mother, Nan and Grandad in the back, and my little sister and brother on their laps. Behind them was my older sister's husband's car. We now had no choice but to pretend everything was normal, to greet them all and usher them in.

Joe slept in his armchair throughout almost their entire visit, which now seemed interminable. I was seething, frightened I might burst into tears at any moment, and was desperate for the family to leave.

I then had to go through the Christmas Eve rituals with the children, helping them to hang stockings on their beds, putting out a mince pie and strawberry milkshake for Father Christmas, not forgetting to add a carrot for Rudolph, and then finally putting them to bed, while Joe continued dozing in his chair.

I went back downstairs on heavy legs, almost unable to stomach the thought that in asking him what was going on, I might get an answer I couldn't bear to hear. But I had to ask, and I got the answer.

'I've met someone else,' he told me quietly, 'who I really love.'

It felt as if my whole world was coming to an end. 'Who?' I said. 'Who have you met?'

'A girl,' he answered. 'A girl I've been driving in my taxi.' She was seventeen, he told me. And very pretty. She worked doing accounts at a firm in the next town, and he would regularly drop her at some disco. I didn't want to know these things, but he told me anyway. I could feel dread engulf me now, suffocating me, a scream of pain and anguish in my throat.

'I think I should leave,' he said then. 'I think it's better. I'll leave tomorrow,' he said. 'Yes, I'll leave tomorrow.'

In my head I *was* screaming now. Screaming *at* him. Saying: 'Please, I *beg* you, don't leave us. I'll do whatever it takes. But, *please*, don't go. Don't leave us.'

But none of that came out. I couldn't seem to form the words. Instead I just sat there and said, 'But it's Christmas tomorrow. What about the children? What will I tell Alfie and Jennifer?'

'They'll be okay,' he said, as if I was making a fuss about nothing. As if him going wouldn't really make a lot of difference. 'They'll be all right with you,' he added. 'And there's your family.'

I was lost for words. How could *we ever* be all right now?

'Joe,' I asked him. 'Do you still love me at all?'

He looked straight at me. But there was nothing in his eyes. Not even a glimmer. It was almost as if, inside, he had already left.

'No,' he said quietly. 'Not any more.'

CHAPTER 22

I went into Alfie's bedroom first. Crept in, as quietly as I could, and left the red punchball, that was to be his big Christmas gift, carefully propped in the corner. Alfie had decided that he wanted to be a boxer when he grew up, and the punchball would enable him to get in some practice before he was big enough for proper classes. It should have been inflated, and its pole fixed onto its base, but Joe hadn't felt like doing it. Looking at it now, I felt utterly defeated. I couldn't work out how to put the thing together, and wished Joe could have bothered to do that one small thing. But he'd done nothing. Not even said goodnight to the children. Just said he was tired and gone to bed.

Next I quietly replaced Alfie's empty stocking with a full one and put a few little presents at the foot of his bed. A book and crayons, some Lego, a few little cars. The wrapping paper crackled and I held my breath. He mustn't wake, I thought, watching him. He mustn't wake. I could feel a familiar hysteria welling up in my throat. How was I going to cope? What was I going to tell the children? What were we going to *do*?

Jennifer was sprawled unconscious in her bed, and I silently put down the little orange-striped doll's buggy we'd got her. She'd love it, I knew. She would so enjoy pushing it around. I placed a little doll in it and tucked a blanket round her, then replaced Jennifer's stocking with a full one, too, and again placed a few presents at the end of her bed; this time a handbag, a few books, a little hairbrush and mirror set.

I then went quietly back downstairs and looked around. At the Christmas tree lights, that hadn't yet been switched off, at the garlands and decorations, at the bowls of nuts, the strewn Quality Street chocolates, and then I sank, ever so slowly, to my knees on the carpet. There, with my hands over my mouth and my forehead on the floor, I cried. I cried silently but non-stop.

It was almost Christmas Day morning before I climbed into bed, where Joe lay, fast asleep and untouchable. I couldn't bear to get too close to him — it was simply too painful. Would this be the last time we slept in the same bed, ever? All I could think was that he no longer loved me and soon, come the morning, he'd be going.

I was scheduled to work on Christmas morning, and I was due there at eight and, having not slept, I felt like a zombie — my head spinning as I pretended excitement with the children, though I could hardly bear to look them in the eye.

Joe was uncommunicative, unwilling to talk, and neither of us spoke as he dropped me at work. The plan was for him to take the children to my sister's for Christmas lunch and then collect me from work when my shift finished at two. We were then due for tea at my mother's. How that plan might now have changed I had no idea. All I knew was that I couldn't think straight.

Walking up the path to the old people's home, as Joe and

the children drove off, I realized I was actually grateful to be there. I would have wanted to work, in any case, as I'd have hated to let everyone down, but now I also thought how much better this was than being at home, waiting for him to leave. But once inside, the enormity of it all overwhelmed me, and I broke down, unable to stop sobbing.

The staff were lovely, and all so caring and sympathetic. Was I so sure? Maybe it was just a silly argument. Go home, they suggested. Sort things out. He wouldn't *really* go. But I knew differently. I worked through the morning, trying hard not to cry, with the thought of two o'clock encroaching ever nearer.

When Joe arrived to pick me up, he was laughing. The children were too – their excitement hadn't lessened – and they were anxious to show me their presents from my sister. Still nothing was said about what would happen. Maybe, I thought desperately, he's changed his mind and is staying. How could he act this happy if he was just about to leave? But the bombshell was quick in coming. As soon as the children had finished telling me what they'd been up to, he said, 'I'll drop you at your mother's and then I'll go.'

Just those few words, spoken quietly while he was driving, that signified the end of my marriage.

I was speechless as we drove to my parents. He wouldn't really just drop us and drive off, would he? He couldn't do that, surely. Yet, he did. He pulled up and as he opened the driver's door, said, 'Here, let me get the kids out for you.' He then lifted them both out, climbed back into the car, reversed it, and drove off.

I stood on the pavement, stunned, the children either side of me, unable to believe what had happened. We must have stood like that, the three of us, for several long seconds, and then Alfie said, 'Mummy, where's Daddy going?'

I took them in then. I had simply no idea.

I spent the remainder of Christmas Day in a fog of misery, feeling devastated beyond words. I sat on a stool in my mother's kitchen, clutching the tumblerful of whisky that I'd been given on announcing what had happened. Nothing had been discussed since. Unable to take part in present opening, because I couldn't stop crying, I remained sitting in the kitchen, occasionally hearing snippets of conversation. 'Why is Mummy crying?' I heard Jennifer ask. I didn't hear my mother's reply. 'Why is she sitting in the kitchen?' I heard my nan ask. But, as was the way with my family, no one talked to me about what had happened, let alone tried to comfort me, and Joe's name wasn't mentioned again.

I was dropped home by my brother at the beginning of Christmas evening and once I'd waved him off, trying desperately to keep myself together, I immediately put the children to bed. Neither of them asked where their father was, for which I was grateful. I didn't think I had the strength to try to tell them. And even if I had, I couldn't bear to. It was Christmas, for God's sake. I couldn't do that to them. I was relieved that they both got into bed without a fuss.

I glanced at Alfie's new punchball as I tucked him in. It was still deflated and unassembled, just as it had been this morning. Joe hadn't even bothered to do that for his little boy. I felt the scream in my throat poised, ready to burst from me.

Back downstairs again, I stood and surveyed the festive living room, which seemed to be mocking me; part of some ridiculous farce. The room was icy and empty, which made a thought suddenly occur to me. How on earth would I manage? I had a little Christmas food, but no money. Joe had gone with all of his and a check of my purse revealed I had just ten pounds in the world. How was I going to be able to pay for things? I only had my part-time job bringing in money, and how could I continue to do that with the children to look after on my own?

I was growing colder as I sat there, both inside and outside, but I didn't put on the heating. I didn't dare.

Where *was* Joe? Where had he gone? To his mother's? It was Christmas Day, of all the days to choose, and I couldn't bear to think he might be anywhere else.

When I woke on Boxing Day, after another night of fitful sleep, I simply couldn't think what to do. I had no energy and no motivation to get up. The silence around me was deafening. I couldn't bear the loneliness that was pressing down all around me, but if I got out of bed I was frightened it would engulf me. Eventually I heard sounds coming from the children's bedrooms, where they both appeared to be playing with their toys. They seemed unusually quiet, however, and when, after a while, they both came in and climbed on the bed with me, Alfie, though Jennifer was chattering away quite happily, just sat there, looking at me.

He knew, I thought wretchedly. He *knew* what had happened. The tears started up again and I brushed them angrily away, as I took the children downstairs and made them breakfast. How could Joe do this to his own little children?

I decided not to tell them anything – not for the moment. Though, even then, I was aware that my not telling them was as much for my own sake as theirs. The imprint of my upbringing ran deep. Nothing painful could ever, or should ever, be discussed. Nothing bad, no matter how great the distress, was ever to be opened up for scrutiny. The death of my little brother, the abuse by my grandfather, the horrible things Daniel had repeatedly done to me, the betrayal by Phillip, the violence of my father – nothing, however dreadful, was to be questioned.

And so with this. In their turn, my two little children, for the moment, were now forced to play 'let's pretend' as well.

As the days went by and there was still no word from Joe, I became increasingly distressed. I also became fixated on trying to track down this girl he 'loved instead of' me. I remembered he'd told me her name, which was Melanie, the type of firm she worked at, and the town it was in. I went through the Yellow Pages systematically, calling any company that advertised the same products and asking for Melanie by name. The last thing I wanted was for her to answer the phone herself, but if I could just find out where she was working, I might at least have some chance of tracking Joe down.

Once again, I'd had no luck with Joe's mother. When I'd telephoned her, she'd just said she didn't want to get involved. But if I could find this Melanie – who I still wasn't completely sure existed – then perhaps I could also find Joe. Perhaps this was just another blip. Perhaps, like last time, he'd come home in the end. I also felt sure that if I could just speak to him, there might be some chance I could make him come to his senses quicker than if I left things to take their course.

It didn't take many calls for me to find out where she worked

– or, at least, someone called Melanie who seemed to be her. It had been a lady who'd answered and I now went through my routine, explaining I was a friend who was anxious to get hold of her, but who had mislaid her number. The woman sympathized and commented that, of *course*, I'd be wanting to congratulate her on her engagement, wouldn't I? She immediately gave me her home telephone number and I wrote it down, both terrified and relieved. Hope sprang in me: if this girl was engaged, then she certainly wouldn't be interested in pursuing things with Joe – if, indeed, she ever really had been. Perhaps he'd been barking up the wrong tree. Perhaps she'd now made it clear she wasn't interested. Perhaps he'd come home after all.

It took a while for me to pluck up the courage to dial the number and to ask the woman who answered, who sounded middle-aged, if I could speak to Melanie. She told me Melanie was out, but that she'd take a message, and it was at this point that I decided to ask the question I badly needed to – was she out with someone called Joe, by any chance?

'Yes, she is,' she answered. 'Is that someone from work?'

'No,' I told her, my heart racing. 'It's Joe's wife, and his two children are missing him.'

There was a long silence, followed by a sharp intake of breath, then she said, 'His wife? His two children? He's *married*?'

There was a pause before she went on. 'But he can't be!'

I assured her that he was, and there was another pause. 'We had no idea!' she said finally, 'but he's a really nice man!' As if she thought that made everything okay.

'But he *can't* be!' she said again, clearly just as shocked as I was. 'He and Melanie got engaged on Christmas Day!'

CHAPTER 23

The day after I found out about Joe's engagement I received a return phone call from Melanie's mother. She wanted to meet me – my mother and father also – and, still not knowing how to say no to anyone, I could do nothing other than agree. It was a daunting prospect, but at least if I *did* see her, I would still have a link, however stressful, to Joe.

It was becoming surreal. In less than a week I had gone from being in a state of blind ignorance about my husband to one in which the mother of a girl I didn't know was coming to see me to discuss his engagement to her daughter.

The visit itself was even more surreal. I had to welcome this woman into my and Joe's home, watch while my own mother insisted on showing her around it and, most bizarre, listen to my father, of all people, talking self-righteously about Joe's infidelity, after he'd been welcomed so wholeheartedly into the family, and given so much support.

Melanie's mother, who'd arranged a special Christmas Day engagement party for the couple, reiterated that they had absolutely no idea Joe was married with children. She was also clear about one thing. Despite her telling us how much time Joe had spent at her house, about the gifts of jewellery he'd apparently lavished on her daughter, even despite telling us how much Melanie apparently loved Joe, she was clear the relationship had to end.

And to *that* end, obviously being a concerned mother, she begged me to let Melanie come to visit me too, hoping that meeting me and the children would make her see sense. 'I have to get her away from him,' she told me earnestly, and I found myself reflecting what it must be like to have such a loving mother take care of you.

I felt powerless, as before, to say no, so at six the next evening, the day before New Year's Eve, I opened my front door and let her in. I'd been in a complete state about what to wear. I had spent all the intervening period in agonies about looking so dreadful. Nothing I could find seemed to make me look nice. I looked frumpy and old-fashioned – twice my twenty-two years – and couldn't look at my reflection without wanting to cut off my whole face and chop off my hair.

I walked to the front door in a state of disbelief. If someone had told me, seven days back, that I'd be opening my door to the girl my husband had declared himself to be in love with, I'd have laughed. The idea was too incredible. Yet here she was, a very pretty seventeen-year-old, slim and smartly dressed, with long blonde hair. She looked so young and confident. I paid special attention to her jewellery because, though understated, it was stylish and gave her presence, the jewellery Joe had bought for her, using money that should have been spent on Alfie and Jennifer. Melanie looked so innocent compared with me. And with what little I already knew about her, that didn't surprise me.

She was terribly upset, and as shocked as I was at the turn of events since her engagement. She asked a few questions, but it was clear she didn't really know what to say. How could she? She was seventeen and the man she had fallen in love with came with a completely unexpected wife and family.

She didn't stay long. In fact, she left somewhat abruptly, as if she couldn't bear to be in my house a moment longer. I watched her climb into a new-looking Peugeot, and felt an awful depression begin to engulf me. The emptiness inside me felt vast. I don't know what I had been expecting, deep down. That it had been nonsense? That there *was* no other woman? That he'd realize he still loved us and come back? That this Melanie would just turn out to be a young girl with a stupid crush?

All these thoughts had flitted in and out of my mind, and all of them had been easier to deal with than the reality, in the deafening silence. It felt incredible that fifteen minutes earlier I had been dreading her visit, and now it was all over all I was left with was the feeling of how much better she seemed than me in every way.

I'd had only one conversation with Joe during all this. He'd called me earlier, not to see how we were, but to warn me, having been made aware of our meeting, that I mustn't do anything to rock the boat. 'Don't you dare,' he'd said. 'Don't you dare spoil this for me.'

Had I? I wondered, as I crept into bed. Would she finish with him now, and would he blame me? I woke up on New Year's Eve with the absolute surety there was nothing to get out of bed for. All hope was gone, and in its place was a void. I had the children, instead, climb into bed with me, and we pretty much remained there all day.

But I wasn't to be left for long. My sister Susan and her husband were off to a New Year's Eve party, and told me I had to go with them. Phillip and his girlfriend were going to the party also, and they then asked if they could sleep over at my house. As ever, I felt unable to say no to either request, but straight away became anxious about my finances. No one was aware that I had absolutely no money – why would they be? Our family didn't discuss anything. And now I would have to turn on the heating, and spend the last £10 in my purse buying food for them.

That evening, I took Alfie and Jennifer to my sister's, and shared the babysitter she'd booked. And for a time, at the party, I held things together sufficiently so no one would know that, on the inside, I was dying.

But by eleven, I could stand it no longer. I left abruptly, leaping up from the table we'd all been sitting around and running out into the street. It had begun snowing earlier and was still snowing now – everything was now painfully pretty, as if contemptuous of me. I ran all the way through town, running down the middle of the empty streets because the pavements were too slippery, aware of that particular silence that only comes with heavy snowfall, and of the fact that I couldn't see another human being.

I knew full well where I was running – I was running home, from the wretched party – but even though my feet seemed to be taking me there, I'd never felt less like I had a home to go to, or more keenly the sense of having nowhere I belonged; that not a single person anywhere cared about me.

I turned a corner, and saw a police car up ahead, lights flashing, sirens blaring, travelling very fast. I wished in that instant I was under its wheels.

Joe never came back. Not that week, or the next week, or any time after, and my depression returned with a vengeance. I took up eating, as a way of trying to comfort myself, tipping very quickly from moderate overeating to bingeing on anything I could find. I would eat whole packets of biscuits at once, dunked in coffee, sweets of any kind; packets of the things, and potatoes and bread in terrifying quantities. I would eat any sort of chocolate I could stuff into my mouth, Crunchies and Mars bars, Toffee Crisps and Dairy Milk, and if I ran out of chocolate I would eat cubes of raw jelly, and devour enormous home-made rice puddings.

Despite a new regime of making myself sick every day – sometimes using washing-up liquid to help me do so – and of taking laxatives and water pills every morning and forever having to rush to the toilet, I went quickly from eight and a half stone to thirteen, a whole two stone heavier than I was when I gave birth to my children.

I would look in the mirror and think, 'No wonder Joe left me. Look at me. What a disgusting sight.'

As well as myself, I found it difficult to face other people, and as the weeks went on I became more and more hermit-like. With so little money to live on, we were forced, when the children weren't in school and playschool, to spend much of our time in bed. Our diet, when I wasn't secretly devouring anything I could lay hands on, was often little more than porridge, made by Alfie.

I couldn't bear going back to the old people's home, so gave in my notice and began working again for the family I'd cleaned and child-minded for before Jennifer was born. I felt more comfortable spending my time with children; no one could judge me or ask me questions. But this too proved short-lived, as one night, when driving me home after babysitting, my employer's husband stopped the car outside some garages near my house and proceeded to kiss and try to touch me.

This didn't come entirely out of the blue. Their marriage was very strained; had been all the time I'd worked for them, and he and his wife slept in separate bedrooms. He was generally known as being a dirty old devil – his reputation for trying it on with women was known by every girl who'd worked there. Plus he drank a lot – had been drinking that evening – but thus far I had managed to avoid him.

Not tonight, alas, but at least one thing had changed. For the first time in my life, in a situation like this, I didn't have that familiar sense of powerlessness. Instead I was imbued with sudden strength. What had happened with Joe had had a powerful effect, and the thought of another man trying to touch me made me feel more like a whore than I'd already long felt, and it repulsed me that this man even tried. I broke free from his arms, flung open the door and ran away.

I handed in my notice the following day, citing the need to find full-time employment. She might have known why – I suspect she knew what her husband was like – but she accepted my resignation without question. I was glad, but also sad to leave a job I enjoyed. But there seemed little choice. After Joe, no man was *ever* going to touch me.

Indeed, touch, in all its forms, was very difficult. I had grown up in a world devoid of *any* affection, let alone the physical affection a parent normally shows their child. And now something similar had started happening to me.

I had always had difficulties relating emotionally – my childhood meant I would find normal physical intimacy confusing and scary. My mother had never touched me with affection, ever – the only physical intimacy I had ever encountered invariably meant something sexual was happening, and though I wouldn't understand how much this had damaged me until much later, it caused me great anxiety in dealing with my children. Though with Joe I had enjoyed my first sexual relationship, I was still unable to do all the physical bonding that a parent would normally make with their child. I couldn't hug them at all. Found it almost impossible to bear them touching me. I couldn't hold their hands, stroke them, or run my hands across their heads – I was so frightened I might hurt them or abuse them in some way. Not intentionally – I just thought it might happen without my meaning to, and the more frightened I was the harder it became.

I shouldered every bit of blame for all this. It was something in *me* that caused men to abuse me, and something in *me* that had caused my brother to die. It was simple; I was bad, but if I kept my distance, then my children would be safer. I couldn't even tell them I loved them.

For a while, with Joe's love, I'd believed we stood a chance. But now he was gone I could feel myself withdrawing from them. I couldn't bear to be touched; I would angrily brush Jennifer's little hands away because the pain I felt when anyone showed me kindness was so immense I couldn't bear it.

My fear of hurting them had also become intense. I had become increasingly angry around Alfie, shaking him by the shoulders, shouting if he was taking too long putting on his coat. I would tug at the hem repeatedly, unbalancing him, shouting: 'We have to put your coat on! Put it on, do you understand? Do up your buttons. Do them up! We have to go out! Do you understand?'

Alfie would just stand there, saying nothing with words, but just watching me, seemingly unafraid. Just sad – terribly sad. I could hardly bear meet his eye, so powerfully did this affect me. It was almost as if I was so useless I couldn't even frighten a small boy. I didn't want him to be afraid of me – of course, I didn't – I just wanted to come across as stronger than I felt so no one would ever mess with me again. Yet his eyes were so assessing. As if *he* were the older one; as if he really had the measure of me.

I knew I must stop crying in front of the children. I had never said – or would say – anything bad to them about their father, but I knew my crying would hurt them even so. So I taught myself not to cry anywhere in the house except the bathroom, where sometimes I would have to clasp the cold enamel basin, just to feel its weight and strength. I couldn't feel my own, and I was afraid I'd just float away, cease to exist.

Eventually, I made myself return to the doctor. I knew I couldn't survive as I was, because it terrified me to realize that the feelings of darkness and futility about everything were so strong that not even the thought of my children seemed enough reason for me to live. This time, I was grateful to be put on another course of antidepressants; to sense some strength seeping back felt like such a relief.

Now stronger, I went to tell my neighbour, Sue, about what had happened, only to find her breathless and coughing. Even so, she was pleased to see me and was very sympathetic, offering help with child-minding the children once again so I could work for a few more hours. She was such a godsend. She had become like a mother to me really and with her help I was able to take on more cleaning work; I needed to work full-time to make ends meet, as I had had nothing from Joe, and I couldn't bear the thought of claiming benefits.

I was also persuaded to start divorce proceedings, by my friend Maria, who now worked for a solicitor. That way, she explained, he'd have to pay me maintenance. By law.

It was while I was doing this that I was given the news that my paternal grandfather – Nan's husband – had died. For all her vitriol, my nan had always adored Grandad, and in spite of all the bad things she'd done to me all these years I went around to see how she was.

I shouldn't have been surprised by her reception. She told me it was my fault that Grandad had died. My fault, for 'making Joe go'. Grandad had liked Joe, had got on well with him, and if I hadn't lost Joe then he wouldn't have had his stroke, and would still be alive. She was really angry. 'This has all happened because of what *you* did,' she told me. 'You're responsible.'

She pointedly ignored me for the whole of Grandad's funeral, and I couldn't get what she'd said to me out of my head. Though any rational person would have taken it for the cruelty it was, I could only wonder if perhaps she was right.

*   *   *

It was still on my mind – very much so – as winter became spring, and I was glad of having a friend such as Sue, who could at least keep me from cracking up. But when I dropped Jennifer at her house a few weeks later, while I went to work, I soon realized I wasn't the only one with problems – she was talking strangely, not making any sense. Concerned, I stayed with her, and telephoned her son, Dick, who was an assistant manager in a supermarket in town, and who I'd got to know well over recent months.

He came straight away, but seemed irritable when I suggested she needed a doctor. 'No she doesn't,' he argued. 'There's nothing wrong with her. She's fine.' He then turned to her. 'You don't need a doctor, do you, Mum?'

Sue shook her head. 'Oh, no,' she agreed.

'That's not true,' I said quietly, not wishing to antagonize him further, but becoming worried. It clearly wasn't just my family who insisted on being in denial about things they didn't want to think about.

'Mum says she doesn't,' he said, making it clear he wasn't about to argue the point. But I knew she did. I'd only had to spend a little time around her to realize that much of what she said made no sense. She had told me, for instance, that his sister, who had only very recently had her third baby, had had lots and lots of babies; that they had just kept on coming out, one after another. This was not only concerning because it sounded so strange, but also because her two young granddaughters were currently in Sue's care.

But there was nothing I could do, as Dick was adamant. I took Jennifer home and called work to explain and hoped that eventually he'd act. And indeed, later that day, Dick called round to let me know that Sue had been taken into hospital. Her confusion was because her brain wasn't getting enough oxygen, due to the chest complaint she had.

I went to bed that night relieved. She'd clearly been more ill than anyone had realized, and now she'd be treated. But it didn't happen, because the next morning Dick called again, to tell me she'd died.

I was devastated. Sue had only been in her early sixties, and had been so incredibly kind to me over the past four years. What was wrong with the world that such a wonderful person should be taken so young?

But as her death sank in, darker thoughts did too. More to the point, what was wrong with *me*? What had I done to cause all these horrible things to happen? First Joe had left, then Grandad had died and, most tragically, Sue had now gone too.

I couldn't go on living here. Without Joe and Sue I had nothing to stay for. I called the council and asked for a transfer. I didn't care where; I'd take any swap they offered, anywhere. I just needed to run and never stop. I needed to get away from my so-called 'home' and 'family'. Get away from everything, everybody, and never come back.

CHAPTER 24

Joe leaving had broken me. He had shattered me into so many pieces I didn't think I could ever put them back together.

For a brief time I'd been able to put my past behind me and to believe in some sort of future. And though putting my trust in Joe had been a mistake, it was also one I was predestined to make. Marrying Joe meant escape from the upbringing that had damaged me; and although I had been naive in not seeing him for the irresponsible person he really was, he still remained the only significant person in my life who'd treated me as if I mattered. Or *appeared* to have treated me as if I mattered − I would find out that in this, as in so many of my interactions with people, I had been woefully misguided. His leaving, therefore, wasn't just about the loss of *him*, it was also about the loss of the person I'd believed I could become *with* him, and now probably never would. How could I ever trust anyone again?

It was fortunate, looking back, that I couldn't yet see the future that stretched before me. All I could see − and manage − were the day-by-day increments of living; of trying to pick up what pieces I could and fashioning some sort of life for me and the children.

In the short term, I found this difficult. The house swap had come through and, with painful irony, I was offered to switch with a family who lived close to both my parents and Nan. Though being physically close again, particularly to my father, made me anxious, I didn't feel as ambivalent as I might have. I still felt terribly responsible for my mother. I still couldn't walk into her house without feeling compelled to start scrubbing and cleaning. It was exhausting, but at least being close to family I might get support; at least it might help me feel safer. It would also, I hoped, make the children feel safer. I was still extremely anxious about hurting them – the feeling simply wouldn't go away.

On the night before the move, feeling overwhelmingly sad, I decided the best way to get rid of the alcohol left over from the previous Christmas would be to drink it all – every drop. I became drunk extremely quickly, as I hardly ever drank, and started crying and crying, completely unable to stop. Then I began vomiting, and couldn't stop that either, so the last night in the house that was our travesty of a home saw me hanging over the toilet, with my children flushing the chain every time I was sick. The worry on their faces broke my heart. I knew I was the worst mother in the whole world and deserved every single thing that had happened to me, including all the things that might still happen, like them being taken away, for their own protection.

I really believed this might happen. I seemed to be in a permanent state of anxiety which I couldn't put a lid on. I began insisting that the children go to bed at six o'clock every night. Though Jennifer didn't make a fuss, Alfie, now six, always wanted to stay up, but I wouldn't let him. If they were in bed, I reasoned, then they were both safe from my screaming and shouting. I was just twenty-three, and I couldn't cope. I had little support, hardly any money, no resources to fall back on, and was completely overwhelmed by the huge responsibility of having sole care of my two little children. I barely felt able to keep myself together, let alone them. At least, if they were asleep, they were safe from me.

I also became obsessed with Alfie going missing. He naturally wanted to go out onto the grass outside the house, and make friends with the other children. I couldn't bear this, because I was afraid he might go missing. He might completely disappear – like my brother Adam did – and it would be my fault, and I'd have to speak to the neighbours, and they'd all know about Joe and think I was a bad mother, and then social services would take my children away, and all my worst nightmares would come true.

Consequently, Alfie spent long periods just sitting indoors watching everyone else playing through the window. I wondered if he was also looking out for his daddy, so that if he did come back he would see him coming.

Finally, under pressure from a neighbour, and also because I couldn't bear Alfie's sadness, I relented, and let him out to play. Typically, he disappeared within minutes. He'd apparently gone with a group of children to play in the field where the corn driers were. The corn driers were enormous, tall, metal containers with chutes for the corn to come out after it had been spun and dried.

I was beside myself, imagining all the horrible ways he could die in one. What if he fell in and choked to death? What if he couldn't get out? What if the machine cut him up into little pieces? Yet I couldn't go down there. I couldn't face what I might find. I also couldn't bear the thought of what I might *not* find. I was literally frozen with fear.

So when, a short while later, I saw Alfie coming up the road, laughing and chatting, I was in such a state I couldn't stop myself. I wrenched open the door, grabbed him, hauled him roughly inside, then began shouting and hitting him repeatedly on the bottom with the little hand brush that belonged with the dustpan, which I'd snatched up in rage from the floor.

His expression changed in an instant from innocent happiness to fear and bewilderment. He must have thought I'd lost the plot. It took me instantly back to my mother's kitchen when I was small, and would watch, horrified, as she slapped my sister. I stopped hitting him abruptly, and threw the brush across the hall, as if, with it still in my hand, I might start hitting him again and never stop.

My despair at Joe then was of such great intensity that had he been there I suspect I might have killed him.

I felt so out of control that I frightened myself. I couldn't be trusted, I realized, after that. I was a bad mother and Alfie knew it, and had become wary around me, and I didn't know what to do to mend things. So I did the thing I was best at, the thing I had been taught to do from my earliest childhood. The thing I needed to do to survive.

I did nothing. I just kept on pretending.

★   ★   ★

Just like I had been pretending about Joe. Not consciously, because I'd believed everything he told me, but on some level I had been in denial since the start, or so everyone started to tell me.

It was Nan who started it. I'd been visiting my mother and was on my way back from shopping for her with Alfie. We were walking along the road, and she fell into step, having just visited an old lady she sometimes looked after, and whose house Alfie and I had just passed.

'Hello,' she said to Alfie. 'Where have you been, then?'

Alfie answered, and she fished a sweet out for him. She passed it to him and then started muttering as she often did; under her breath but still designed to be heard. 'Poor little devil,' she said, looking down at him. 'You really should have made your marriage work. Tried a bit harder. Marriage is for life, you know. Not something you can just discard when you feel like it.' She didn't seem to want an answer, and I didn't have one anyway. 'Your mum and dad,' she went on. 'They've quite enough to do, without having to worry about *you*.' Since what she said still didn't require an answer, I didn't give her one.

I felt overcome by hopelessness as always. And injustice, though at the time I didn't recognize it. I couldn't fathom why no one ever really seemed to want to know how I felt. All everyone seemed to want was to remind me how *they* felt. How they knew Joe leaving was my fault, and how much they disapproved. Why wasn't *he* here to give them the answers they wanted?

'You know,' Nan said, stopping on the pavement in front of me. 'I knew what he was up to all along.'

I was taken aback. 'What?' I said, conscious that Alfie could hear.

'The other women,' she said. 'Everyone knew. Even Grandad knew.'

What was she talking about? I just looked at her, shocked and confused. Please don't do this, I thought. *Please*. I really don't feel up to one of your tellings-off today. But, of course, I said nothing, because to do so would only give her further opportunity to tell me things I didn't want to hear. Or *not* tell me. Just leave me hanging, which she often did. 'What did you expect?' she carried on. 'You should have looked after him properly.'

We'd reached my mother's now, and she stomped straight off up the road, head held high, all self-righteous, sniffing her disapproval. I could still hear her as I walked through the gate.

When I got inside, I still felt knocked for six. But there was more. My older sister Susan had arrived since I'd left, and she and my mother were clearly talking about Joe too.

I asked them what they'd been saying about him, and my sister's expression spoke volumes.

'You live in a dream world,' she said in a superior voice. 'Honestly, if you only knew the truth!'

'What truth?' I demanded, becoming even more upset.

'Listen,' she said, as if I was stupid, 'your Joe even tried to get *me* to go to bed with him. When I was *pregnant*. That's the sort of man you married.'

That's the sort of man you married. I couldn't get my sister's words out of my head. Was there really so much more than I already knew? Who *were* all these women he'd been seeing?

I tried to call him when I got home, desperate to know the truth but, as usual, I couldn't get an answer. I then called his old manager, Bernard, who I'd only ever spoken to on the phone, and arranged that I would go and meet him.

He expressed surprise when he saw me – couldn't believe I was Joe's wife – he'd always been under the impression that I was a 'right piece of work'. As if that would have made Joe's behaviour acceptable.

But Bernard spelled everything out. There had been no apple-picking. Joe had been sleeping with the wife of a pilot whenever her husband was away on long-haul flights. There had never been much taxi-driving either. He used to go to nightclubs to pick up girls. He mentioned the groom at the stables I'd known about – the girl Joe had left me for the first time. She'd been one of many; apparently the husband I'd trusted often picked up women at bus stops and chatted them up, hoping for sex.

Bernard told me how Joe had laughed when describing the various women who'd come to see me at the first house, how he boasted about 'having both the mother and the daughter'. And so it went on, revelation after sordid revelation, plus the news that the reason Joe never earned very much was not because they were laying people off – that was just the lie Joe had asked Bernard to tell me – but because he rarely showed up for work.

I left Bernard stunned, but soon rationalized it the way I knew best. It was all my fault, every last bit of it. How could I have been so trusting, so naive?

But by now, for all my need to know the truth about the past, it was the present that was causing me the most pain. We hadn't long settled into our new home, and Alfie into a new school, when he became seriously ill, with vomiting and diarrhoea. My brother and I rushed him to Casualty. He'd been sick for five days, and was now so dehydrated that they needed to keep him in. Various tests were carried out, but when all of them came back negative, they decided his illness must be stress-related. They suggested Alfie have a chat to a child psychiatrist. Stressed myself by now, both at his condition and by the guilt I felt for having caused it, I was even more stressed when the psychiatrist arrived and he was the same man who had seen me when I was a teenager. The same man who'd betrayed me to my mother. Before I could stop myself and regain some composure, I had already angrily blurted out how much I felt he'd betrayed me.

Taken aback by my outburst, he didn't allow me the courtesy of finishing what I was saying. I was clearly a mad woman and a nuisance, and for someone who knew my past, as well as the current situation, I was – and still am – flabbergasted by his lack of compassion. My opinion was that he expressed complete indifference towards me, and acted as if there was no reason for my anger. He seemed to imply that unless I basically 'shut up', he wouldn't treat my son. It was as stark a choice as that.

Which meant there was *no* choice. So I submitted to Alfie being assessed, and diagnosed, as suffering from the trauma of his stressful situation, with no treatment apparently available.

Feeling completely responsible, I carried on looking after him as best as I could, watching both his weight and health fading away. But as the weeks passed, I decided I could accept things no longer. I took him to my GP, who referred him to another hospital, to see if they could help him there. It was here, on an adult ward, that he was tested more and found to have severe Crohn's disease.

Alfie would have to take pills for the rest of his life, but at least I now knew what had been wrong and was in a position to help him.

About my guilt, though, I could do nothing.

CHAPTER 25

September 1979 saw me at rock bottom. Everything seemed to be going wrong. I had no money for bills, a messy house, upset children, and I couldn't seem to see my way out of it. I'd got a job, working as a bookkeeper, but couldn't concentrate, and was making mistakes all the time. As a consequence, they'd decided they had to let me go, plunging my self-esteem even lower. And now I had problems even thinking about a new job, as the childcare I'd arranged with a girl in the village, for Jennifer, hadn't worked out either, since I'd heard reports that she would stand at the front gate of the girl's mother's house, crying out 'Mummy! Mummy!' for long periods.

I was supposed to be taking antidepressants still, but wasn't, and was having to keep out of the way of my parents, as I was terrified of my father's 'whore'-based tirades. Nan had decided to have nothing more to do with me, unless she saw me in public with one of her friends, when she would deign to speak but only to say horrible things. I was twenty-four years old and I see-sawed between feeling like a ten-year-old, unloved and abandoned, and a bone-tired person of a hundred.

So when Phillip suggested I go out with his friend, to 'start over', my principal reaction was one of gratitude that at least someone was looking out for me. But I was still so devastated about losing Joe, so in love with him still, so bewildered by what he'd done, that I felt there was nothing to go on living for, and the prospect of trying to start a relationship scared me. It was all I could do simply to function day to day, and to do the best I could for my children.

I had seen virtually nothing of Joe. Indeed, it would be two years before I did meet him again, and that meeting would distress me. In the meantime I reluctantly agreed with my brother's suggestion that 'starting over' would be a good idea.

His friend was called Gary. He was fourteen years older than me, divorced with two adopted children, then three and five, and he was the ugliest man I'd ever met. Perversely, this pleased me – I was glad he was so ugly, because I was determined never to let any man close enough to hurt me again. I didn't fancy him at all. In fact, physically, he made me feel sick, and his company, though intelligent and worldly-wise, was nothing like Joe's. Joe had been exciting and, when he wasn't behaving oddly, such fun. Gary, in contrast, seemed dull.

But also safe, which was crucial; an old-fashioned bastion of the community. He played football, cricket, golf and darts, chaired committees, ran sports teams, and was often called upon to make speeches at social events. Everyone liked and respected him. He was very popular in the local community, and was seen by many as a positive role model.

In the first few weeks, I processed all this information about him almost forensically – trying to weigh him up. I couldn't begin to imagine why a man of such standing would be interested in me. Had I the wisdom I'd eventually acquire, in so many hard ways, his interest in me would have been all too obvious, but at the time all I could think of was the word 'safe'. He must be safe or all those people wouldn't look up to him, and he wouldn't be asked to do the things he did. And, crucially, his presence in our lives would make my children safer around me.

Things hadn't improved with the children. I still felt crippled by anxiety about looking after them, weighed down by fear whenever we were alone. If someone like Gary had a place in our lives, wouldn't everything be so much better for my children?

I finally arranged for him to meet them, and though I was upset at how distant and unnatural he seemed around them, I told myself this was because he wasn't used to them — when he got to know them better it would be fine. It had to be, because Gary was good for us, despite my continuing worry that, when he was around, Alfie really wasn't himself. He always seemed aggressive and demonstrably anxious.

But it would be fine. As would sex, I kept hoping. I had to hope, because it took me straight back to the horrors of my teens, before Joe had chased the demons away. I felt nothing. Completely empty. Revolted. I had to go back to pretending, which made me wretched. But what should I *do*? This revulsion about sex was obviously my problem. Something *I* had to sort out. But I sometimes hated it so much that I felt physically sick, and would count the seconds till he left in the morning.

I also worried about his meanness. He was well aware how dire my circumstances were. When he stayed over I always felt I should give him a full breakfast, so entrenched was my belief that I must give, give, give, whether I had the means or not. I didn't have the means and he knew it, yet he'd never offer to contribute, nor did he the first time he spent Christmas at my house, his only contribution being three leftover chipolatas and half a loaf of bread, as he was concerned they'd go off. So difficult were things money-wise that when on a Saturday, after football, he'd turn up, expecting dinner, I'd hide behind the sofa and pretend I was out, not only because of how queasy he made me feel about sex but also because I had nothing to feed him with.

There was a voice inside me too – a voice so quiet, I rarely heard it – telling me I shouldn't let him bully me. He'd begun to seem all too sure of me, too soon. Too ready to take my acquiescence to his needs for granted.

The first time Gary took me to his flat, I felt overwhelmed. It was so posh, I felt completely out of place. I didn't know if it really *was* posh, but it was certainly the poshest place *I* had ever been in. There was fitted white carpet throughout, even stuck onto the side of the bath. It had elegant patterned tiles on the kitchen and bathroom walls, and the main walls in both the living room and bedrooms were covered in beautiful, expensive-looking wallpaper with tiny flowers. I felt so poor when I compared my situation to his. Why would he want to be with me? I couldn't work it out.

Gary was well liked by the middle-class people in the village, and began taking me to parties where we were usually one of about ten couples, who got together regularly. They all had lovely homes too, and were all equally well connected. There was the chair of the local chamber of commerce, the chair of the parish council, a businessman, a TV artist, a local police officer. They were all very welcoming, but I felt an impostor among such successful people.

But this was as nothing to how I would soon feel. Early on, at the very first party I attended, I was asked to dance by a good-looking, interesting man, who I didn't realize initially was married to a lady dancing with Gary across the room. Seeing my mistake, I became anxious. Wouldn't Gary get cross? Or the man's wife? But then I realized everyone was dancing with other people's partners, and seemed not at all concerned.

Straight away I felt uncomfortable. Something just didn't feel right, but I didn't dare ask in case I seemed stupid — perhaps this was what all middle-class people did. It took a couple more parties before I noticed something else: that couples who weren't couples would periodically disappear, only returning towards the end. Now I did question Gary, who explained patiently that these were swapping parties, that his ex-wife and he had always gone to them, and that they always slept with other people. It was fun, he said, mentioning that they'd swapped regularly with a local accountant and his wife. They would apparently put both couple's children to bed, swap for the night, then make sure they went back to the right bedrooms before the children woke up. It had only ended, apparently, for technical reasons; his wife hadn't fancied the accountant as much as Gary had fancied the accountant's wife. I asked Gary if he'd hoped we might do like-wise and he said yes, which meant I had to put him straight right away. The whole thing made me feel sick and dirty, and my negative feelings were increased when I heard, a few weeks later, that the man I had danced with at the first party was now dead. He had apparently committed suicide.

There was no way of knowing whether the two things were related, but everything about it felt horrible. Could it really be such fun if the people doing it were so unhappy? I didn't think so. Even less so when Gary commented later that they had all laughed and joked together during the funeral service, as if that was perfectly okay.

I made a decision to end things with Gary. He was making me feel ill. I introduced him to another young mother I knew he fancied, and he started going out with her instead. Perhaps she'd be happier doing the 'wife' swapping with him. I found all of it revolting and unfathomable.

My decision wasn't popular with my mother, of course, who made it very clear I was wrong; that the best thing for my children had been, and still was, for me to be with Gary. And perhaps, given that I still talked to him on the phone now and again, he knew he should bide his time and wait.

In the meantime life was getting worse. I met another man, called Malcolm, who reminded me of Joe, and who I immediately fell for, but in doing so made myself ill. Having feelings of such strength about another human being plunged me immediately into more anxiety; I was so stressed about losing him, I could barely function, and began binge-eating and taking laxatives again.

My mental ill-health impacted on everything. It was as if all my life I only knew one way of being; that I was on my own, unwanted, that no one would ever care about me.

I was also in debt, living hand to mouth, feeding the children on cheap jam or lemon curd sandwiches, living in terror of social services finding out and taking the children away. Paradoxically, at no point did it occur to me I had lived my whole childhood in far worse conditions and no one in authority had ever noticed.

Ironically, I came perilously close. When my younger sister, perhaps taking pity on me, offered to babysit one night, so I could go out with Malcolm, I jumped at the chance. While I was out, however, my sister and her friends decided to light a bonfire, and the blaze became so dangerously out of control the fire brigade had to be called.

Typically, my father came to hear about it. As soon as I walked into my parents' house the following day, he started shouting. 'You fucking cow, you fucking stupid little shit!' he yelled. 'What the hell did you think you were fucking doing?' Unable to face the barrage, I stepped backwards down the steps, but he followed, his breath hot on my face. 'That's it,' he said. 'That's right. You fucking well walk off. Leave your fucking mess for everyone else to clear up. You're nothing but a fucking whore!'

I rushed home, blinded by tears. I couldn't bear to think what all the neighbours now thought of me, having heard all the foul things my own father had called me. I arrived home feeling I didn't have anyone anywhere to turn and, in desperation, I telephoned Gary.

He immediately calmed me and made me feel better and then suggested that the best thing would be for him to take me away for a couple of days. My older sister offered to have Alfie and Jennifer for the weekend and we went to stay with Gary's aunt in Herefordshire.

It was there, once again, that my life turned on a moment that would haunt me for ever. Once again I found myself making a life-changing decision based on the deeply troubled relationship I had with my mother.

When Gary asked me to marry him – which he did almost as soon as we arrived – I instantly decided to say yes. Not because I loved him – I didn't even like him – and not because I felt grateful either. I mostly did it because in the very instant he asked I recalled that when I'd first told my mother I was going to meet him she had declared him (having already met him, through my brother) to be 'a bit of all right'. I felt the same sort of inexplicable rage about that now, as I had when I'd seen Joe on the arm of a girl who had reminded me so much of her.

Years later, it remains no less inexplicable. I still have no understanding of why I did it, other than to recall that my anger was immense, and made me hate her so very, very much. Perhaps it was just one of the few ways I could get back at her for my childhood. Looking back, perhaps the rage was more to do with my feelings about how useless she'd always been; just blind anger about how I felt she'd failed me. Yet I didn't get back at her by acting as I did, did I? On the contrary. I just harmed myself and my children.

'And let's do it quickly,' I added as, even as I nodded, I knew that if I had any time to think about it, the wedding would never take place. And it did have to take place. I didn't want to be with such an ugly, mean-spirited person, but I also knew it was possibly the only way out of the abyss I was falling into. He would take control. He would sort my life out and all would be well.

When we got home, I immediately got in touch with Malcolm and told him our relationship was over. Doing so distressed me greatly, and also made him incredulous and, I heard later, terribly upset. Had I any idea then of how much he apparently cared for me, would my life have panned out completely differently? Perhaps if I had realized – not been so convinced of my worthlessness – I could have told him how I *really* felt about him. But I was too far out – drowning in the sea of my self-loathing about the mess I was in. Being with Gary – so controlling, so ugly, both inside and outside – was what I was used to, what I knew; which made me feel safer. At no point was this conscious – it was just instinctive and unthinking. All I knew was that around Malcolm, I felt so vulnerable, but with Gary I felt nothing. How sad to know now that my anxiety around Malcolm was just love manifesting itself – was *normal*. Whereas what I felt with Gary – his emotionlessness, the dead-ness between us – was not normal at all. But what it *was* was the mirror of my emotionally void childhood, which is why it *felt* normal to me.

If ever a person was given opportunities to reflect on the folly of their decision, it was me. Right away, the wedding plans made Gary irritable. While the family endorsed my decision (I was doing 'the right thing', I was 'doing what was best', how lucky it was that I had 'seen sense', and agreed to be with someone who so 'graciously' was going to 'take on' me and the children') I was increasingly aware of his annoyance. He knew I had no money, but he still couldn't help reminding me. He was angry about having to dip into his savings, particularly when I asked if

I could perhaps have a little cash to buy Jennifer a dress. 'Why can't you buy it yourself?' he demanded. 'Where's *your* money? What contribution are *you* making?'

But what could I say? Nothing. All I could do was reflect on how unfathomable it was that the man who would vow soon that he would cherish me, thought so little of me that he didn't care about how I or my children looked or felt.

In the small hours, I'd panic. But in the daytime, with everyone around me reminding me of my luck, I just accepted that I was a burden on everyone and that having me married off again would address that. It's the right thing, my mother kept reminding me. The right thing to do in your circumstances. And perhaps she was right. My circumstances hadn't really altered. I was still that same woeful Wednesday's child I'd been born. A useless waste of space and a failure.

Energized, my mother started arranging the reception.

CHAPTER 26

I spent the morning of my second wedding, just as I had my first: sitting on my mother's filthy kitchen floor, crying. How ironic. Because all I could think about was Joe. How if Joe hadn't left us, I wouldn't have to do this. How we'd still be a happy family. How if Joe hadn't left us, poor little Alfie would be well.

'It's for the best,' everyone kept saying, and I believed them. It *was* for the best. I *knew* that. I did. But it didn't make me feel any less heartbroken.

I had a simple cream dress, with little brown flowers on it, and when my brother and his wife arrived they gave me a handful of carnations to hold during the photos, which were gathered together in a piece of foil. Once again I spent both the service and the reception in a daze, unable to believe what was happening. What was wrong with me, I thought, that I had to settle for this terrifying, cold man?

Yet settle I must. How could I pass up this one chance for my children? How could I let this go knowing the alternative was just a big, terrifying void? I truly believed I was just a piece of rubbish, my heart was broken, and I felt like the whore my father had called me. Who else would want me? I really felt Gary was the only thing that stood between me and some terrible end.

I woke the next morning, after a sleepless night, and felt I could hardly bear being in the house with Gary, let alone accept that I was married to him. He had gone through the service like an automaton himself, and I wondered if he felt as horrified as I did. For me, it was like having a complete stranger move in, but how did he feel about it? I realized we never ever talked – about anything – and that I didn't know him at all. Why had he married me? Was it just because I was so much younger than him? Was it the idea of having someone young and sexy on his arm? The one thing I'd come to learn about Gary was that sex was a huge part of his life. And not in a healthy way.

He behaved inappropriately, be it around women, who he was always chatting up, or around men, when he sometimes told filthy jokes. Yet, at the same time, he had this guilty air as though he was ashamed of himself, and acted as if he expected his mother to appear, and tell him off, like a naughty little boy.

Perhaps I recognized something horribly familiar in Gary – I didn't know. What I *did* know was that the four walls of my house were closing in. Needing to get out, and it being such a balmy September day, I suggested we take the children to the beach. I felt so sorry for them, and so guilty that they were stuck in all this.

It was only a short drive to the nearest seaside town and we soon arrived and drove into the multi-storey car park. It was here, less than twenty-four hours after I had married Gary, that I saw something that made me understand, chillingly, what a terrible mistake I'd made.

We'd got out of the car, gathered our beach things, and set off to the exit and stairs. I was walking ahead with Jennifer, helping her negotiate the steps, and happened to turn around to check that the others were behind us. What I saw made my blood run cold.

Gary had Alfie's ear twisted between his thumb and forefinger, and was banging his head against the brick wall. He was leaning over him as he did so, saying something I couldn't catch.

My stomach felt as if it had plummeted to the floor, to be replaced by a rising wave of horror. What was Gary doing to him?

I tried to shout but no sound came out. And, at that moment, Gary looked up and saw me. He immediately let go of Alfie's ear and smiled.

'What were you doing?' I asked, my voice wobbly.

'Nothing,' he answered. I walked back towards them. 'Yes, you were,' I said. 'I just saw you.'

Gary shook his head. 'No I wasn't,' he said. 'You're mistaken.' He turned to Alfie, placing a hand on his shoulder and smiling again. 'We're all right, aren't we, Alfie?'

He laughed then, passed by me, and we all carried on walking, Alfie completely silent, looking scared.

As I sat on the beach watching them both play cricket, I began to question myself about what I'd seen. Alfie looked fine now, and Gary was throwing the ball for him, and it was a lovely day, and . . . well, had I got it all wrong?

No, I hadn't. I knew exactly what I'd seen, but even as I thought that, I thought something else too. I could hear a familiar voice inside me, one that was always louder than any other. The one that kept saying, 'Who'd believe you, anyway?'

'Gary wouldn't do that,' everyone would say. 'You must be making it all up'; 'Gary is a good person'; 'Gary agreed to marry you'; 'Gary has heroically taken on your children'. Oh, God, I thought, sitting on the shingle with Jennifer, watching her throwing pebbles into the sea. I really *had* made the biggest mistake of my life, and now I was trapped. I could already hear everyone clamouring to blame me, just as they'd done when Joe had left me. 'Such a nice bloke,' they'd said. 'I liked Joe – such a shame.' 'Is there nothing you can do? Isn't there anything you could change?' 'You used to shout at him sometimes – admit it. You can't really blame him for leaving, can you?'

I watched Gary now, looking every inch the kind stepfather, and I knew I had messed up our lives. How could he just blithely *do* that to Alfie? The bastard. I hated him. Yet how could I escape? Where would I find the money? The courage? The wherewithal? I had nowhere to go and no one to go to, and the alternative – being alone with the children – was unthinkable. I really believed they were not safe with me alone. That I had to stick this out so that my children could be safe. Only then, when they were grown up, and safely away from me, could I run away from this terrifying man.

I saw all this so clearly, on the beach, that autumn day. I wanted to scream and cry, shout out my pain to the heavens, but I knew I mustn't do that. I must keep my head.

I tried very hard to get on with being Gary's wife, but it was hard. He was such a cold man. And also frightening. Unlike my father, who was like a volcano that could blow at any moment, Gary was ice cold – like someone who was already dead.

Our marriage very quickly became one of extremes. Around people, Gary played the part he had always played, carefully editing his words and behaviour around me and the children so as not to expose his coldness and cruelty. At home, by contrast, we lived this strange, barren coexistence, punctuated only by frequent rows. I always felt physically afraid of him, just as I had my father, and it wasn't long before he confirmed my fear as rational. When I once spoke about his mother hitting him with washing tongs when he was small (something he had mentioned to me early on in our relationship) he grabbed me so hard around the throat with one hand that he was able to twist and throw me down on the bed. He then kneeled beside me, his hand still clasped tight around my throat and said, in a quiet but incredibly threatening voice, 'Don't you *ever* mention my mother again. She was the salt of the earth, do you hear?'

He then added that she only hit him – and on the most painful place she *could* hit – so that he'd know how to behave. Which he patently did in public, but, I remember wondering, even as he was drumming this point home, what she'd have thought if she could see her son now.

It was one of the few things Gary ever told me about his childhood, but it was enough to make me even more wary. It certainly explained the coldness and cruelty of which he was capable. I had terrible nightmares throughout the whole of our marriage – of men in visors and armour whose faces I couldn't see, clutching guns, out to shoot and kill me.

Outside the house, I felt safer. So I threw myself into getting involved in village matters and found I was good at, and enjoyed, fund-raising. I also had a talent for putting on events, and both wrote and directed a well-received pantomime, based on characters in the village, that all the locals, including children, starred in.

I learned later that most had given our marriage six months, me being so patently not good enough. Behind closed doors, however, things were different and though the children wouldn't actually say he was unkind to them until years later, Alfie's behaviour was becoming a cause for concern. He would tease his sister and be generally disruptive and unhappy, both at home and school. At the time I thought this was because he was sad about his daddy, and the fact that Joe didn't bother with him. But I later found out that when I was away working (which by now I was, often, as I had work as a peripatetic care assistant for residential homes) both children were terrified of Gary, and would keep out of his way. Indeed, he apparently often threatened to assault Alfie, and though less physically aggressive around Jennifer, acted in other ways that made her feel very uncomfortable.

Yet again, however, I failed to take heed of what stared me in the face.

Gary, like every male from Grandpops backwards, on my mother's side, was a drinker with a problem. Gary drank alcohol most nights and could out-drink pretty much everyone. He would drink with some of the men from one of the committees he was on, and one of the villagers told me he had a bit of a reputation for telling the filthiest jokes and singing the filthiest songs, which embarrassed and surprised me. How could someone be so admired and respected and yet so boorish and drunk and uncouth? It puzzled me how society seemed to operate.

What I should have known was that when someone was telling me something I ought to take heed. For a while one of the teachers at the children's school was giving Alfie and Jennifer some extra maths tuition. They'd go to her house after school twice a week, and their treat, once they had finished the work she'd set them, was to go and feed the fish in her pond.

One day, as they finished feeding the fish, she suddenly said: 'Be careful with the children. Watch them around Gary,' prompting me to ask her what she meant. 'I used to live next door to him when he was married to his first wife,' she explained. 'I saw how he behaved with those children.'

At the time I thought her comments a bit odd, and she didn't elaborate. How tragic I didn't heed her warning.

Joe came back into our lives when I'd been married to Gary for a couple of years. It was a weekday, and Gary was at work, when the doorbell rang and Joe was on the doorstep. He was apparently passing and thought he would stop by to introduce me and the children to his new daughter.

I knew Joe and his girlfriend had had a baby. His sister had telephoned me during the pregnancy to tell me, and the idea had really distressed me. I'd been particularly upset by the news I'd kept hearing about what a lovely couple they made.

Yet here he was, two years later, with the news that the mother had left them shortly after giving birth. As divine justice for Joe, had my mind worked that way, that situation couldn't have been better.

But I gained no satisfaction, just felt great sorrow about another young life now in tatters. What I didn't expect was the bombshell. I asked them in, and tried to speak to the little girl, inevitably asking what her name was.

'Lee Jennifer,' Joe told me. 'We called her Lee Jennifer.' And not for an instant did he express anything at all about how incredible a thing that was. How could he call this new daughter *exactly* the same name as his first daughter? All he'd done, after all, was to switch her first and middle names around. Did he just have a complete lack of imagination about names?

Joe didn't hang on to Lee Jennifer for any longer than he'd kept in touch with his first daughter, Jennifer Lee. Shortly after his visit, the mother came back, and was reunited once again with her daughter. We saw nothing of Joe then, for years. Indeed, Alfie's next meeting with the father he so missed wouldn't happen until he was thirteen years old.

And when Joe was in prison.

Meanwhile, in the personal prison that was my marriage to Gary, life continued much as it always had.

By the early eighties, when Alfie was eleven and Jennifer seven, we'd bought a large house which we'd adapted so I could run it as a residential home for older people. Though desperately unhappy in so many areas of my life, at least one thing had given me purpose. One thing marriage to Gary had given me was time, and I'd been working hard at reclaiming an education. I'd passed my driving test, completed an O level in English language, and done courses in bookkeeping, shorthand and typing.

My mother's life, though thankfully no longer so enmeshed with my own, continued as chaotically as ever. By now my father was pretty much a part-timer at home (the reasons for which would become all too evident) and though she functioned well as administrator of his haulage business, her weird behaviour had become ever more pronounced.

When cleaning her house – which I couldn't seem to stop doing – I'd regularly find food tucked away in corners of the spider-filled larder, dating as far back as 1968. As well as hoarding food as old as I was, my mother had recently taken up collecting Avon toiletries. The kitchen cupboards and surfaces were now stuffed with lotions and potions, with the overspill hanging from door handles in bags. There was so much stuff piled high on the freezer that no one could access all the food stored inside, so that too just sat until it was inedible.

The whole house, in fact, was growing ever more packed. When Jennifer used to go over to stay the night – which she enjoyed; her grandmother, for all her eccentricities, being the only kind she knew – she'd wash before bed with my mother's slimy old flannel, then go to sleep in the little third bedroom. As with everywhere else, it was chock-full of stuff: ornaments and crockery, suitcases, newspapers, coats, piles of bedding and old toys, and the only place to sleep was on the little camp bed, pushed as far into the room as it would go. Wedged between twin towers of ceiling-high clutter, it could only be accessed by climbing onto the foot end and crawling up it to get inside. She would, when grown up, liken the business of being in the bed to being in a valley, in the middle of two hills; a landscape of clutter so vast that she couldn't see the walls, the hills of junk sloping from the ceiling to the bed, like snow in the corner of a window.

It was like being in a tunnel, she said, or the middle of a bonfire, and she'd fret, when lying there, reading her Famous

Five and Secret Seven books, that the whole lot might come down and bury her alive.

For all that, however, she enjoyed being with my mother, her relationship with her comfortable and easy. My mother, who'd never touched me in tenderness from birth, was able to hug her and enjoy her company. She would rouse her at dawn and they'd leave for jumble sales at seven in the morning, so she could have the first pick of all the bargains. The bargains were invariably more carrier bags of rubbish, but she'd also do things like buy ten loaves of bread 'for the birds'. She'd have Jennifer help her stir up big dishes of leftover fat for them, mixed up with bread and porridge oats. She had huge amounts of fat at her disposal, as she still fried vast amounts of food.

She'd also enjoy sitting watching videos with Jennifer, though as there had been no diminution of her obsession with sex and filth, many of these were entirely unsuitable for a child. One in particular – by a comedian called Jethro, I recall – would leave me horrified to think my nine-year-old daughter had been watching it. Yet, as ever, I felt completely unable to take action and tell my mother to stop. Nor did I when I'd watch her pull Jennifer's pants down and smack her bare bottom, as if she'd been naughty – even traumatized as I was by the fact that as she did so she would sing songs to her at the same time.

I suppose my abiding memory of Jennifer spending time with my mother was that it was fine, despite everything I'd endured in my own childhood, because if Jennifer was spending time with her, it meant that she wasn't spending time with me. I still so feared for my children whenever they were around me, and it never once occurred to me that one of the principal reasons for my own emotional frailty as an adult was the woman my daughter called Nanny.

My mother was still very close to Grandpops, who was now in his early eighties, and who still visited her with vegetables once a week. He became ill, though, quite suddenly, and she was terribly concerned, and insisted that the family – which included myself – take turns to stay overnight at his house, as he was too ill to be left on his own.

As was – and I think still is – the situation with my family, no one, least of all me, questioned this. And so, revolting as it was, I took my turn staying in the filthy, foul-smelling, junk-crammed house of the man who'd caused me so much anguish for my entire childhood.

A few days into this arrangement, which was fast becoming untenable, my mother was getting more and more anxious. And, as ever, feeling predictably concerned for her welfare, I suggested that he should come and stay with us. I didn't think this through at all before suggesting it. Didn't think beyond the fact that I hated – really hated – going to his house. And besides it was a home for old people, wasn't it? What better place *was* there for him to go? So he came, and we put him in the only bedroom that was available, a bedroom which actually joined onto *our* bedroom, and which you had to pass through to get to ours.

I was almost thirty now, but however much I knew he couldn't hurt me – indeed, I now saw him very little – the knowledge that he lay in bed, so close to me physically, made me feel unwell. I was unable to sleep knowing he was lying there so close, and after rushing around all day, looking after all the residents, I'd lie in bed listening out for him and getting in and out of bed. I was scared I wouldn't hear him, and of what might happen if I didn't, and I was scared that he might come into my bedroom while I slept . . . I basically felt sick all the time.

And over the coming days I was forced to be physically intimate with him too, which was something I hadn't thought about before either. I had to help him to the bathroom, pull down his long pants, help him sit on the toilet, hold him so he didn't fall off, and then steady him when he stood up again. I felt sick doing all this, dirty all the time, and chronically anxious about what might happen. I'd no idea what might happen, only that something was making me apprehensive, and that the sense of apprehension was making me feel guilty. Why did I feel like this? I was caring for my grandad. Why should doing that make me feel so dreadful?

I was still a long way from acknowledging and accepting the things he'd done to me in childhood, but what I *did* know was that I felt exactly the same cocktail of emotions I always had when around him. And I didn't like that feeling at all.

And the feeling worsened, especially as he grew sicker and frailer and I had to empty the bucket when he vomited and put his penis in the bottle for him to wee. How had it happened that it was *I* who was dealing with all this? Somewhere deep inside I was screaming.

Finally, eight days later, when he could no longer eat or drink, I called the doctor out to see him. My mother was there and after examining him the doctor asked her if she wanted him to give Pops an injection to ease the pain for him – he was so obviously dying – but it might also make him unconscious. He explained this would be a very strong injection – one which, realistically, he might not wake up from.

My mother immediately turned to me, saying, 'I can't make that sort of decision. You decide.'

Floored by being given the responsibility, and seeing the doctor was waiting, I felt unable to decide what to do.

'Yes, do it,' I said, suddenly, not realizing when I spoke how much those three words would come to haunt me.

The doctor duly injected him and I took him downstairs and showed him out, leaving my mother sitting holding Grandpops' hand and putting wet cotton wool in his mouth for him to suck on. By the time I returned he was already unconscious, giving me no chance to do the thing I desperately wanted, which was to apologize for doing what I now realized I'd done – I had killed him, just as I had my little brother.

My mother called the vicar and the rest of the evening was taken over with last rites and family prayers. I felt sure Grandpops could hear all the commotion that was going on but, because of my actions, was unable to communicate he wanted them all to shut up and go away.

He died later that night, at 3.45, having never, as predicted, regained consciousness. I felt completely drained and shockingly responsible for it all. I had ended his life. I was a murderer. I knew I was a murderer because I was glad he was dead now, and though it would be many years before I was able to acknowledge that what he'd done to me since I was tiny was abuse, I still felt this strong sense that I might have said no to the injection that killed him if I hadn't felt so bad being around him.

The next day, my father, who'd been away somewhere, turned up, grabbed my hand and sat and wept like a baby. What was all that about? He had hated Pops, always. My grip on what was right and real and normal, always tenuous in recent years, felt completely skewed by this incredible display.

My mother bustled off then, to be comforted by my sister, leaving me, the murderess – stunned and emotionally exhausted – with the empty bed, the smell of Pops, and all my memories.

I sat down and started crying, and couldn't stop.

CHAPTER 27

The death of Grandpops plunged me into another downward spiral. I couldn't seem to reconcile my completely conflicting feelings. I felt profound relief he had gone, but at the same time couldn't understand why. I also felt loss and anger at the incredible grief everyone else seemed to be feeling.

Naturally, being so at odds with myself made me feel guiltier still. I remember watching my mother and sister sitting for hours with him after he died, as if he was sacred, and not understanding why I felt so much anger. It all felt so false; like my marriage to Gary, it seemed a sham – like they were pretending something that wasn't true. I didn't yet understand why I felt that so strongly. But I did. Which completely perplexed me.

I felt dead inside. It felt as if my marriage to Gary was killing me, and Pops' death had brought it home to me there was no escape. *He'd* escaped now, but I was still trapped here, and I couldn't see any way out except the obvious one – my own death. Seeing the contrast between how I felt compared with the other members of my family only served to reinforce the idea that I was wrong about everything; that I was constantly being judged and put down.

The pretence – that I was coping – was becoming more difficult to maintain. Consciously, I was desperate for affection, to have a voice, but unconsciously I was harbouring secrets too big to push down, and I was becoming increasingly aware that my distress was destroying the people I *really* cared about – my children.

After Pops' death, I couldn't bear to be in the house and immediately insisted we move. We continued to move house – twelve times in eleven years – always driven by my need not to find something I was seeking, but just because I needed to escape. I couldn't, of course, because the thing I was escaping was any notion of us being a family and, ultimately, probably myself.

Phrases such as 'living in a loveless marriage' are bandied about all the time. That I knew I was living in one had never been in question – I'd known from even before we'd married there was no love between Gary and me. It was the ultimate marriage of convenience; though he would, over the years, have all sorts of questionable relationships with other women, what he most seemed to want in me was an obedient 'trophy' wife and the domestic comforts of home. I wanted a rescuer – from my grim situation, but mostly from the terrifying alternative – that of being alone and destitute, trying to raise two children I could barely cope with. That I now lived in a house that wasn't a home, with a man who didn't love me, in an atmosphere of chilly dominance, touched with a permanent overlay of anxiety – none of these actually felt abnormal. Where some might scream, 'Why on earth DID you marry him, then?' my answer, had the question been asked, was simple. Almost *every* man in my life, for *all* of my life, had taught me this *was* normal. That I had no right to expect anything different. This was what men were like and what I deserved; my experience with Joe – initially my salvation – had rammed home a point already made.

But I felt heartbroken for my children. They hadn't asked for this, and didn't deserve it. Didn't deserve the harsh words, the threats, the air of menace, the knowledge that whenever I wasn't there they'd be in a house with a man who treated every small transgression (putting out the bins, Alfie's chore, for instance) with violence, either threatened or, oftentimes, actual – he would regularly hit my children around the head. A man who'd insist on absolute silence at every mealtime as if neither children nor wife had a single thing to say that wasn't annoying in some way. Who fostered an atmosphere of miserable mean-spiritedness, that meant nothing they could do was ever right, ever good enough, ever able to meet his expectations.

They hadn't asked for any of this and I hadn't wanted it for them. This had been the miserable story of *my* childhood, and it haunted me that the legacy of that childhood had made me shackle myself to misery, and was making them endure miserable childhoods themselves.

And it wasn't just my own marriage that was a sham. My parents' relationship, always so one-sided and antagonistic, had become one in which one party – my father – appeared to have given up being part of a 'family' of any sort, as I was eventually to find out.

It had been happening for decades, of course, and looking back it now started falling into place. There'd been a woman, for example – much older than my father – when I was eight or nine, whose house he took me to on two or three occasions. I'd be told to go and play with her daughter, who seemed to know my father really well. But I hadn't minded because, when my father and the woman returned from doing whatever they were doing, she'd make us lunch, with mash she served from a scoop, giving me two perfectly formed rounds of potato.

As the years had passed, there'd been no diminution of my mother going on about my father and 'his whores'. Now I could drive, and had use of a car, I'd often drive my mother around. One day, after nagging me endlessly, she persuaded me to follow my father. I couldn't bear to think about my parents' relationship; the other women, the lack of love. All I wanted – still wanted, even knowing it would never happen – was to be part of a normal happy family. It made me feel profoundly uncomfortable to be doing it but, as ever, I couldn't bear to see my mother upset and I reluctantly agreed to go along with it.

I followed my father in his lorry on a number of occasions, watching glumly alongside my mother as he entered houses she said he had no reason to be visiting. One house was of particular interest, being that of a woman with whom he'd been having an affair for years. My mother said he had two children by her, a boy and girl, and the latter had the same name as me.

In the end, I couldn't stand listening to this any longer and, embarrassed and anxious, but feeling unable to say no, I climbed out of the car and walked up to this woman's front door. By the time she opened it, my anxiety had increased to the extent that I could barely string a coherent sentence together. I accused her of having an affair with my father, told her how much it was upsetting my mother, and made it clear that unless she stopped seeing him forthwith, I'd come round again and 'sort it out'.

I left her doorstep feeling angry and useless. Useless for failing to speak more eloquently – I must have sounded, after all, like one of the bullies who used to taunt me at school – and angry at my parents for putting me in the situation where I had to do such things. Would there ever be a time when I wouldn't feel I needed to be a mother to my own mother?

Naturally, my father found out a few days later having presumably been to visit his 'whore' and been told of my outburst. His response was entirely as expected.

'What the fuck has she been up to?' he demanded of my mother, while I stood there. 'She should learn to mind her own fucking business! Fucking interfering bastard!' he added, for good measure, once again without once addressing me directly.

My mother, however, did address me. Having nodded her head along with every word, she turned to me and said, 'Your father's right, Faith. You really must stay out of what's not your business.'

To say I was astounded would be such an understatement as to render the word useless. But what was the point of taking them on? It had always been this way. So I dug in and got on with the business, like my parents, of just living, unhappily, day by day.

If there is virtually nothing in these pages about the decade I was married to Gary, it's because that's exactly how it was. The word 'nothing' is deeply significant. Gary was so cold, so emotionless, so unlike a living, breathing human being, that it was almost as if a part of me just withered away, the part that still had the capacity to love. I knew that I loved my children, but I also knew my mothering of them was, then, deeply flawed. We moved house so many times they could never settle and on top of all they'd faced in losing Joe, and enduring Gary, they were constantly having to make new friends. They also had a mother who was struggling with mothering them. I didn't know how to cuddle them, cherish them, fill them with confidence and laughter. I couldn't even say the words 'I love you' to them. Because those words had never once been said to me, ever, I couldn't force them, however fervently I did love them, to actually come out of my mouth. How profoundly a lack of love from those you depend on when small corrodes so much that follows as an adult.

That I can never forgive those in my family who damaged me so deeply is in great part because of what they did to my children, in causing me to fail them when they needed me. I have always felt deeply sad and distressed that I failed to give my children the care they so desperately needed and deserved. It's a child's birthright, this entitlement to love and nurturing, and being *my* children denied them this right. They didn't even have freedom of speech in their own home. I couldn't teach them the basic things, like how to protect themselves from harm, how to be confident, self-assured, to know that they mattered – to know they had a right to be here, that they were loved; all things most other children take for granted. That I didn't experience an iota of joy in being their mother breaks my heart, but is still as nothing to the pain they were put through.

★   ★   ★

But the vast and chilling void I had thought I must drift through for ever, was to be eventually, and dramatically, filled. Unexpectedly, in 1990, after eleven years of marriage I was invited out for a drink by the most amazing man.

I knew Warren already – had done for three years. He'd been chairing the panel that had interviewed me in 1987 for my first management post. His voice, I remember, was particularly mesmeric. He spoke quietly and in tones that couldn't help but command your complete attention and respect.

I'd been overwhelmed by him the first time I saw him, as was I think every woman who met him. He was so handsome, so fascinating, so knowledgeable and so, so sexy he took my breath away. Ironically, in the three years we worked together, I was never truly comfortable around him; his charisma and charm were so disarming that together they had the effect of rendering everything I said to him a self-conscious, clumsy, garbled mess. He was also mysterious; his personal life – about which he barely said a word – attracted constant speculation from the staff.

Warren had gone on to become my mentor. Two years after I'd started working in my management position, I applied to train as a social worker. I had long been forming a desire to do such work and though I didn't yet understand why I felt as bad as I did, I'd always felt I wanted to work at something where I could help others be treated both fairly and with respect. I was very committed to justice and the concept – alien in my own family – that we were all responsible for one another.

However, I was told that because there were others who'd been waiting longer than me, my application couldn't be

I knew Warren was married with three young children, so I naturally convinced myself that it must be work-related. After all, why else would he want to spend time with me? Besides, he was my mentor, so it was reasonable.

We arranged to meet at the Blue Dragon, a pub in the next village. I had thought it would be a location where no one I knew would see me; despite my reassurances to myself, I think deep down I knew something was going to happen and I was already feeling uncomfortable.

As it turned out, I arrived before Warren, only to find Gary's friends from the darts team there – they were playing away to the Blue Dragon team. I quickly pointed out that I was meeting a colleague regarding a work matter, my heart all the time pounding in my chest. But my fears that our assignation would seem furtive were unfounded. At no point did Warren so much as hint at a relationship; he just blew me away with his charm. He spent most of the evening asking me about myself, and doing something I'd virtually no experience of – listening to me and seeming fascinated and interested by my answers. He was disarming, kind and very sensitive, which was the most captivating thing he could have been.

Over the following three weeks we talked in the office every day, and he engaged me in conversation at every available moment. Yet, for all that, he always seemed very slightly out of reach, playing with me, tantalizing me, enticing and tormenting me – just enough to keep me hooked, and off balance. We met again in the evening a further four times. My head was by now whirling with him, even though the knowledge of his family was ever-present. It was as if I'd been taken over by some powerful drug and was unable to do anything about it. Even so, any relationship with Warren was still just in my head.

Not that Warren was the first man I'd strayed with. Three years previously I had got involved with two other men: one an impulsive one-night stand, and one for about two months. I hadn't felt guilty, exactly – by now it was clear Gary maintained relationships with several women – one of them from back before we'd even married – but both had made me feel dirty and sad, and every inch the 'whore' my father had said I was.

This was different. This was not some desperate craving for physical affection. This was a whole other level of intensity of feeling, which had completely swept me away.

The fifth time we met he dropped a bombshell. We were in another pub, near where he lived, and I was, as usual, sipping red wine; not because I liked it, but because it was what *he* liked. He'd already hugged me, and told me how beautiful I looked, but there was still nothing remotely sexual about his actions.

And then, all of a sudden, his tone changed. 'I've been seeing someone,' he announced. I felt my stomach plummet into my shoes. I felt terrified, and also shocked by the strength of the feeling. Why had he suddenly told me this, out of the blue? Why hadn't he mentioned it before? My thoughts raced. Would this mean he wouldn't want to see me again? Of *course* it meant that, I thought. I tried to gather my face into some sort of mask to hide my devastation. 'Oh, are you?' I answered, trying, though probably failing, to keep my voice light.

He nodded. 'I've been seeing her for about five years.'

My stomach, with nowhere lower to go now, turned over. 'Who is she?' I asked. 'Do I know her?'

He nodded again, and after a hesitation told me it was Sarah, another of the managers he was responsible for, and who was on the social work course with me. I couldn't believe it. 'You've been having an affair with Sarah for *five years*?' This shocked me too, because when we'd first met he'd told me when he and his family had moved here five years ago, it had been following an affair he had had, and the move had been so they could 'make a new start'. If what he'd just said was true, then that 'start' had been a short one. He must have started seeing Sarah straight away. It felt too much to take in. 'And you're still seeing her?'

'Yes,' he confirmed, and my immediate thought was how glad I was that so far at least my relationship with him hadn't been sexual. I had *so* wanted it to be – for the first time since Joe I had felt desire for a man – but in this case nothing had happened. I could hardly even get him to kiss me.

In an act of bravado I didn't feel, and clutching at straws, I took a breath. 'I wouldn't have an affair with you. I couldn't,' I told him. I swallowed again, my mouth dry. 'I would want *all* of you.'

As if what we'd been doing wasn't *already* an affair, in my heart, if not actually in reality. He considered me for a moment, as if weighing me up.

'Do you really mean that?' he said quietly.

I nodded at him. 'Of course I do.'

He looked hard at me. 'Because if you do, Faith, then I'll finish with her.'

And so it was I fell in love with Warren. I didn't even know if it *was* love, not really – it was more like an intense infatuation. My feelings were so strong they terrified me, but this time I wasn't going to run away. This was my chance, there was no choice – it *had* to happen. I simply couldn't believe any man as perfect as him could be interested in someone like me. To gaze on someone so perfect, after so much ugliness, was wonderful. To look at beauty, and not ugliness, was such a relief. Warren was everything I could ever have wanted, and was completely different from any man I had ever known. He was always really interested in everything I had to say, and spoke to me as if I was the most important person in the world. He would throw his head back when he laughed, and he laughed such a lot. There'd been no laughter in my world for as long as I could remember and it was so wonderful I never wanted it to stop. For the first time in my life I could look across a room and see my partner, and feel optimistic. When I saw Warren, I saw someone beautiful.

Alfie was almost eighteen now, Jennifer fourteen. I could do this, I thought. At last my children and I could be happy.

Once decided, I couldn't run away from Gary fast enough. Nothing and no one could stop me.

PART TWO

Four years later . . .

CHAPTER 28

It is the 5th of November 1994, and I am thirty-nine years old. I'm lying in a bed, and I'm feeling very drowsy, but somewhere in the background I can hear someone crying really loudly, and disturbing my sleep. I want to tell them to shut up, and stop bothering me, but then I become aware there is someone bending over me, saying: 'It's okay, you're in recovery, you're just coming round. It's okay, the operation is over.' It's the voice that makes me realize. It's the voice that brings me round. The person I can hear crying so hard is me.

With consciousness comes the realization I feel absolutely dreadful, and my body, of its own volition, starts to heave. I have to keep swallowing, fast, to keep myself from vomiting, and I become fearful about choking because I'm lying on my back, and I can't seem to get enough air. I take panicky shallow breaths, which only make things worse. It feels like I'm going to suffocate and die.

Eventually, though, I settle, and the next time I wake up I look around and see that I've been moved. I am now back in a two-bedded hospital ward that I recognize. I am still groaning from the pain, and a nurse soon appears, telling me to press the little button I have strapped to my finger; she tells me this will help stop the pain. Outside I can hear noises – lots of screeches and loud bangs – that I realize are fireworks going off. I recall that the 5th of November is Bonfire Night, before drifting off once again into sleep.

The next time I wake up the ward is in darkness, though the dim lighting feels soothing and comforting. My bed is snug, and my thoughts are ephemeral – everything feels numb and slightly dream-like. But then, without warning, a bolt of pain shoots through my body and I cry out again, loudly, in agony. Now, all at once, my thoughts begin crowding around me, and they scare me – I just wish they'd go away. I know something dreadful has taken place – I can feel it – but I still cannot bear to think about it. Perhaps if I think hard – about other Bonfire Nights, crackling flames – then the horrible thoughts will keep away.

It's then that I look up and see my left arm suspended above me, clamped to a tall metal contraption. My arm is covered, from my shoulder to the tips of my fingers, in a huge, heavy, double plaster cast. Seeing it is enough for all the horrible thoughts to crowd me, and I hear myself howling louder and louder. It's not that loud – intuitively I know I'm not screaming – but inside the noise of it is deafening.

Along with the panic – I feel trapped because I am attached to this machinery – comes a great wave of shock and grief and sorrow. I can't make sense of it. How did it happen? It must be a mistake. It just must. Warren loves me. What he did to me must be a mistake. He could never hurt me like this. I must have done something to make this terrible thing happen. I can't think about it. As soon as I do I can't get my breath. I feel jumbled, confused, all mixed up in my head, and there's this emptiness where my stomach should be. I can't believe what is true: that I am lying in a hospital bed, in recovery from emergency surgery, because my hand has been so badly injured.

And I have lied to them. To the doctors and nurses. I've told them

I did this by tripping on a rug while walking with a glass in my hand. I've lied, and I can't bear to think about why. And yet I must. It was Warren who did this to me.

How obvious it all seems looking back. How readily I can see, now the process of chronicling my life is coming to an end, how some might read what I've written and feel incredulous. How did I let the damage done by childhood destroy my adult life so comprehensively?

But that is the central tragedy. That the scars inflicted on me as a result of my childhood left me too broken to make rational adult choices. It could be argued that *all* the choices you make when in the grip of passion are irrational, but mostly – for people with a healthy self-esteem – they are tempered both by self-respect, and experience of what's appropriate and what isn't. For me, though, if anything inappropriate ever happened, I would naturally analyse what had occurred and reach the conclusion – always, because I was programmed to do so – that *it was me*. That *it must be my problem*.

Back in the November of 1990, however, I thought I had, in choosing Warren, made the very best decision ever.

I left Gary very quickly. And it had been a shockingly straight-forward business. Afraid of his reaction, I was absolutely stunned when his response was simply to shrug and say 'okay'. All that mattered, it seemed, was that I sign over everything: the property, insurance policies, any claim on his pension – all of which I did. He would very soon hook up again with the now ex-wife of the accountant who he'd wife-swapped with long before he first met me. He is still, I believe, with her to this day.

I left with just two bin liners of clothing, and was happy to do so. After Warren's declaration about his feelings we very quickly went away together and, though we didn't see much of each other over that Christmas, had already planned our escape. The one time we did, though – we went to midnight mass together – we were, of course, spotted by some colleagues.

That was it – our secret was out, and on his return to the office Warren was summoned by his boss for a meeting to discuss what to do. Affairs between staff were a difficult business, and once Warren told him that this was no idle fling we were both given two weeks' leave while the fuss all died down.

I was completely besotted. So much so that the first of many warnings about him sailed, completely unnoticed, over my head. We'd already decided to move in together, but first of all, at his insistence, we attended an appointment at a clinic, to book me in for sterilization. Warren had, he explained, been tricked by his first wife, who'd said she'd used contraception but hadn't. He'd reluctantly agreed to having one child, he told me, but her dishonesty meant three further pregnancies, one of which she'd aborted.

I recall thinking at the time if this was something that mattered so much to him, then why didn't he take responsibility for it? But, of course, I wouldn't have dreamed of saying that. Instead, though I told him I couldn't have any more children – I'd known that since Jennifer's birth – I agreed. As it turned out, however, it was Warren who was sterilized, as I don't think he trusted that I would go ahead with it.

He had the operation and then rolled around in agony all that evening, then became angry that he had to have it in the first place and applied, less than three months later, to go on the waiting list to have it reversed.

It was a year before the reversal itself happened, and it wasn't long after that he changed his mind and decided that he'd quite like to have a son, by me.

In keeping with everything between me and Warren, if he wanted something – in this case, the baby he now wished for – then it was my absolute priority to give it. I would have had Warren's child like a shot. In this case, I knew it was never going to happen, but I would have, had nature allowed it. Once again, that now astounds me. I'd found everything about motherhood impossibly difficult, and could barely cope with the children I had – what on earth was I thinking, wanting to have another? Much as I told myself that with Warren as the father, things would be different, what would it do to the children I already had?

And right now – and this is almost impossible to write – I was about to hurt my precious children further.

Straight away, logistically, we had a problem. Warren and I had found a flat to rent but it only had one and a half bedrooms. He had made no secret of the fact that he didn't want my children – he was leaving his own, after all – but had reluctantly agreed that one of them could come. As Jennifer was the youngest – she was fourteen now – it was obvious it should be her. I could hardly bear it, but I kept telling myself it was just till Warren could be talked round, and we could find a bigger place, and he could be persuaded to find room for Alfie, now eighteen, as well. In the meantime perhaps I could find somewhere else for him to stay – how could he bear for me to take Jennifer and leave him with

Gary? There was also the question of Jennifer's beloved dog, Polly. I agonized about separating Jennifer from Polly; they'd spent every day and night together for eight years.

It was a terrible mess. All of it of my making, and impossible to reconcile. When I told the children I was leaving, just the day before I did, they both just sat and looked at me, stunned. They couldn't understand how this was happening. They'd had no warning, or time to prepare – just the news that I was leaving, the very next day, to live with a man they'd never met. Jennifer, shocked and angry, refused point-blank to come with me, while Alfie just sat and stared.

As well he might. I was, in every way imaginable, abandoning them. And whatever their home life, it was all they'd ever known, and this was something they could make no sense of. It was madness, but I did it even so; so powerful was the hold Warren had over me, nothing else mattered as much as he did.

Jennifer, realizing she had little option, finally packed, and the three of us moved into our flat on 5 January 1991, leaving Alfie and Polly with Gary. I should have realized he wouldn't abandon Jennifer's dog; she was perhaps the one thing he could cling on to. He slept with his baseball bat under his pillow, ready, he said, to kill Gary, if needed. Looking back now it's almost too much to contemplate – but the person who had most hurt him now was me.

Warren's children, too, were struggling, and would come to us after school, looking bewildered, a couple of nights every week, and cram in with us every other weekend.

That all of this happened – that I let it happen – still feels unbelievable, and will haunt me for the rest of my life.

And the warnings about Warren began coming thick and fast. Within days of us moving in, things felt uncomfortable. I'd frequently wake in the night to find Warren thrusting away inside me. Not just once, either – up to three times a night. 'I fancied you,' he'd tell me, by way of explanation. 'But you were asleep so I thought I'd do it anyway.' He'd suffix all this by pointing out that I 'shouldn't be so alluring', and though I was reassured by the compliment, I still had this feeling of anxiety about it – about him doing it being once again *my* fault.

There were lots of things Warren did that made me confused and discomfited, but I naturally reasoned them away. I'd been born a Wednesday's child and I remained one; who was I to think I could do a relationship properly? I was just being silly and naive.

And there were aspects of Warren's behaviour that did nourish me. When he slept he would wrap himself tightly around me – both arms and legs, so I was pinioned. Far from this making me feel claustrophobic, however, it made me feel cherished.

So when he was controlling and difficult I forgave him. When he came home, as he did most nights, and drank whole bottles of brandy, I reasoned that was just what he did. I thought that was what *all* middle-class people did. I felt wholly inadequate around middle-class people, generally, and when we went shopping I'd let him choose most of the food. I felt too embarrassed to admit the food he liked – fresh olives, garlic, pasta – were things I'd never eaten before.

After six months we bought a little two-bedroom house, but still Alfie didn't move in. There was insufficient room – I couldn't ask him to share with Jennifer, and, in truth, too much damage had already been done, and I didn't have a clue how to mend it. The only way I could fix things with my sad, angry son would have been to leave Warren, and I simply couldn't do that. Already I was trapped, by the strength of my need for Warren's care and attention, a terrifying need – almost a compulsion – and one that would serve me very badly.

Alfie was working as an apprentice bricklayer by now, just down the road. He'd been advised by the doctor not to do something so physical, because of his Crohn's disease, but he was determined, and I remember sadly wondering if it was perhaps because that had been what his daddy had done.

Having found lodgings, Alfie could at last leave Gary's house. However, this raised the problem of what to do with Polly, who was now growing old, thin and, understandably, depressed and wouldn't be allowed in his digs. I couldn't bear leaving her with Gary because he'd always been cruel to her, and I knew Warren, who didn't want her, would be unkind to her too. In desperation, therefore, I made another terrible decision. One which at the time seemed the only rational course but that I instantly, bitterly regretted. I decided that the kindest thing for poor Polly would be for her to leave this miserable world altogether.

It was the spur of a moment I fervently still wish had never happened. I didn't discuss it with Jennifer, I just telephoned the vet and made an appointment to have Polly put down. I then took her, with Alfie, for a walk across the common, reached the vet's and in no time the job was done.

Even as it was happening I knew I'd done a terrible thing; it was just like when I thought I had 'killed' my little brother all those years back and, more recently, hastened my grandad's demise. But it was too late. The injection was already going in her leg.

My poor son, moreover, had to witness this, and I still had to break the news to my daughter. What had happened to me? Who was I to say who should live or die? I sat, head in hands, for a long time afterwards and sobbed. What *was* happening to me? What had I become?

CHAPTER 29

The repercussions of adultery are huge in any situation, and ours was no exception. Things quickly became very difficult, both in doing my job and on my social work course.

Warren remained in his job, as if nothing had happened, but I, being the 'home wrecker', was told that as Warren managed the areas I worked in I would have to be deployed somewhere else. I was offered two roles, neither of which I wanted, but I'd no choice but to take one – it had been my choice to cause all this, hadn't it? Later on I would come to question how meekly I just accepted this – after all, he was the one in the senior position and I wasn't the first member of staff he'd had a relationship with – Sarah, I found out, hadn't been the only one besotted with him as I was – but at the time I just blamed myself. I also had to take the flak from the general assumption that he'd been seeing me for much longer than was the case. Of Sarah, no one knew a thing.

As a result of everything, I failed the first year of my course, and had to spend the summer working for and re-sitting my practicals, or I wouldn't be allowed to join the second year. I did manage to get through, but the second year was even worse. During it, Warren's wife divorced him for adultery and, quite understandably, named me, then compounded my already sorry situation at work by becoming a tutor on my course, responsible for supervising students and grading their work. I felt strongly that other tutors – friends of hers – were marking my work down to punish me. I felt defeated by this – guilty, yes, but also angry that everything seemed to fall to me, while Warren was able to carry on as before.

Meanwhile, he was becoming a very possessive partner, and increasingly jealous of the male students on my course. He'd accuse me regularly of wanting to go to bed with them. When we were out socially he'd often make sure he stood in front of me, explaining that he needed to hide me from other men, and so protecting me from unwanted male attention. It got to the point where I went everywhere with my eyes fixed on the ground, feeling ashamed of even existing.

But I was also grateful for his attention because, at the same time, where other women would have felt stifled by his behaviour, a part of me was glad he cared so much about me. This protective behaviour was no small thing – no one had ever done that in my entire life.

Not that I ever felt anything but inferior to him. I felt inferior to almost everyone, of course, but with Warren it was more intense. Warren was a terrible snob, and had an obsession with class. I'd never really thought too much about class – as in the class that I was born into – but it was a very big issue for him. He was disparaging about the values of the working classes – somewhat strange, given the work he did – and told me if I was successful in acquiring an education, my own values would change and I'd be in the happy position of moving from lower working class to lower middle class. This really upset me. I wasn't trying to get an education to move class. His assertion made me angry that he felt I wasn't good enough for him, though I later realized it wasn't my class I was ashamed of, it was the way I'd been made to feel as a child.

I did try, early on, to articulate my feelings about my family to him, but Warren didn't want to know. If I tried to talk to him about my early experiences, he'd start pretending to play an imaginary violin, which just confirmed my feeling that I was a piece of rubbish, always trying to compensate for my upbringing.

I tried very hard to be what Warren wanted me to be, but I was no match for him academically. I thought compared with him I had so little to offer.

And little by little, I began to get to know him even better. Or, more accurately, to get to know two different people, one of whom was as essential to me as the air I breathed, and the other, who was terrifying.

I wonder, looking back, why I couldn't see what was so obvious. I was in a relationship that, in some ways, resembled the one with my mother, in my childhood. I was often bewildered by Warren, who could change in an instant from loving, caring partner to this cruel monster, treating me like dirt. He really was an archetypal Jekyll and Hyde. If I pleased him, he was attentive and charming, complimentary and affectionate, behaving as if I was the love of his life. But if I displeased him he would treat me as if I was not even worthy of a glance; blowing up into terrifying rages and rants, and then not speaking to me for days and days.

I suppose the truth is that he was not at all like my mother. When he was happy (about me, life, or anything) Warren's love for me shone like a beacon – why on earth else would I endure the horror of his other side?

Of course, it never occurred to me to question there *were* these two sides. As he began pointing out early on, and continued to insist, it wasn't *him* – this man who meted out such breathtaking cruelty – it was all about the way *I* behaved.

Today we are all so aware of abusive behaviour in relationships. Women know (for it is still mostly women who endure domestic violence) that when a man says 'It's *your* fault – it's *you* that drives me to this anger' the problem of the violence is the man's. We know because young people are being told this now, repeatedly; we know there is no justification for it – *ever*. Until recently hardly anyone dared speak about what happened to them. And, naturally, I had a prior disposition to believe I was wrong, so looking back it's no wonder that I did.

Warren and I stayed in the house for two years, and during this time it became clear that our relationship was becoming extremely challenging. Little things would cause him to fly into terrible rages. Early on, I dared to question why when we were having sex he would clamp his hands round my throat so tightly that I couldn't breathe. This terrified me, as did his absolute silence when he did it, and it took a lot for me to bring the subject up. He immediately became angry and dismissive and then cold, and didn't speak to me for several days. Feeling unhappy, and guilty for making him so cross, I eventually tried to get close to him again. His petulant response was one that would be repeated many times. 'Oh,' he said, coldly, 'I thought you didn't like what I did. Why do you want to be around me now, then?'

Warren's silences were by far the worst things I experienced – every bit as debilitating as anything he could do to me physically. When he was ignoring me it was like another chilling echo from my childhood; I couldn't function, felt anxious, and couldn't eat or sleep. It wasn't just his insistence I should be slim and perfect that made me lose two and a half stone in as many months. It was the ongoing torture of being so ruthlessly ignored – something that got worse and worse throughout our time together. But when Warren was happy, it was the best feeling in the world. If I pleased him he was so kind, so sensitive, funny and attentive – a completely different person. When he was nice to me I felt amazing. He was so gifted and he would lavish those gifts on me. He used to read to me, recite poetry to me, make up funny little stories, leave me silly little notes, and when he played his guitar and sang to me I was in heaven. I felt so honoured he wanted to be with me, and that he cared for me sufficiently to want to introduce me to a life I'd never known. We would often sit, him with his Sunday paper and me with the supplements, and I'd pinch myself that this was really happening.

But even then, there was a part of me that continued to feel anxious and sad. How was it no one had ever treated me like this before? That no one had ever taken the trouble to point out the sky and clouds and flowers, and the sound of birds singing in the trees? It did make me happy, but it also made me depressed; how come I'd always been so blunted to such things and had this core of deep misery still inside? And that in turn made me anxious – why *was* he bothering with me? I owed so much to this man, I really did.

So busy was I trying to please him – living this see-saw existence of attempting to maintain harmony and keep his temper at bay – I continued to ignore further warnings. Another of these came when we'd been together eight months and the phone went. It was the woman he'd been seeing before me – Sarah. She told me she was very upset, and really needed to speak to me, and that because she was married and no one knew about their affair she didn't have anyone else she could talk to.

I didn't want to speak to her – it felt all wrong – and mouthed at Warren to come and talk to her instead.

Warren refused, and she went on to give me more details. He'd apparently told her he loved her, just before he left her, and asked her to leave her husband and move in with him. She refused, feeling ambivalent about breaking up her marriage, and told him she needed time to think. It was then, she explained, that he abruptly ended their relationship and immediately moved in with me. She also added she'd been interviewed by him only a few days previously, for a promotion, and he'd humiliated her in front of the other panel members and been really unpleasant.

I was staggered to hear this, and wondered why she was telling me, but then she blurted out she still loved him and really didn't know what to do. Did I love him too, she wanted to know? Because she was sure I couldn't love him as much as she did.

I ended the call but when I challenged Warren about the declaration of love, he completely dismissed it. He apparently never said it, much less asked her to move in. But on the charge of his horrible, unprofessional behaviour his response was one that I should have heeded. He just laughed, dismissing her as if it had been all she'd deserved; she was, after all, so 'pedestrian'.

He had a similar tone when speaking about his ex-wife, who he readily conceded he shouldn't have married, as he 'couldn't stand either her or her values'. So irritating did he find her that he began an affair within weeks of their wedding, and said she annoyed him so much he mostly ignored her.

Indeed, he admitted he grew to hate her so much he'd planned to kill her by cutting the brake lines on her car. I recall at that point remembering how he liked to squeeze my throat during sex – would he soon start planning *my* demise?

But, as ever, I stored that thought into a box marked 'Don't be silly' and carried on as if all was just fine.

There were plenty of distractions from thinking in any case, as Warren soon decided he didn't like his job. He wanted to apply for something more suited to his skills, something in which he'd be top dog. It meant financial instability and another round of changes, not least of which was moving to a new house some way away, which needed serious renovation. Crucially, it also meant another move for Jennifer, one that would take her away from her friends, which she was very unhappy about. The only plus was as we weren't going to sell our existing house Alfie could move in and save on rent.

It was about this time that I got a call at work from my young sister telling me that my nan had unexpectedly died. She'd had a fall at home and had died there a short time later. She was in her eighties, so it wasn't completely out of the blue, but the circumstances were a little strange. She'd had a fall eighteen months before and hurt herself badly, and her GP – who was also a longstanding friend – had prescribed her pethidine for the pain. She was still taking it, in apparently increasing quantities, and it appeared she'd taken so much of the stuff that she'd become dizzy and fallen over. But it turned out she'd left a letter, detailing both her feelings in recent weeks, and her wish that the family 'let her go now', all of which made it sound like suicide.

After her funeral it turned out that she had been well prepared. As well as the note she'd left detailing how she wanted things at her funeral, she'd also labelled almost everything in her possession with the name of the family member for whom it was intended.

There was nothing whatsoever for either me or my children.

I felt glad she was dead. Glad and relieved I would no longer be made to feel bad and bewildered by the way she treated me. But also sad that, even in death, she wanted to punish both me and her great-grandchildren. I still don't, and probably never will, know why.

Thank goodness, I recall thinking, as another link to my unhappy childhood was severed. Thank goodness I had a new life, and Warren.

CHAPTER 30

Despite all the changes and my tempestuous relationship, in 1992 I divorced Gary and completed my social work course and so finally obtained my diplomas. I was so pleased that I couldn't stop looking at the certificates. I couldn't believe I'd managed such a thing.

I was all too aware I didn't do it alone. Yes, I'd done it, but it never would have happened without Warren's support. Even here, however, I was blinded by love, because in truth his help had always been grudging; he always seemed cross if I solicited his input and when he did read what I'd written he mostly told me it was nonsense, substituting my words for his own, longer ones. I couldn't always understand what he'd written – nor his complicated language – and would have to rewrite it so it made sense to me again. But his input did help, and I remembered to feel grateful. Perhaps his dismissal of my skills had been what spurred me on. Certainly no one in my family bar, ironically, my mother, who was pleased, passed any comment, despite my being the only family member to have had any sort of higher education.

It was tragic that for all that education I was failing to be educated in other areas. Warren didn't like the new job he'd so wanted and was becoming increasingly irritable. The silences, always frequent, had become an everyday torture, as well as his habit of, when he'd decided he was angry, physically removing himself from me, in order that I couldn't beg him to talk.

This behaviour sent me into frenzies of anxiety, and I recall often being marooned on the other side of a locked door, shouting every obscenity my father had ever taught me, just to get a response. I wouldn't, and the inevitable outcome would be that I'd fall to my knees, mentally and physically exhausted, unable to stop the big choking sobs. I went to work in a complete daze, couldn't settle, couldn't focus; all my energies were channelled into one thing – wondering when next I would displease him.

It got so bad I became hyper-vigilant. I would wait anxiously for him to return home and see what sort of mood he'd be in. It got so acute that I could tell, just from the way the key turned in the lock, how hard he shut the door, how and if he said 'hello'.

At this point, three years into our relationship, physical violence was just confined to 'sex games'. But one day I had the most chilling exhibition of what, if I stayed, was to come. He was ironing in the kitchen during one of his long silences and I, as usual, was trying to talk him round. He grew angrier and angrier, but I clearly hadn't noticed how much, because entirely without warning he suddenly threw the hot iron at my head, so hard the plug was wrenched from the socket. It missed me by so little I thought at first that it had hit me, so hot was the blast of heat that came off it against my cheek. But it missed and hit the wall behind me leaving a big indentation in the plaster. My hand flew to my face, which was just as well really, because seconds later he threw the ironing board at me too, which, unlike the iron, did meet its mark.

I was utterly in shock, the ironing board clutched to my chest, as he stomped out and slammed the door, hard.

He returned two miserable, soul-searching hours later. What had I done to provoke such terrifying fury? How could he do something so dangerous? By now I'd packed some clothes and transferred them to my car, and was just about to leave when he walked back into the house, with not a single word spoken. He completely ignored me.

I drove off, stunned that he hadn't acknowledged anything, and stayed overnight at my sister's. I didn't tell her what had happened – she didn't seem to either care or want to know – I just told her we'd had an argument, which, oddly, seemed to please her. I went to work the next morning with my heart in my mouth, and spent the whole day trying to hide the fact that I was crying. Thank goodness, I remember thinking, Jennifer had been away on a two-day college course. There was still no contact from Warren, and I drove home again feeling awful, terrified about what might happen next.

He eventually came in, his only comment being 'Oh, so you've decided to come home then?' and I nervously suggested we talk. To my shock, he agreed. It was my fault, he told me, because I deliberately wound him up, and when he was wound up he just saw red – he couldn't *help* it – *everything* became red. He admitted that he shouldn't have thrown the iron at me, but said he had deliberately aimed it to miss me – he was a good shot, he added, so if he *had* wanted to hit me, he most definitely could have. I asked him why he'd want to frighten me like that – and how could he be so sure it actually *would* have missed me? His answer was clear. He never had *any* doubt it wouldn't hit me.

At no point did he apologize. It was as if the word 'sorry' simply wasn't in his vocabulary. And I – and I can barely believe this now I write it – accepted that, yes, it was as much my fault as his and I must try and modify my behaviour. Yes, I did feel the first stirrings of resentment, but leaving him simply wasn't an option. I still felt that I was lucky to have him at all. After all, when he was lovely, he was very, very lovely and like an addict I could never have enough of him.

There were to be two further warnings of what a risky road I was walking, and the first of them, again, was about sex. Despite my conversation with him about his violence in the bedroom Warren continued to be rough. I hated it – I felt frozen; felt just as I'd done with Pops and Daniel, as if sexual attention was an ordeal to be endured. It probably didn't help that he was drinking a great deal and had also resigned from his job. He was spending more and more time drunk and lying on the sofa, often waking and storming out soon after I came home, driving his car while way over the limit.

Sex seemed one more expression of his anger, and he'd use intercourse as a way of physically demonstrating his power and control. He'd have sex with such force it took my breath away, literally, but I, so well used to being an empty vessel for men's gratification, now did what I did best, simply got on with it. I had completely given up trying to reason with him.

However, my body had other ideas, and I began developing symptoms in my bladder. Increasingly I couldn't empty it, and became worried about my symptoms – I was also beginning to have trouble with my bowels, increasing my anxiety even more.

When I found one day I couldn't pass urine, I finally told him about my problems. He was predictably dismissive, aggressive and defensive, so in agony with my stomach blown up like a balloon I drove myself to the local hospital.

Here they examined me and inserted a catheter, and my relief at this vast volume of urine coming out – jug after jug of it – meant I actually found myself laughing along with the nurse, almost as if this horror was happening to someone else. Naturally I did not tell them how I'd got into such a state.

But the truth was, I *was* in a state and they couldn't understand what was going on. With every key question, particularly about difficulties with sex, I gave my stock answer 'No'. I couldn't bring myself to tell them the truth for fear of repercussions and denial about Warren, and also because it was what I'd spent my whole life doing – protecting the perpetrator. Blaming myself. They decided they'd need to perform a keyhole procedure, and I would need to remain in hospital.

I saw Warren once during that time. He arrived, then remarked that he hated hospitals and left. He didn't want anything to do with it. I wasn't the only one in denial. Eventually I was sent home with a catheter and a leg bag and, over the next few weeks, my body repaired itself. He didn't want anything to do with me while I was attached to my catheter, and, important though it was to the process of healing, not being able to have sex with him troubled me. Much as sex with Warren made me feel under stress, and was often so painful, I hated us *not* doing it even more, because sex was the only way I knew to be close to someone – my childhood abuse had taught me sex meant someone loved you and cared about you, and I thought I had nothing else to offer.

Ironically, at around that time I saw Daniel for the first time in years. Warren and I were attending a family party being held in the school hall where my sister worked. I watched him arrive and make a beeline for the two of us, his eyes never leaving my face. So focused on me was he that he even tripped and stumbled, sending the little infant-school chairs and tables flying.

He gushed over me, kissing me and cupping my face in his hands, and sending me straight back to the sense of complete powerlessness that he used to invoke every time he came near me.

'I don't know what you're doing to her,' he said to Warren as he released me. 'But it's certainly working. She looks wonderful. *Wonderful.*'

I wasn't sure which of them was worse to behold. The abuser who'd stolen my innocence and trust, or the one I was currently in thrall to, and who was apparently 'doing' something so right. Remembering these feelings today feels so tragic, but I was actually glad when the catheter was removed and Warren and I could be physically intimate again. However, just two weeks after resuming sex, I was back with the same problem: doubled over with a hugely distended bladder and driving myself to hospital again.

I was fitted with a longer-term catheter which was inserted, very painfully, through my stomach, watched by a group of junior doctors, and held in place via stitches in my stomach. This time I didn't even tell Warren I was in hospital so naturally he didn't come to visit me, and when Alfie and Jennifer did, looking concerned, I told them absolutely nothing about it.

It would be years before I told Warren the cause of all my problems, and his response then was not 'I'm sorry I hurt you' but 'You should have said if it was hurting. How was *I* to know?' As if he really, really couldn't tell.

I became expert at explaining things away. I was working full-time as a social worker by now, travelling a great deal and responsible for a large team. I was not in a good place at work. The title of being the boss's 'other woman' had stuck fast and it was generally believed among some of my staff that I had been promoted ahead of other people who should have been considered before me. Once again, I knew I had brought all this on myself, and instead of holding my head high and proving my value, I found myself feeling I must apologize for my existence. It was almost as if, subconsciously, I'd managed to recreate my place in the family as a child – the person designated for ignoring or blaming, the one it was okay to dismiss.

One afternoon in particular, I left work early after an upset in the office, hoping to get some sympathy from my partner. When I arrived at about three o'clock it was to find him prostrate on the sofa, clearly having been drinking – and a glass of red wine on the floor beside him. Straight away he was irritable and confrontational, as if I had no right to turn up at my own house. I was really scared, so much so that when he went out to his car to see if he could find some cigarettes, I quickly went and locked the back door. He often stomped out angrily to do something or other, as a prelude to getting into his car and driving off. Hopefully, I wouldn't see him again for a while, and when I did perhaps he'd be nicer. Locking the door felt safer.

But my relief, as I flopped down on the sofa, was short-lived. Almost immediately, I heard a loud banging at the front door. I jumped up and ran towards the kitchen, not sure what to do, and as I did so I saw him walk past the kitchen window, moving fast, with a big metal thing over his shoulder, which looked like a car exhaust. I had no idea where he'd got that. The next thing I heard was the sound of breaking glass as he smashed it into the conservatory door. He then put his hand through and unlocked the door, and then went through to the back door and smashed the window there too, once again putting his hand through and unlocking it. Next thing, he was in the kitchen, angrily walking towards me, with the metal thing on his shoulder, aimed right at my face. 'Oh, my God,' I thought, terrified. 'He's going to kill me.' But he didn't. He came right up, so his weapon was mere inches from my face. 'Don't you *ever*,' he said coldly and very quietly, 'lock me out of my own house again, *ever*. Do you understand me?' I nodded, petrified, unable to get a sound out of my mouth. He then threw the metal thing down and stalked off through the back door. I heard the car leave a few moments later.

I stood there, in the sea of glass, shaking and stunned, repeating to my own shocked reflection, 'I thought he was going to kill me. I thought he was really going to kill me.'

By the time I'd gathered myself together enough to find a broom and start clearing up the broken glass, Jennifer arrived home with a friend. I couldn't stop crying, so I didn't dare look up, and just muttered something about doors slamming in the wind. I didn't think she believed me – as she stepped over the glass she looked angry and embarrassed – but at the same time I knew she didn't want to know. Not that I wanted her to, in any case. I wanted my children shielded from all this.

Warren arrived home again, two hours later and, as usual, completely ignored me.

After several days he finally agreed to talk about it, and made the usual array of non-apologetic proclamations, all of which I swallowed. We then got a firm in to fix the broken windows. But it wouldn't be the last glass he smashed.

CHAPTER 31

The incident with the metal thing – I never did find out what it was – really shook me. I'd been so sure I was going to be killed, and was repeatedly having nightmares, and when awake was constantly jumpy around Warren. Though on the surface I carried on as though everything was okay, inside I was completely screwed up. I decided I needed to find somewhere else to live, and went to the council to see if they could find somewhere for me and Jennifer, telling Warren that I was doing so on the basis of our finances; now he was earning so much less, I told him it would be better if we rented somewhere smaller and sold our house. We'd already sold the one Alfie had been staying in, as now that he'd finished his apprenticeship he'd gone to work abroad for a while.

The woman I saw at the council was very understanding and though I didn't tell her anything about what had happened she was obviously aware something was going on. This wasn't surprising, as I couldn't stop crying, but when she said, 'You're a victim of domestic violence, aren't you?' I was completely in shock. 'You'll get priority, of course . . .' she began to explain, but I interrupted her. 'What are you talking about?' I said. 'I'm not here because of domestic violence!' And I believed it, as well. I thought she was mad. How could she think such a thing? I wasn't a *victim* – how dare she suggest it!

She carried on writing, nevertheless, and then added that, in order to be made a priority, Jennifer and I would need to be homeless too.

And so it was that we spent two nights sleeping in a hostel for the homeless, and then were given a brand-new two-bedroom house to rent, close to where the children had grown up.

But still my dream of making things right with Warren persisted; it was as tenacious as ever and I still believed it. Thus when Jennifer and I moved into our new home, Warren, unknown to the council, came too. I'd by now forgiven him, having once again talked myself into minimizing what had happened, and also accepting that it had been my fault. A new start, I believed, was just what we needed – less outgoings, less stress. And when Warren got a new job – agency work – that seemed to suit him really well, I felt sure I'd made the right decision. The money would be less, but the pressure would be less also, though something inside me must have felt less certain as I still kept the tenancy in my name.

And I'd been right to. It wasn't long before I realized little had changed. Every time Warren got angry – which was often – he would throw things at me using anything he had to hand. Cutlery, crockery – anything he was holding, though on one occasion it was even worse. We were in the kitchen, and I'd upset him, and I watched, stunned, as he calmly walked over to the cupboard and took out a jar of mayonnaise. He half turned and threw it. It connected with my foot, smashing really hard into my instep. I watched the mayonnaise splash up onto my skirt in great blobs, which then began sliding slowly down. He said nothing – just barged past me and marched off upstairs, and I remember standing there, sobbing, as the mayonnaise and my blood mingled together, falling over the kitchen tiles.

I can't do this any more, I thought. I really can't. I had no energy left, and no will to fight on. I felt the same useless piece of rubbish I always had done. Why else had my life come to this? It was just like being a little girl all over again, I thought, as I wiped and mopped and tidied, weeping. Doing my job: cleaning up mess, just like my mother's.

Things were not improving for Warren with his job either. The agency work wasn't proving to be either sufficient or less stressful. With his high-ranking position at social services just a memory, he was increasingly angry about going for interviews to be grilled by those he considered 'lesser' people.

I actually admired him for putting himself through this repeatedly – even if he *had* put himself in this position – but with every rejection he became angrier and it was beginning to spill out, not only towards me. He became more and more rude to the children, to whom he spoke dismissively and critically, as if his problems were somehow their fault.

Alfie, who was now working in Copenhagen, had escaped him, but Jennifer bore the brunt of Warren's anger whenever it wasn't directed at me. It was just such an incident that put me back in hospital in late 1994, this time for emergency surgery.

Warren had returned home after attending yet another

interview, and I could see he was in a bad mood. Jennifer had cooked for us – spaghetti bolognaise – and when Warren came in she had just opened a bottle of red wine, so she went into the kitchen and poured us both a glass. By the time she returned, he'd gone upstairs, so she handed me mine – I was sitting on the sofa – and put Warren's on a side table, ready.

Like anyone who lives with someone who has a temper, I imagine, I had a sixth sense there was trouble brewing. That horrible hollow feeling in the pit of the stomach told me to tread carefully. I could tell, just by the sound of Warren's feet on the stairs, that he was returning downstairs in a worse mood. He entered the living room. 'Your room is disgusting,' he told Jennifer, who'd just come back in. 'It's a pigsty!'

Unlike me, Jennifer wasn't afraid of Warren. 'What were you doing in my room?' she shot back.

He muttered something about checking a radiator, which didn't impress either her or me. I realized he was simply trying to pick a fight. Using Jennifer as a target for his frustration. 'There's nothing wrong with my radiator,' she went on. 'Why were you in there?'

'Never mind that!' he retorted. Now he was shouting. 'Your room is disgusting.'

This was my daughter he was yelling at. I couldn't help but speak. 'Look,' I said, trying to keep my voice level, 'why go in there? If you can't stand the mess, just don't go in there. I don't.'

He saw his wine then and, muttering angrily, came over to the sofa, sat down beside me, and picked it up. He hadn't calmed down but perhaps he had accepted this was not a fight worth picking.

Jennifer went back into the kitchen and dished up the spaghetti bolognaise.

'TV dinner!' she said brightly, now recovered from Warren's outburst, and taking her place on the sofa alongside us.

What happened next happened very quickly. The first thing I heard was Jennifer scream out, 'No, no, no!' as Warren leapt up and threw his dinner plate down on my lap with such force that it broke not only his plate, but also the wine glass in my hand. The next thing I heard was the cry that escaped my own lips, as a bolt of almost unimaginable pain shot through my wrist and up my arm. When I looked down, there was blood pumping out of the back of my hand. My fingers were locked in a bent-up position, and for some reason I couldn't move them.

I stared at the blood, transfixed – it just wouldn't stop pumping, and was mingling with the spaghetti sauce and wine. Jennifer stood wide-eyed in front of me. 'What shall we do? What shall we DO??'

I tried to think. 'Get me a towel,' I said. 'Yes, a towel.' I had to ask her several times before she moved. Warren, meanwhile, was now seated again, his silence saying I was making a big fuss.

I must get out of here, I thought, rising from the sofa. I must get Jennifer out of here too. I must, above all, make her safe. She brought the towel and I wrapped it around my wrist and hand, propelling her back into the hall as I did so.

I shut the door, then, and went and sat on the stairs. 'Call 999,' I told Jennifer, 'and ask for an ambulance.' She just stood there, looking horrified. I repeated the instruction and now she did move towards the phone. 'Pick it up,' I said softly. '999.'

Once again she just stood there. 'Push 999,' I repeated gently, and this time she punched out the numbers. I felt relief, and my old friend hysterical laughter rising up in my throat. I swallowed. Warren still might charge out of the living room at any moment. I really hoped there was an ambulance nearby. I was also aware that if I moved my hand even slightly, the blood, which was still pumping from the wound, would start spurting.

I could tell the call had been answered. 'Ask for an ambulance,' I told Jennifer. 'Tell them Mummy has fallen over and cut her wrist badly.' I found out later that what they'd recorded was that I'd actually attempted suicide and hadn't a clue what to expect when they arrived.

But they were quick – within minutes we could see the blue lights flashing in the road – and their demeanour, which was upbeat and jolly, soon had Jennifer coming back to life. They wrapped my wrist – the gash was pumping in time to my pulse; they couldn't stop it – in an enormous quantity of wadding, and quickly transferred us both to the ambulance. At no point during all this had Warren emerged, and I was glad. The ambulance men probably didn't even know he was in the house. But once speeding to the hospital, shock set in with a vengeance, as the enormity of what had just occurred began to sink in. I couldn't breathe, couldn't seem to inhale enough air, and the pain in my wrist – which was now a powerful throbbing – was beginning to make me feel I might be sick at any moment.

The paramedic, unaware of the true cause of my injuries, was jollying me along, making jokes about me tripping, saying, 'You want to take more water with it next time!' but by now I could barely function, so intensely was I in shock.

I had another shock soon after. After they'd X-rayed my arm, a surgeon came in and, taking my wrist and looking at me with a serious expression, he explained the severe nature of my injuries. There were apparently two tendons for every finger of my hand, and six of these eight had been severed altogether, with a seventh hanging just by a single thread. The snapped tendons had, of course, pinged back up my arm to my elbow, and he'd have to operate both to locate the severed tendons and to pull them all back down individually, at which point he'd attempt to re-attach them as best as he could.

The operation was scheduled for the morning, and, in the meantime to minimize the bleeding, my arm would be encased in a full plaster. Thankfully, I was given morphine for the pain, and transferred to a small two-bedded room, where I telephoned a trusted neighbour I'd known for many years, and asked her if she'd come and get Jennifer. She was still just eighteen, and in great shock herself, and the last thing I wanted was for her to go home to Warren.

I watched her leave, finally, all out of strength, the morphine making me drift in and out of consciousness. But when awake I felt Wednesday's child grim: wound up, afraid, and full of woe.

CHAPTER 32

Having spent most of the day after my operation in a blur, and having fallen asleep to the sound of more fireworks, I woke on 7 November 1994 to a very different sensation: that of someone stroking my hand. It was my right one – the left was still strung up above me, following the surgery. It would be the first of several operations.

I opened my eyes. It was Warren.

'I'm sorry,' he said. 'It was a stupid argument. You just wound me up. I didn't mean to hurt you – I just saw red and wanted to shut you up.' He stroked my hand some more. 'I really didn't mean to hurt you.'

I was wide awake now – I felt such fear when I saw him, and I couldn't help but jump at his touch. I watched him in silence for some time.

'That's not true,' I said. 'You *arrived home* wound up. You were angry and just wanted to dump your mess on me.'

He shook his head. '*No*, Faith, that wasn't how it was.' He looked down then. 'But I'm going to move out.'

I would learn later that I wasn't the only one shocked. Seeing the extent of my injuries was a big shock for Warren too. It was this that had prompted the spur of the moment decision to tell me he was going to move out. He really had thought I'd been making a big fuss about nothing – well, if not nothing, not terribly much. I knew this already, because Jennifer told me. The previous night – the night after the operation – when she'd gone home, he'd sat downstairs watching TV late into the evening. She could hear him from her bedroom, and he was laughing really hard. In the end, she'd gone down, unable to contain her fury at his lack of concern. 'Mum's in hospital!' she'd shouted at him. 'She's had a big operation!'

But he'd just looked at her. 'Oh, is she?' he'd said, his voice indifferent. He then went back to his programme and resumed laughing.

Looking back, his reaction in the hospital makes sense – despite maintaining the blame still lay with me for making him angry, he still couldn't bear to look at what he'd done.

I felt a range of emotions as he sat and spoke those words, but my principal one was of huge relief. This meant it was a decision I didn't have to make. It was over, at last it was over. I didn't need to be in this nightmare any longer. I felt so worn down, depleted, so tired of trying to make sense of it, that I felt genuinely relieved.

Just at that moment, Jennifer arrived. 'Get out!' she screamed immediately, her anger voluble and intense. 'Get out! Stay away from her, you hear me?!' She threw herself across the bed, forming a barrier between us. 'Just get out!' she said again, arms tightly around me, now sobbing. 'Just get out and stay away. Right away!'

I tried to soothe her, reassure her that he wasn't going to hurt me, while he just stood there impassively, with a slight smile on his face, which I couldn't quite read. Did he think it was funny or was it just anxiety?

Whatever he felt, Warren, true to his word, moved out the next day and moved into the other house we hadn't managed to sell yet. He took plenty with him, too, including pot plants and pictures. And, naturally, the television.

My period of reflection following my return from hospital and Warren's leaving turned out to be quite a short one. I was still, at this point, regularly seeing the therapist I'd been with since 1989, and it was to her, having told all the medical staff otherwise, that I told the whole truth. She was horrified. She told me that if I didn't stop Warren it would happen again, and next time how did I know he wouldn't kill me?

At this time I trusted my therapist completely, and it was she who informed many of my decisions. When I finished telling my story, she told me I must tell the police, and that I should also get legal advice. It was at her suggestion that I finally called the police and told them I needed to speak to someone about an incident in my home in which I had been hurt. I also got in touch with a female solicitor, who was kind and very helpful, and very shocked about what she also termed Warren's domestic violence, and keen to start proceedings against him.

But to me it didn't feel quite so straightforward as it appeared to my therapist. We'd also talked about the problem of Warren's extreme temper. She pointed out he clearly had severe problems of his own, which was what was leading him to behave as he did. And, in contrast to what she'd said to me about informing the police, she also speculated that perhaps it was more my duty to *help* him – to make him better, and so heal our relationship. Having him arrested, in that case, could actually be seen as a way to help him, by calling a halt to any escalation of his violence. After all, she said, you wouldn't treat an animal like that, would you? If it was lashing out because it was wounded, you'd try to help it. And because it was so ingrained in me to help other people before myself, her words really stuck. So though I felt dread at having to go back to him, and fear that in having him back there was no longer a way out, I essentially did what I was told. I also felt some relief that our lives weren't going to separate completely, and there was at least a chance of putting everything right.

So it was that by the time the police officer called round to obtain further facts, Warren had already moved back in, and we'd begun the process of trying to move on. Which meant I didn't *want* him arrested. I still felt unsure – a part of me wanted him to take responsibility, and to be made to see what he'd done; for him to hurt as he'd hurt me. But with no support I just didn't have the strength to see it through – I was too afraid of the consequences. Warren was so credible, so charming, so quietly spoken, so respected and liked by everyone who knew him superficially and professionally – if I told the truth, who on earth was going to believe me? And what else might come out if I opened this can of worms? What impact might it have on my career? I was also afraid for *him* – I didn't want to get him into so much trouble that it wrecked his whole life. Quite apart from anything else, he had children to consider, too – would it be right for me to do this to *them*?

Thus I sat with him as he patiently explained to the officer there was absolutely nothing to worry about; it had all been a mistake; it had just been an argument that had gone too far. In fairness, the officer did press me; he needed my firm confirmation that I absolutely did not want to press charges. I gave it. He left. That was that.

And that really *was* that, for a time. We settled back into a routine, as before, without anything having really changed. Warren found a job in the city that meant he left home very early in the morning and didn't return home till late at night. I was still committed to us making a go of things – what choice did I have? – but with my ongoing wrist problems, and still being in the huge plaster, I was finding day-to-day life hard. I was left-handed, so losing the use of that arm wasn't just inconvenient, it was really debilitating. I couldn't perform even the simplest of tasks, like making a sandwich, or doing up my bra; every tiny thing was really hard.

Though Jennifer helped when she could, Warren, of course, avoided the whole issue. Where he could easily have done a few things before leaving in the mornings that would have helped, it was as if he couldn't face even accepting what had happened. I was desperate to talk about it, but he was adamant – and became angry every time I brought it up – that the only way forward was to put it behind us, and how could we do that while I kept going on?

So once again it became *my* problem. My problem emotionally, because I kept wanting to talk about what happened, and my problem, how to cope with the day-to-day chaos. All I wanted was for him to apologize, like he really meant it, but I soon realized that wasn't going to happen.

I had to arrange my own transport to the hospital for my initial daily check-ups and ongoing physiotherapy – even when he was at home and could have taken me. Everything was my problem, as though what had happened to me wasn't really anything to do with him.

The one really hard time in the early days following my surgery was when I had to have the plaster off so my stitches could be removed, after which they would put it back on. This was one appointment I really didn't want to face without him – I was terrified of coming face to face with just how bad the injury was.

But he wouldn't come, and when I saw my hand the trauma of the whole thing came crashing back, and while the nurse looked on, bemused – she obviously didn't know the circumstances – I burst into tears of real distress that I found very hard to stop.

It was awful not being able to talk about what had really happened, though I think the physiotherapist assigned to me might have had an inkling, as there was no logic to the state I found myself in when she sat and manipulated my fingers.

They say life begins at forty, but my fortieth birthday was the biggest hint possible that mine wasn't about to. My lovely daughter had arranged a surprise party, arranging beautiful food – an incredible spread – that she'd organized through a part-time job she had at a local caterers and deli. All Warren had to do was get me out of the house on the day so she could set everything up. As it was, he made such a fuss about how difficult this would be that she had to tell me.

She'd also invited some of my family, and they'd all said they'd be coming, meaning there was little room to invite many more. Needless to say, on the day, none of them showed up, leaving just six guests to share in my birthday celebrations, and a lot of magnificent food wasted.

It wasn't long after this debacle when Warren arrived home from work and announced that we should marry. He had spoken before about this over the past couple of years, but understandably with my experience of marriage so far – not to mention our tempestuous relationship and his temper – I'd naturally been reluctant. Now, however, he also added an ultimatum. We were 'going nowhere' apparently, and unless we got married should call it a day.

To this day, I don't understand what prompted this. Was it control? He was, after all, a very controlling person, used to getting women to do as he told them. Was it that he needed me? If so, I had no indication. Loved me? Did he even understand the concept? All I knew was this made everything between us different. This was a declaration of commitment. Faced with an alternative scenario – us splitting up – I felt I had no choice but to say yes. I was on antidepressants, and feeling so low already, life without him didn't bear thinking about. I looked into a future on my own and all I could see was, well, nothing. I certainly didn't feel any of the things I thought I should feel; when I thought about Warren I felt fear and uncertainty. I didn't trust him and I felt completely mixed up. But then, I'd spent my entire life in damaged and damaging relationships so this was nothing new. But neither did I agree to it blindly.

By now I had an ally. My therapist had originally suggested that I write to the hospital and tell them the truth, and confide in my GP. My GP became my confidant – he was so kind when I went to him, and so angry when he read the notes about the injury sent by the hospital. He said it was a horrific injury and, unknown to me, contacted a respected psychiatrist, begging him to see me, because he thought I was in danger and needed help to realize how important it was that I get out. Unfortunately, the psychiatrist had a conflict of interests at that point, and because of this had to refuse. (I would find him again a decade later, when he'd come into, and remain central to my life.)

At this time I had a revelation. I was attending meetings of the group Al-Anon, who counsel families and loved ones of alcoholics. I began to go because I'd become increasingly concerned about Jennifer's relationship with alcohol. From the age of sixteen – not surprisingly, given the nature of our home life – she had been drinking at dangerous levels. She'd be drunk at weekends, and sometimes even during college, and she'd been left by her friends in my car after a Saturday night out, unconscious, with a blanket over her. Sometimes, she wouldn't come home for two or three days. I had joined Al-Anon so that I could deal with being 'co-dependent' and help her deal with her problems. At that point I had little understanding of what that meant, only that I felt responsible, frightened and guilty. My life was apparently so consumed with trying to please Warren – particularly now – I'd neglected my own flesh and blood.

During my visits, I wouldn't speak – I would just listen to others' stories, and became upset to the point of crying. I cried through almost every meeting I attended – and these were tears

I didn't feel safe enough to cry anywhere else. Being in such a caring, non-judgemental environment gave me hope that, in time, my life could be better, that I'd finally find somewhere to belong.

But I was beginning to notice something odd happening. I would listen to people's stories and all the time think not about Jennifer but, 'That's Warren. That's what Warren does. That sounds like Warren.' It wasn't long before a huge revelation came to light. It was around four in the morning when I awoke to the plain fact. It wasn't Jennifer who was the alcoholic, I realized. It was *Warren*. Suddenly everything became clear. Why hadn't I seen this before? It had never occurred to me that Warren might be an alcoholic. Yet he so obviously was. All those bottles he brought home, the fact that he drank every night – and sometimes at lunchtimes too. The way he knew the location of every pub for miles, the way his mood changed and he'd become so aggressive. The way I'd behave too – it was all so blindingly obvious – how I would be so anxious around him and also around alcohol, keeping an eye on how much was in bottles, and pouring alcohol down the sink when he wasn't looking. It was clear. It wasn't Warren that was the problem – it was drink. If I could help him get free of it then I could help *him*.

But even in this I felt guilty. Because when I ventured to suggest that drink might be his problem, he, of course, ridiculed me. 'Oh, it's never *you*, is it?' he said. 'It's always somebody else, me. It's always Little Miss Perfect with you.'

And despite my knowing that I didn't have a drink problem, he still made me quite sure that if he *did* have a problem, which he doubted, then it was obviously *me* who'd caused it. 'No wonder I drink,' he pointed out more than once. '*You* wonder *why* I need a drink?'

But it was this very sureness about the drink problem that made me accept Warren's proposal. That and the fact that splitting up from him – being alone again – was unthinkable.

I didn't want any fuss though – I wanted just the four of us attending: him, me and, as witnesses, Jennifer and Alfie – the latter would have to be brought home from Copenhagen. Ironically, since none of them could be bothered to attend my party, my elder sister insisted the whole family come, and suddenly everything grew bigger.

But not wholly bad, even though I ended up rowing with my father, and felt once again in a daze during the ceremony. Warren genuinely seemed to want to show me how much he loved me, by arranging a surprise honeymoon in Jersey. He also had a really striking wedding ring made, though I could only wear it for short periods as my fingers were still always swollen. Two weeks after the wedding I had to leave it off altogether, as I went in for a second bout of surgery.

Due to the injury, I'd not been at work for many months, but soon after we married Warren said he'd found me a job, with lots more responsibility, and encouraged me to apply. It wasn't really the sort of work I wanted or thought I could do, but I applied anyway, had an interview and got it.

It was work involving protecting vulnerable adults and children and came with a dizzying array of legal powers. It seemed a job much more suited to him than me, and, indeed, when I quizzed him about why he didn't apply himself, he admitted perhaps he should have. As it was, it was me doing it, but I would naturally defer to him, feeling woefully inadequate. And it often seemed as though, far from supporting me, he was really setting me up to fail. I persevered and though it would take its toll on me eventually, by working sixty to eighty hours a week, I could just about keep on top of it.

And then in June 1997 my beautiful granddaughter Melli was born. In Copenhagen, obviously, since that was where Alfie had made his home. I was genuinely reluctant to go and see her, fearing the same things that had haunted me all my life. Of what I might feel when I met her, and held her; that I wouldn't like her – that I actually might harm her.

But I was persuaded to go, when she was three months old, and flew to Copenhagen with Jennifer. From that moment my world changed. I set eyes on my granddaughter and it was love at first sight – the biggest revelation of my life. I was captivated by her and wanted to hold her all the time, even though doing so, inexplicably, always made me cry. With hindsight, I was crying for the childhood neither I, nor my children, had had – for the enormity of being given a chance to help make one for Melli.

Her circumstances weren't good either. They lived in an apartment in a grey and grim part of the city and I could hardly bear the thought of them being there. Her own mother, Anna, was very damaged. Like me, she had had a terrible childhood, and as an adult was in and out of psychiatric hospital and strug-gling to cope. I resolved that my job must be to persuade both her and Alfie to come back and live near us in England.

Happily, they agreed, and my beautiful little granddaughter came to live in England when she was five months old. From that day she was a part of my life almost every day. I couldn't do enough to help Alfie and Anna; it was so wonderful to feel I mattered. I would look after Melli all the time and loved the things we did together. I'd teach her songs, point out birds and insects and flowers, and show her clapping games like pat-a-cake. When she began speaking the thrill of having her call me Grandma was the most wonderful thing in the world.

Not that all in my garden was now lovely. In 1998, while Melli was at our house one afternoon, she pulled something out of Warren's briefcase. It was a Valentine's card, with a poem handwritten in it, which started: *You are my oasis in the desert.*

Warren denied everything, just as I'd imagined he would; he was now supplementing his income by working weekends and overnight with an emergency team, and said this was just some silly joke from the girls in the office. I believed him until a few days later, when I got a call from someone who worked with him, telling me he was having an affair.

Once again he denied it and it was only when I threatened to call the office that he caved in and confessed. It was my fault again, of course, for arguing with and shouting at him; he just couldn't stand it any more.

I was stunned, but at the same time I felt numb – he'd done everything he could to hurt me over the years – this new thing wasn't very new at all. When it was compounded by another discovery, two weeks later, that he'd borrowed and lost £20,000 gambling on shares, it was beginning – though more shocking, and with worse implications – to seem par for the course. He'd always gambled – had done ever since I'd known him – but I suppose, looking back, I hadn't seen it as such, because it didn't fit with my idea of what gamblers were – they were like Pops: to my mind, rough with smelly breath and brown teeth.

But the biggest shock was just around the corner. I don't think I realized just how vital was my relationship with Melli, until the day of her second birthday party. Alfie and her mother hadn't been getting on for some time, and Anna told me she and Melli were returning to Copenhagen.

Watching the two of them leave for the airport was worse than anything Warren could do to me. Just knowing how much I loved my granddaughter and not knowing when or if I'd see her again was like the worst bereavement imaginable; almost like losing a part of my own body – a precious part that I'd only just discovered.

Alfie, of course, was completely distraught to be waving his daughter off from all she knew – beside herself, distressed, crying 'Daddy! Daddy!' He'd felt it incredibly important for his daughter's well-being that she remained in the UK. It was mostly all she'd ever known; we were her family, who loved her. It was a place where she'd felt safe, and had love and support. We didn't realize until after she'd already gone that, under the Hague Conventions, she was entitled to stay here. We pursued every avenue, and she should have been returned to the UK, but Denmark wouldn't uphold the decision.

It would be four years before I saw her again.

CHAPTER 33

It is difficult for me to describe, to anyone who hasn't experienced it, what an appalling form of torture being ignored is.

My marriage to Warren had fallen into a pattern that was the same, only worse, as it had always been. Ignoring me, pretending I didn't exist – these were the chief weapons he liked to use. Those who are familiar with relationships like this will know how destructive such tactics can be, and how completely they can crush another person.

Warren had always acted in a superior manner, of course, because he felt he *was* superior, and I mostly agreed. I'd been programmed from early childhood to think *everyone* superior – or at the very least more important. Nothing Warren ever did challenged that. His manner had always been offhand; he'd correct me when I spoke, and either laugh in front of people at my unintentional misuse of a word or became exasperated with me for my 'inferior knowledge and tastes'. I was often a source of great annoyance to him, and as a consequence I tried excessively hard to please him. I felt that I couldn't get anything right; even the food I was used to eating Warren said he didn't like. He didn't like my taste in music, my reading material, my interest in and sensitivity to other people, or my increasing need to understand myself and why I was like I was.

Lying in bed enduring one of Warren's cold silences was the most challenging thing imaginable. I used to feel I was going mad. The longer it went on the more worked up I became. It felt almost as if I was being physically tortured; I'd get into such a state I couldn't relax. I'd keep talking to him, endlessly, but he still totally ignored me so, eventually, I'd start raising my voice. Sometimes he'd laugh, like he was really enjoying it, but still wouldn't engage with me. This would tip me over the edge and I would begin swearing at him, using the most offensive words I could remember my father using to me as a child.

Using such words naturally made me feel even worse, and reminded me of all the reasons Warren must hate me, but he'd carry on ignoring me or, sometimes, leave the room altogether, going into the other bedroom or to the sitting room. I'd follow him, still trying to get a reaction – till I was completely exhausted, and usually ended up crying, feeling defeated. How I functioned in my demanding new job, I do not know. It was like living in the middle of a war zone all the time, not knowing when to expect the next bombardment.

By the end of the nineties, Warren was almost permanently angry. He'd spend a lot of time walking around in a mood, wanting to know why he had to live in 'this house' and why he was condemned to doing his 'shit job', when he was so obviously meant for better things. He'd become bitter about everything, and knew the reason. Women, he said, had been his downfall. He had had what is termed a 'clean break' divorce, and it was anything but. In exchange for him keeping his pension, his wife had kept the house, virtually mortgage-free, and it'd made a big dent in his finances. He'd hurt and humiliated her too, and she wanted revenge. Sadly, she also turned his children against him, which helped nobody, least of all them. It was all just a horrible mess.

In September 1998, a house came up for sale down the road, and as it needed renovation it was well priced. As ever, I was concerned mostly about pleasing him, so I overrode his moans that we couldn't afford it, as I knew it would make him happier; it was spacious and had a huge garden. I was also concerned that we put something into bricks and mortar, as even though he protested about affording it he always seemed to find money for gambling.

I also persuaded him to go to marriage guidance sessions with me, as I was becoming so worn down by his constant moaning and the tortuous silences. Once again, now I'm putting words on this page, I can't help but question why I was trying so hard to please him.

We only lasted two sessions at marriage guidance, because it was obviously going to achieve nothing. All I wanted was for him to accept some responsibility for what he'd done, to accept that his behaviour was unkind, to embrace the idea of at least trying. But it was pointless. Emboldened by there being someone present, I'd get increasingly vocal when asking him these questions, and his response, which would be quiet, and civilized, and measured, would be to say: 'Faith always wants to pretend I'm a bad person. But I'm not. I am a decent person. She just wants everyone to believe I'm bad.'

And, of course, he was always convincing. Who'd ever believe this charming, urbane man could inflict so much cruelty on another person?

In the meantime, though things had been so tough for my children, they were trying to make good lives. Alfie, who'd been so upset about losing Melli, had managed to buy himself a two-bedroom flat, in the hopes she'd be able to come and stay. He also decided he must get out of bricklaying and get himself more education. He did a number of college courses and after two years of hard work, he went on to win a place at university to study nursing. He'd been through so much in his young life, and I was so proud.

Proud of them both – because Jennifer, too, had begun to turn her life around. Her problems with drink had continued to be troubling, and we knew she needed to find direction or else fall very heavily by the wayside. In this, at least, Warren was helpful. He went with her to look at several different universities, and she eventually got a place in London.

The day we moved her into university digs was one I shall never forget. A big part of me wanted to bury my head in the sand and keep her close, because I was terrified about how she'd cope. I could hardly bear driving off and leaving her there, but at the same time I knew it was make or break. After a rocky first year, she began to adjust and settled into university life well.

I too had been continuing with my education. It was one area that I thought I must do well in, partly because of how they treated me at school, and partly because it gave me a sense of self-worth. Also I thought it would enable me to make change happen. I desperately wanted the people I was paid to work for to feel protected and get a better deal. For them to have a voice that was listened to. Mostly I wanted them not to lose faith; to believe there were people out there who would work on their behalf to ensure they got the best possible care.

My knowledge had come to be respected as by now I had been promoted to senior staff, and was offered the opportunity to go to university and study for a degree in social work. I was also offered the chance to do a diploma in the regulation of health and social care. I was worried about how I'd ever manage the huge workload, but I said yes – it could only be a good thing to do this – and through everything that was going on in my personal life, I studied as hard as I could. I'm still not quite sure how I did it, but in October 2001 I was awarded a BSc (Hons) 2:1.

My presentation ceremony took place in Cambridge, and I remember that day very well. It seemed almost unimaginable that I, of all people, should walk robed, with the other students, through a city like Cambridge, to receive a certificate saying I had a degree.

Perhaps made bolder by this, I decided to do something useful with the strong feelings I'd always had about trying to get justice for other people, and applied to become a Justice of the Peace. Part of this process would prove painful – I was asked to attend a series of interviews, and it was asked whether I had anything I needed to tell them, about either myself or my extended family, that could bring the magistracy into disrepute. I didn't know where to begin. By now my family, always dysfunctional and unhappy, had grown, and there were even more skeletons in the closet.

I asked tentatively if it would make any difference if a close family member was a convicted burglar. There was also the matter of the heroin addict and convicted criminal, and the small detail of the one who was serving a life-sentence for murder. That these people were all closely related to me felt desperately sad – the younger ones were victims, indirectly, just as I was – and it was almost, as I sat there, surreal.

But I had to finish, to my distress, with one of my own children – prosecuted for possession of cannabis.

As it turned out, they weren't that interested in the roll-call of felons, but more interested in how I managed my own child through that difficult time. But my overriding feeling was one of anger at a family whose history I'd have to drag around with me for all time and whose legacy it seemed I'd never escape. I didn't think they'd want to touch me with a bargepole.

So saying I was surprised to find I'd been accepted would be the biggest understatement ever. I must be the only JP in the country with such a chequered past.

One member of my family who was central to this was my mother, whose behaviour was increasingly bizarre – if that were possible – though as my experience as her child was the only one I'd known, it was difficult to be objective. I'd always tended to accept it and think it was normal.

But now I was approaching middle age, and with the benefit of distance, I really began to question it. I was puzzled by all the strange allergies she had, and by her depressed and odd demeanour generally. Her repetitive behavioural tics had increased greatly, to the point where she couldn't do anything at all without tapping or humming at the same time. She'd begun sporadically giving strange gifts to people, some of them through the post: a 'willie stretcher', a picture of a topless woman on horseback, a monk whose willie stuck out when you pushed his head, and a lump of pretend poo were examples. She continued to laugh till she cried at anything sexual or to do with bodily functions, and had numerous 'page 3' pictures stuck up on the kitchen walls, accompanied by really filthy jokes.

She'd also purchased a parrot which she was trying to teach to swear. This bird was allowed to fly free around the sitting room and kitchen, so, naturally, its excrement fell wherever it was. Although there was some newspaper on the floor where it sat, there'd be poo stuck to the wall, running down the fireplace and in a heap on the floor. The perching area was also strewn with nuts and crisps and bits of fruit.

Most rooms in the house were as full as ever with junk, and although there were only my mother and father living there, it had spread to almost every corner. Every horizontal surface was covered with pictures and ornaments, and carrier bags of food and junk were propped up in rows across the floor in both the sitting room and kitchen, and before anyone could sit down it was always first necessary to locate a big pile of newspapers or clothes. The stairs were also lined, on either side, with further rubbish, and on some treads there wasn't even room to place a foot – you had to climb them two steps at a time. Upstairs, the room Jennifer used to sleep in was full to the ceiling, and the third bedroom completely out of commission; my mother had made a ceiling-high tower of books right in front of the closed door. My parents' bed could only be accessed by a narrow walkway on one side, unless you climbed in via the foot end, and the room was festooned with my mother's clothes, on hangers – things she hadn't been able to fit into in years.

My mother still had her dolls stationed next to the bed, though; her row of seven ugly, raggy dolls (there were never eight, which always made me think of my dead brother – why was there no doll for him?).

My mother told me, one day, that my father had announced he was going to end his womanizing ways, and stay at home full-time to look after her. The truth was, other women were not so interested in him now. Not now that he'd had a double hip replacement and was walking with a stick, and taking pills for all sorts of health problems. I think the fact was he'd become afraid of dying, and making sure my mother in her chaotic, eccentric way would look after *him*. But his constant presence wasn't what she was used to and she really didn't want it. 'He's killing me, Faith,' she said desperately.

I was to remember those words when, on one spring day in 2002, my phone rang at 6.30 in the morning. Just like any mother, my thoughts went straight to Alfie and Jennifer, and I became anxious – who'd be calling me at this hour? But it wasn't about them. It was my brother.

'Can you come, Faith?' he said. 'Mum is dead.'

CHAPTER 34

'My mother's dead,' I told Warren, as I began getting dressed. 'That was my brother. My mother's *dead*.'

'I can't believe it,' I continued. 'I was only speaking to her two days ago, and she was fine. And now he's saying she's dead. It must be a mistake.'

Warren stayed in bed, so I had to drive myself there, wishing he was with me to support me, as I felt really shocked. As I drove there, along familiar streets, seeing familiar sights, it didn't seem possible. What could have happened, I thought to myself, to make my brother think she was dead? Because she couldn't be. It had to be a mistake.

When I arrived, there were police cars and ambulances outside, and inside my father was sitting in his chair, with a policeman opposite.

When he saw me, my father immediately started crying, grabbing hold of my hand, and really sobbing. He took me upstairs to where my mother was still lying in bed, lay down on the bed next to her and grabbed her pyjama collar. He grabbed it really hard, and bunched it up between his fingers, pushing her chin so that it was raised up at an angle. 'You bitch,' he said. 'How could you do this to me? How *could* you?'

Her eyes were open and she was staring straight ahead. She was, very definitely, dead. I couldn't stop staring, and I felt anger. How could he *do* that? Even in death, he was still abusing her. So aggressive, so possessive, so completely self-absorbed. Thinking only of what she'd done to him by *dying*!

But mostly I couldn't understand how she could be dead. She'd been fine. There was absolutely nothing wrong with her.

'What happened?' I asked my father. He said he didn't know. He said she'd been talking and was going to get up and get him a cup of tea. And then she'd tried to get up and, well, she'd just died. He'd called my younger sister, who'd tried to get her breathing, and then apparently the ambulance men had tried too, but it had been no use.

I went back downstairs, but my father remained up there for some time, only coming down to answer more questions. I found out that she'd apparently died from choking – that much they had established – and because of the circumstances there'd be a post-mortem. Her body was then taken to the hospital mortuary, where she remained for the next few days. My father proceeded to visit her daily – this woman who he'd treated so appallingly for fifty years, who he'd bullied, maligned, threatened, never helped, who he'd been unfaithful to, having affair after affair – and cry like a baby. I was, and still am, speechless with exasperation. What a travesty. What a farce it all was.

I was the one who went to register my mother's death and, following the post-mortem, the death certificate arrived, which said she'd died from respiratory failure, chronic obstructive pulmonary disease and bronchopneumonia – her childhood neglect had finally killed her. Apparently, as soon as she'd moved in bed to get up, something related to the disease – pus, most probably – had lodged in her throat, completely blocking her airway, and killed her instantly.

My father grieved like a man utterly devastated by the loss of a woman he adored. It was all, every bit of it, about him. What was *he* going to do, how was *he* going to manage, how could she do this terrible thing to *him*, surely she would have known how difficult it would be for him? On and on, endlessly, while we all had to listen, and it sickened and distressed me to hear it. He was such a pathetic, useless, entirely selfish man. Except he wasn't a man – he never had been. He was a self-centred, narcissistic little boy. Particularly when he started one of his bouts of self-indulgent reminiscing about this wonderful woman he'd been oh-so-happily and devotedly married to for half a century. No Holocaust denier could have rewritten history so passionately.

One thing, once the practicalities were dealt with, came to light. My mother had left money in a building society account for the children of one of my sisters. It was the sister she always used to hit so hard. None of the other grandchildren got anything.

In the days following my mother's death, I walked about in a daze. Something had happened to me through my mother dying. I was desperately sad, incredibly shocked and, day after day, couldn't stop crying. But there was something else, too; something I couldn't quite verbalize. My mother's death, and my jumble of feelings about it, was the very last thing I had expected. It had happened without warning like all the other major things that had happened to me: the deaths of Adam and Pops, Grandad, my friend Sue, and, of course, Nan. Also Joe leaving me, and all the other distressing things – I had not seen any of them coming. It seemed life was just a series of shocking things that harmed you, and it felt as if I'd suffered far more than I could cope with. Being that Wednesday's child, and so bad and inadequate, I was simply unequal and unprepared. Retrospectively, it now seems clearer. Change – shocking change – *is* a part of normal life, but because such things were never ever discussed or explained, I had no tools whatsoever to deal with it.

The funeral – my mother was to be cremated – was led by the family, and Jennifer agreed to go up at the start of the service and read out a poem written by her cousin. But it was Phillip who had the task of telling everyone about the kind of person she was, and how much she'd be missed. As he spoke it was as if he was describing a different person. He described his memories of her as being very loving, warm, gentle and caring, and how she 'was always there' when he needed her. Such a different experience from mine. I simply didn't recognize the person he was talking about. My mother had been remote, detached, physically undemonstrative, and not loving towards to me. Certainly 'gentle' or 'caring' or 'always there' wasn't how *I* would have described her. Why had his relationship with her been so very different from my own? What had I done for these qualities to miss me?

I look back at my brother's life today and one thing is very clear: it has always been so much happier, so much more stable, than mine, and this, I imagine, is why. But then it was really no secret that my mother preferred boys – particularly her eldest, who was perhaps the flesh-and-blood replacement of the brother she had so loved, and lost. He died around the same time as Tony.

On the day of the funeral I cried non-stop. Huge tears, the size of saucers, that flowed and flowed and flowed. It was as if I had no conscious control; as if a tap had been turned on and couldn't be shut off. As if, on that one day, I was crying for everything that had ever happened between my mother and me. And also, I think, I shed tears of relief too. Somehow I think I knew that, from this day on, it was over. Over, or just starting: I wasn't sure which. All I knew was my life would never be the same again.

I didn't know it at the time, but my mother's death would be the catalyst for everything that followed. Now that she could no longer hurt me – or, crucially, I her, by confronting all my child-hood abuse – I knew I had to do something about my own life.

The day after my mother's funeral I had been scheduled to attend a second interview for a promotion to a management post, a post I'd already been told was mine, following an 'excellent' first interview. I'd telephoned to explain my mother had died suddenly but was told I must either still attend, or miss out. That was simply the way things were in the so-called 'caring' agencies. The interview, unsurprisingly, went very badly, and I was told that I hadn't got the job.

It was here, perhaps, that the strong feelings now being churned up about my mother were first channelled and put to some use. I immediately appealed, as I felt I'd been treated without compassion, and that a post I had been told was mine had then been taken away. The appeal went on for six months.

Eventually, at the very final stage, my appeal was upheld and I was given the post, plus awarded back pay from the time I should have had it. My feelings about this were strong. It was almost a metaphorical chance to say 'Up yours' to both those in authority who'd tried to deny me, *and* my mother.

Within a few months I was in a very demanding role, managing a large team of staff. My work was intense. I attended child and adult protection meetings, and oversaw the gathering of evidence. As soon as one appalling case was successfully prosecuted, and my team's evidence upheld, the next appalling case would be stacked up behind it. At the time I saw no connection or irony in doing a job so closely tied up with the childhood *I'd* had. All I knew was that, to the exclusion of any other part of my role, bringing people who harmed others to account for their actions was my most powerful driving force.

But there were no winners in cases such as these, and both this and the hours I was working were beginning to take their toll. It was made worse by the fact that my employer wouldn't meet their commitment to my role as magistrate, and I was regularly having to work weekends as well, to make up for the time I spent sitting on the bench. Yet I couldn't stop doing it – I was a woman possessed. I had no idea why I so desperately wanted to make people safe – but I passionately wanted *everyone* who didn't look after the people in their care prosecuted – and to make sure nobody got away with harming any adult or child.

My need to help people had already begun to spill over into my personal life. The Christmas before my mother died, Alfie met a young girl, called Amber, in the pub, and had asked me if she could join us for Christmas lunch, as she had nowhere else to go. A few months after that first meeting, around the time of my mother's death, she told me she'd given birth to a baby boy the previous September. She had turned eighteen only a month earlier, and the baby had been put into foster care; he was now due to be adopted by a nice young couple, who could give him everything she thought she couldn't. She told me her own mother had had the baby taken away at birth and she hadn't even seen him. Her choice had already been made abundantly clear: she'd been made to choose between either keeping her baby, or her family; if she chose to keep her child, they'd disown her.

Of course, being so young, and so vulnerable, she'd chosen to follow her mother's ideas, and her mother, who'd hidden the pregnancy from everyone, told people that she'd brought her daughter home to convalesce because she'd been kicked by a horse.

I was so moved by Amber's story, and her very palpable anxiety, I told her that if she decided she wanted to get her baby back, I would try to help her.

Several chats later, she reached the decision that she just wanted to see him before he was finally adopted – she couldn't bear the thought that she would never see him. But, of course, when she did see him, it all became clear. This was *her* child and she desperately wanted him back, so over the next few weeks wheels were put in motion for this to happen, and he was finally returned to her at just eight months old.

Sadly, when her mother found out what had happened, she moved to France shortly after and, true to her word, has had almost no contact with her daughter and grandson to this day.

I, however, very much have. Feeling so involved in their lives, I felt I couldn't abandon them and when Amber reclaimed her son, who she decided to call Cameron, I found them a little house, close to where I lived, and they became – and still are – very much a part of my family.

It was this experience, perhaps, that was one of the key nails in the coffin of my continuing travesty of a marriage. Ever the upstanding member of the community, and still a respected professional in social care, Warren wanted nothing to do with Amber or Cameron, and was routinely rude and unwelcoming. He made no secret of the fact he didn't want them around, citing 'Whatever would I have in common with them?' as his reason for treating them badly. Indeed, for someone who made so much of his superiority, his lack of charity towards others he deemed of lower standing was breathtaking. He used to treat Amber as if she was less than human, and would also punish me for continuing to associate with her, by ignoring me and them when I had them in the house, which I did often. As Amber had only the reading and writing age of a child, she'd come to me for help with her paperwork. Warren would continue to be cruel to Cameron when he was older – promising he wouldn't let him go, if pushing him downhill on his little tractor, and then laughing as he did so, despite Cameron's tears.

Yet still I couldn't find the wherewithal to leave him. By now, his anger spilled out everywhere; sometimes passively, sometimes scarily and openly aggressively. Looking back, I realize it had always been like this, but perhaps I needed to change myself in order to see it.

When we were out socially he'd routinely drink so much that

his abusive comments to me must have embarrassed everyone around him. Once he came home and was sick on the floor. One day, we had a few people around for lunch when, midway through the meal, he disappeared. Embarrassed and flustered, I made my excuses and went to look for him, only to find him in another room watching television.

And his anger was no longer just directed at me. One day, on a train, when we were returning from lunch with his daughter, he got angry with a young man sitting opposite. He had his feet on the seat, which annoyed Warren greatly, but instead of just saying something, quietly and *to* him, he began talking in a loud whisper, in a really aggressive fashion, saying: 'Someone has to sit on that seat – fucking rude bastard. No consideration for others!'

Already anxious about his temper, I gently suggested that if it was really annoying him, it might be sensible to actually ask the man to remove them, or tell the guard, or even change seats. But Warren didn't want to do any of those things. He just continued to sit there, getting angrier and angrier and staring continually at the man.

I'd known Warren for many years, and through many bouts of violence, but even I wasn't prepared for what he did next. When the man stood up to get off the train, Warren suddenly leapt up from his seat. He would later claim – though I certainly hadn't seen it – the man had deliberately shaken his water bottle so that a couple of drops fell on Warren's arm, but whatever the reason it was as if Warren had gone mad. He started shoving the man, and punching him, over and over, while the man looked at Warren in complete shock. He didn't retaliate, just put his arms up to protect himself from the blows. Eventually he managed to stumble to the exit, while Warren, now seemingly spent, sat back down. I was so shocked that I could only sit and stare. Warren's face was by now scarlet. But it wasn't over yet. He suddenly jumped up again, and began running up the train towards the exit, passing the shocked faces of the completely bewildered passengers, and reaching the man just as he alighted. Once again he started hitting and trying to wrestle with him, and I watched in horror as he half picked up and half pushed the man through the now open door and onto the platform. The man landed on his hands and knees and eventually scrambled up and staggered off, thinking, I imagine, that he'd been attacked by a lunatic and had better get away as fast as he could.

I remember being surprised that at no time did he retaliate, particularly as he was both taller and younger, but what I most remember thinking was how astonished I was that an apparently sane and sober, smart, well-groomed, middle-aged man could behave in such an appallingly violent way.

When indoors, Warren wasn't any less scary. He'd taken to spending his evenings upstairs, on the computer, apparently working. But it soon became apparent something wasn't right. Whenever I entered the room, he'd quickly click his mouse so that whatever was on screen would disappear. Before long I found out his 'work' wasn't 'work' – he was looking at particularly disgusting kinds of pornography. Feeling predictably, and ridiculously, dirty myself, I eventually confronted him, only to be told that if I gave him more sex he wouldn't need to look at it. When I pressed him, he also showed me, and it really was truly disgusting, and I asked him what he got from seeing it.

'It's curiosity,' was his considered response. And it was this, I think, this simple thing (and its implications – where would his curiosity lead him – us – next?) that made me realize I had to act. I had to find the courage to make a new life for myself and my grown-up children, and begin the process of finding out who I really was. I could no longer countenance the terrifying prospect of going to my grave without doing so.

CHAPTER 35

My mother's death affected everything I did. I'd been so tightly enmeshed with her I couldn't imagine never seeing her again and every time I thought about it I panicked. During this time my therapist, without warning, sent me a letter saying she was no longer practising. As I'd been with her for ten years, this was a huge shock. Finishing without notice and without having made provision for continuing care was the last thing you'd expect from a professional engaged in this kind of sensitive work.

Following this, and still clutching at straws, I suppose, I persuaded Warren to attend couple therapy with me. We saw a therapist weekly for about a year in all, but she appeared unable to hear what I was trying to tell her and seemed, as usual, to be completely taken in by Warren's quiet, engaging, good-humoured manner. He'd blind her with his knowledge and views on various things until in the end I started shouting and Warren would tell her how awful he found it. She'd then, of course, ask me to try not to do it. It ended suddenly one night with Warren refusing to go back, saying it was a complete waste of time. Nothing, he'd decided, was ever going to change. I felt he'd sabotaged it intentionally from the very beginning.

I continued with my work and coped with it well over the next two to three years; it was actually a welcome distraction. My workload was massive though and increasingly it began to engulf me. It overwhelmed me to the point where even moving from my desk took effort I didn't have. I'd shuffle papers and put them away in my drawer and get them out and reshuffle them, sometimes throwing them away if they weren't important, in order to maintain my feeling of being in control. I was continuing to work seventy hours a week, but it still wasn't enough. I began dreading having to supervise my staff and found myself unable to end the meetings. Consequently they'd go on and on. I felt too dreadful to write up their supervision notes afterwards. This made me feel even worse – the safety of children was at stake here. Children like the child *I* had been.

I'd been managing a ground-breaking case and my staff and I had just completed most of the work for a big prosecution. It was complex and exhausting, but even before it went to court another was dumped on my desk. I really don't know how I managed this second case; I was breaking down in tears before court hearings and breaking down again afterwards. It was as if my whole body was refusing to function, either professionally, or in my disturbed marriage. I went to my GP where, once again, I couldn't stop crying, and she straight away signed me off work, with severe stress and depression.

It was around this time that something else happened that might have signalled all was far from well. I unexpectedly ran into Daniel one day, while visiting one of my sisters. I had, at the time, begun growing out my hair, from a short layered cut to one all the same length – I had intended to grow it to my shoulders. At that time, however, it was halfway between the two; all one length, almost, but still not that long.

On seeing Daniel in my sister's house, I stiffened, as ever, as he approached with his customary speed. Only this time, his expression was different from usual. 'No no no no!' he whispered, with great intensity, intimately, in my ear. 'Your hair! It looks terrible! You must either have it long or short. You can't wear it like this!'

I was immediately mortified. It was like being a child again. And knowing I would be seeing him a week later, at a family christening, I rushed to the hairdressers and had it cut really short. There was no time to grow it, so I felt compelled to have it cut off. I simply couldn't countenance displeasing him.

I attended the christening, as did Daniel. 'Much better,' he crooned in my ear as he greeted me. He kissed my cheek. 'Yes,' he purred. 'Much, much better.'

Immediately after that I had a nervous breakdown. A full breakdown; the most terrifying sensation imaginable – to feel so overwhelmed by every little thing, to be unable to do anything, even move. Movement, even movement around me, made me feel like I was falling, and was never going to stop, going down into a black nothingness.

I just sat there, staring straight ahead, gripping the chair arms, afraid to move because I was sure if I did I'd fall to pieces – literally – and never recover. I couldn't stop crying, and was in the grip of a dangerous depression. Needless to say, the whole thing made Warren cross and he ignored me most of the time.

'Do you know,' he asked, 'how awful it is, having to live with someone who's depressed?' I had no answer to that, even if I had had the mental energy to answer. Which was probably why he also commented that he'd always promised himself he'd never live with a depressed woman – as if I'd planned it. Even so, he was still there.

I begged Warren to stop ignoring me, and I begged him in earnest. I knew – and I told him – that I was in such a bad place that, if I had a knife, I was afraid I would stick it in him. I was terrified by how much I wanted to do that – to kill either myself or him. Naturally, having listened to, and dismissed me, for so long, Warren didn't take any of it seriously. Though he seemed to hear me, nothing changed.

For two months I existed in this horrible place, being seen by the doctor every week, and with the medication I'd been on since the injury to my hand being increased dramatically. Then, on the spur of the moment, I acquired an eight-week-old puppy. Amber had got a puppy, Buttons, for her little boy, Cameron, and asked me if I'd go with her to collect her. Unfortunately, perhaps knowing his sibling was about to leave him, the other puppy left in the litter became so upset I said we'd take him too. He was called George, and he was such a comfort. It was a bit like having a baby. I'd wrap him in a blanket, and sit and stroke him, feeling not quite so alone. I had really got him for Jennifer, to say sorry for having Polly put down.

Warren was furious that I'd got George without consulting him and so another marital battleground – how to look after a puppy, of all things – gave my tenuous grasp of emotional stability another bashing, and my mental state went back downhill.

I became so ill again my GP wanted me to see a psychiatrist – one she believed was the best in the business. She made arrangements for me to attend one of the Priory Hospitals, and to meet with the same psychiatrist who had been unable to take me as a patient eleven years previously.

This time, to my undying gratitude, he was able to help me straight away. For the first time in any sort of therapy in my life, I felt a real sense of protection. The staff at the centre treated me like I mattered, like I wasn't just a condition, but a human being, and never made me do anything I didn't want to do, both in terms of taking medication, and with my treatment. When he encouraged me to become an in-patient and I refused, he respected and trusted my decision. Despite his serious concerns for the way I was thinking and feeling, he arranged for me to attend the hospital for as many days – for day care – as I felt I could manage.

Attending day care terrified me. It meant admitting I was unwell, but as time went by I realized that the therapists and patients just accepted me as I was. They didn't judge me, bully me or expect me to do anything I didn't want to do, and though I couldn't speak in groups they encouraged me in other areas, and I found an emotional outlet in painting. I was no artist, but that didn't matter in the least. It wasn't about becoming the next Monet or Picasso. While the tears flowed incessantly, I had no words to articulate my distress. With painting, however, I had a voice. I painted in red and black – I didn't want pretty colours, and my paintings were always of body parts: hands, fingers, mouths making noises, dirty teeth, penises – and when I could no longer stand looking at each picture I used to roll it up and go with the therapist to the shredder and watch while she shredded it for me. I couldn't seem to cope with doing this task myself, and would just watch as the picture turned into scores of tiny strips and fell into the bin.

I did this for many weeks, until eventually I could bear it if other members of the group looked at my pictures. I still couldn't talk about them, as they did – both theirs and mine – but somehow that didn't seem to matter.

Despite the support I received from the team at the Priory, my recovery continued fitfully. At the same time I was undergoing a further frustrating eighteen months of therapy with a private therapist I'd found, but I no longer held out hope anyone could help me. I truly believed therapy didn't work for me, because I was too pathetic to engage properly with the process, and because my problems – I was beginning to realize – were so severe.

My private therapist told me I wouldn't get better unless I left Warren and attended a group she supervised. I did attend the group a number of times, but I still couldn't talk about my experiences. Looking back on that time, I don't think even *I* knew what those experiences were. In any case, it was too soon for me to attempt to share such things with a group of people I didn't know.

Yet again, this ended abruptly. Ended with the realization, with the help and support of Jennifer, that if a therapist started crying and telling me she wasn't up to her own job, then she wasn't going to hear *my* cries for help. Stopping seeing her, having invested so much time and money, was a real watershed moment – especially as I'd been a decade with the one before.

However, I still failed to leave Warren. I knew we couldn't continue living as we were, yet again and again I convinced myself of the fiction there was still a chance we could mend things. It's odd, reconsidering that time, but I really seemed unable to grasp I could have any sort of future without him. I didn't *want* to leave him, despite everything he'd done to me. I still hoped the tiniest crumbs would come from his direction and sustain me sufficiently to continue. I was just like a small child listening intently to a fairy tale: I *had* to believe in the happy ending.

Only now do I realize the extent of my denial. Of *course* I couldn't confront why I let him treat me as he did – doing so would have exposed all my earlier abuse and the floodgates would surely have opened. So perhaps, in staying in such abusive adult relationships, I was keeping those gates locked, for my own emotional protection.

Once again, I felt the best thing was to move. Financially, our position felt precarious. I was worried I might not get my early retirement pension, and Warren was already carrying on about my not working. There wasn't a shred of reassurance from him about how we'd cope if we stayed where we were, and as usual it was only once I set wheels in motion to downsize that he was suddenly full of ideas about staying, and therefore recriminations about the action I'd taken. It was almost as if he wanted out of the marriage himself, but was waiting for me to make the decision and the move, solely so he could act the wounded party.

It was heartbreaking selling my home. Having lived in it for eight years and done so much to it, I couldn't bear the thought of someone else living there. I cleaned it lovingly for the last time before I handed over the keys.

Though even as I was packing, there was a tiny spark of strength growing inside me. Because as I did so, I was secretly packing 'mine' and 'his' boxes, perhaps as a way of being ready when I did find the strength to get away. It was a very conflicted business; I did it because I knew I must acknowledge the possibility, but at the same time I kept alight the flame of hope he'd change and these separate boxes wouldn't be needed.

I was preparing in other ways too. My therapist had previously advised me to open my own bank account and to ask our solicitor to split the proceeds of the sale between us, thereby protecting my share. This annoyed Warren greatly, but I stood firm, and we moved into a rented house, just down the road, on a six-month lease, while we decided what to do next.

It was during that time the decision was made that we should move to London. I had barely ever spent time in any city, let alone the capital, but London was where Jennifer lived, and I wanted to be close to my daughter.

It was Jennifer, who, encouraged by my belief, was by now having therapy herself (unsurprisingly, given all the traumas of her young life), that provided the final key to my recovery. She encouraged me to embark on new therapy myself, with someone who came highly recommended by her therapist. Warren was characteristically furious at the expense, but it was my money and I no longer cared. I felt so suicidal that doing nothing was not an option, and no price would be too high. Before we made the move to London, I would drive there twice weekly – a round trip of 160 miles – just to see her.

Straight away I saw what therapy should be like, and how what I'd been receiving for the last thirteen years couldn't be classed as 'therapy' at all. Initially this revelation made me angry and despairing for the many years I'd wasted. But even then I realized I mustn't allow such feelings to take over. I had never been taught to trust myself or my feelings, and routinely accepted everyone else knew much better than me, when they didn't. Indeed, I soon understood that the 'therapy' I'd received was abusive in itself. But just when I'd started to make inroads into my psyche, I received the final push to take the step that would undo the continuing damage my marriage to Warren was still creating.

We had found a house together in London and the week before we were due to sign the documentation before moving a letter arrived, correctly addressed but to Warren's brother. I couldn't believe how something like this could have happened. Why would anyone connect our address with Warren's brother? Warren's brother lived miles away. Some sixth sense telling me all was not well made me decide, then and there, to open it.

Inside was a summary of shares Warren's brother had sold, together with details of the payment that had been made – to *Warren* – of £25,000. Confused, I confronted him when he got home, only to be told he *had* planned to tell me – he'd lost some money gambling, and had borrowed this from his brother in order to make up the shortfall. I couldn't believe either what he'd done, or that he had intended to tell me, and asked him if he really believed we could have a life together if that life was to be built on more lies.

I insisted Warren pay his brother back straight away, and it was when I was checking we still had enough money to complete the purchase that he was forced to confess he'd lost even more money and had actually already borrowed on a credit card in order to ensure we had enough. The loss, in total, came to at least £40,000 and it was hard to find words to convey how I felt. Thank God my half of the money was still safe.

Warren was predictably defensive. Why should I be so upset? It was, after all, *his* money he'd lost, not mine – his to do whatever he liked with. And when I suggested words like 'betrayal' and 'trust', he got angry and just said the same again. With hindsight, I don't believe he had any intention of completing on the house, but at the time it was simply the route to clarity. I knew I had to move to London for my sanity. Similarly, I had to escape *him*.

At long last, finding a courage I didn't know I had, on 4 June 2008, I finally left Warren. I was fifty-three years old, and this was the most significant thing I'd ever done for myself in my entire life.

On arriving in London I rented a small flat because I'd elected to spend my share of the house proceeds on daily therapy – without it my emotional sickness was still so great I was afraid not only that I'd be tempted to return to Warren, but, worse, I might take my own life. And as I did so, the enormity of what had been done to me gradually, and painfully, became clear. The sadness and betrayal was enormous, almost too much to bear – and for the most part I felt incredibly alone.

Even so, I made the decision, if I was going to heal properly I must give up contact with my birth family. It was the first time

I'd walked away from an abusive situation, but instead of feeling free I felt desolate. The feelings of loss following this decision were immense. I had given up my home, the county I'd lived in all my life, the countryside, my husband, my birth family, my job, my income – my financial security and my career. It would be just me and my children from now on.

London was different in every way to anything I'd ever known. So many people, houses, noise – everything felt so fast. The only people I'd see who I knew were my daughter and her partner of seven years, Oliver, a nice guy who over the years I have come to respect and rely on. Without them I really, honestly feel I wouldn't be here now to tell my story.

I needed justice to be done, and I needed to be heard, and I decided to start writing down the events of my life. I did this initially to help both myself and my children come to terms with the reasons why our lives had been so unhappy, unsettled and distressing. To write about the abuse and the inevitable chronic domestic violence I went on to suffer was painful but also liberating; I found a peace and calmness I'd never had before.

Throughout this ongoing process I acquired a diploma in psychotherapy, which helped me understand what psychotherapy was. My thesis – and one could say the topic chose me – was on the responsibility therapists have to ensure they are 'up to the job'. But writing this book was also to take back responsibility for the events of my life – to finally, unequivocally, tell the truth.

And now, here I am, in the spring of 2010, and the process is all but complete. Except, as it turns out, not quite.

I don't know why – it's just a niggle in the back of my head really – but one day in 2010 I decided to check the day of my birth. I suppose I think if I actually see it, written down, it might be in some way cathartic. Might help me to finally internalize the travesty of being told (and so having always lived my life in the belief) that I was born a Wednesday's child, full of woe. It takes little time to check it and even less to take it in. I had actually been born on a Monday.

AFTERWORD

The purpose of this book was to help me and my dear children understand our lives better, and, with the help of my therapist, I believe we have achieved that. She has been and continues to be considerable in my life. Without her wisdom, compassion and recognition, and the great mercy she has shown me, I could not have come close to sharing with myself what my life has really been like. By moving away from all the chaos and abuse of how my life *was* and acknowledging and beginning to come to terms with my experiences, a huge empty space has been created – *a space I can at last reclaim as belonging to me.*

Why *did* the people I should have been able to trust the most end up hurting me the most? The reality is that there *is* no reason. I didn't even exist as a person to them. I always wanted just one of them to acknowledge what they did and say sorry. Now, for the first time, I recognize that no amount of apologizing, which none of them will do anyway, would make any real difference. Nothing can ever justify what any of them did or make up for the enormous upset and injustice that has taken place. My new maturity, and acceptance of my right to life, has given me back the power they took from me.

For my family, Alfie, Jennifer, Melli, Oliver, George and me it is a new beginning, a beginning in which we do not have to hold back, we can say what we believe and feel without fear of punishment and riposte. We can for the first time be a family, an honest family, with no more secrets, no more make-believe and no more betrayal.

I am about to start sitting as a Justice of the Peace again and am actively looking for a new job in advocacy or something similar. I have purchased my first home on my own and I own a little bit of a two-bedroom house with a garden that George and I are working on.

Jennifer was rewarded with a BA (Hons) 2:1. She then started a year-long trip, backpacking round the world with the girls she shared house with while at Uni. When Jennifer returned, Ozzi, the landlord of the house they had rented for their time at Uni, and who she also worked for during weekends and holidays, asked her to go into a business partnership with him. She had been planning – and had an interview – to work as a diplomat, so it was a big decision and an opportunity she hadn't been expecting. But Jennifer decided to take up Ozzi's offer and go into his hair and beauty business. I am very grateful that Ozzi and his family have always been there for Jennifer and have treated her as one of their family. They have together gone on to make a good and prosperous business partnership, developing and expanding their company and, more importantly, remain best and trusted friends.

After three years' study and obtaining a diploma in nursing,

Alfie has worked his way up to team leader. He now manages a team of staff who care for children who have mental-health needs. Alfie has a lovely two-bedroom flat, and when Melli, who is now nearly thirteen, comes to see her daddy, she has her own bedroom ready and waiting. We have been lucky enough that since she was seven years old she has been flying over from Copenhagen, on her own, and spending every Christmas, Easter and summer holidays with us. She is athletic, and an amazing swimmer, and despite our enforced absences we have a very relaxed and close relationship with her.

I cannot finish without mentioning Lynne Barrett-Lee, notable published author and my collaborator in the writing of this book. Lynne is extremely funny, making me laugh when all I wanted to do was cry, showing me great respect, compassion and sensitivity throughout. Her resoluteness, energy and commitment to making sure every word, every sentence, every meaning was as I wanted it to be, even when I and/or she had written and rewritten it many times before, is to be endorsed as rare; only a few like her exist.

Faith Scott, April 2010

WHY DOES IT MATTER?

Because it does.
It matters, because you stole what was
Only mine to give
To the right person
At the right time.

It matters because what you did to me
Affected how I saw myself
And how others saw me too.

It matters because of what I was denied
Then and now.

It matters – and don't let anyone
Least of all you
Think that it doesn't.

It matters that today
Children are still unseen and unheard and
That Judges and the law of the land
Blame them for what others
Have done to them.

IT MATTERS – and it always will!
Gillian (00), CIS'ters, May 2009

Sources of further information and help

Childline – **0800 1111**

The United Kingdom Council for Psychotherapy (UKCP) –
0207 014 9955

The Priory Hospitals Group – **0845 277 4679**

24-hour National Domestic Violence Freephone Helpline –
0808 200 024711

CIS'ters – PO BOX119, Eastleigh, Hants SO50 92F